Nietzsche's *Ecce Homo* and the Revaluation of All Values

Nietzsche's *Ecce Homo* and the Revaluation of All Values

Dionysian Versus Christian Values

Thomas H. Brobjer

BLOOMSBURY ACADEMIC
LONDON • NEW YORK • OXFORD • NEW DELHI • SYDNEY

BLOOMSBURY ACADEMIC
Bloomsbury Publishing Plc
50 Bedford Square, London, WC1B 3DP, UK
1385 Broadway, New York, NY 10018, USA
29 Earlsfort Terrace, Dublin 2, Ireland

BLOOMSBURY, BLOOMSBURY ACADEMIC and the Diana logo are trademarks of Bloomsbury Publishing Plc

First published in Great Britain 2021
This paperback edition published 2023

Copyright © Thomas H. Brobjer, 2021

Thomas Brobjer has asserted his right under the Copyright, Designs and Patents Act, 1988, to be identified as Author of this work.

Cover design: Charlotte Daniels
Cover image © Baivector / Shutterstock

All rights reserved. No part of this publication may be reproduced or transmitted in any form or by any means, electronic or mechanical, including photocopying, recording, or any information storage or retrieval system, without prior permission in writing from the publishers.

Bloomsbury Publishing Plc does not have any control over, or responsibility for, any third-party websites referred to or in this book. All internet addresses given in this book were correct at the time of going to press. The author and publisher regret any inconvenience caused if addresses have changed or sites have ceased to exist, but can accept no responsibility for any such changes.

A catalogue record for this book is available from the British Library.

Library of Congress Cataloging-in-Publication Data

Names: Brobjer, Thomas H., author.
Title: Nietzsche's 'Ecce homo' and the revaluation of all values: Dionysian versus Christian values / Thomas H. Brobjer.
Description: London, UK; New York, NY, USA: Bloomsbury Academic, Bloomsbury Publishing Plc, 2021. | Includes bibliographical references and index. | Identifiers: LCCN 2021004551 (print) | LCCN 2021004552 (ebook) | ISBN 9781350193741 (hardback) | ISBN 9781350193758 (ebook) | ISBN 9781350193765 (epub)
Subjects: LCSH: Values. | Nietzsche, Friedrich Wilhelm, 1844-1900. Ecce homo.
Classification: LCC B3318.V25 B76 2021 (print) | LCC B3318.V25 (ebook) | DDC 193–dc23
LC record available at https://lccn.loc.gov/2021004551
LC ebook record available at https://lccn.loc.gov/2021004552

ISBN: HB: 9781-3501-9374-1
PB: 9781-3501-9430-4
ePDF: 9781-3501-9375-8
eBook: 9781-3501-9376-5

Typeset by Deanta Global Publishing Services, Chennai, India

To find out more about our authors and books visit www.bloomsbury.com and sign up for our newsletters.

For Marika, Max, and Mattias

Contents

1

The Revaluation of All Values as the Purpose of *Ecce Homo*

1.1 Introduction: The *Revaluation of All Values* as the Purpose of *Ecce Homo*

What an extraordinary coincidence that just months, weeks, even days before Nietzsche's mental collapse in early January 1889 he wrote a summary of his life and reviews of all his books! What other philosopher has done that? What remarkable luck! Less fortunate is that the text is marred by Nietzsche's excessive sense of self-importance and possibly by other signs of mental confusion and impending collapse.

This, I believe, is the view of most readers and commentators of Nietzsche's last book, *Ecce Homo*. However, I no longer believe that this is an accurate description of what happened. Nietzsche did not at the end of 1888 primarily look back and summarize his life. He looked forward. He looked forward and used *limited parts* of his life and writings for the purpose of preparing his readers for and drawing attention to what was to come. Such a realization has consequences for how we read and interpret *Ecce homo*.

There are strong reasons to accept that the primary purpose of *Ecce homo* was to prepare for and attract interest in Nietzsche's "revaluation of all values," which was both a philosophical (axiological) project and the title of a literary project. Nietzsche had worked on this theme during the previous five years (from 1884 until at least December 1888) and planned to present and develop it in a four-volume work with the final title *Umwerthung aller Werthe* (*UAW*), *Revaluation of All Values*, a work which was now coming to fruition.

Nietzsche states this aim explicitly in the first sentence of the book: "In view of the fact that I will shortly have to confront humanity with the heaviest demand ever made of it, it seems to me essential to say *who I am*." In the second section he claims to be a disciple of Dionysos, who later in the work is contrasted with Christianity and Christ, and he asserts that our present values have become fake and false, and are the "opposite to the only ones which would guarantee it [humanity] a flourishing, a future." In the third section he contrasts his forbidden truths with moralism and idealism.

The "revaluation of all values" is the *leitmotif* throughout the work; it contains eleven explicit references to the planned work with the title *Umwerthung aller Werthe*, and many more implicit ones. Still others, explicit and implicit, can be found in his concept and theme of "revaluation of values." In the first two chapters, Nietzsche describes the revaluation as the goal and meaning of his life, and he attempts to show why he is able to see and do what no one else sees or does. In the very first section of the first chapter he writes: "I am handy at *inverting perspectives*: the foremost reason why for me alone perhaps a 'revaluation of values' is even possible."[1] At the end of the second chapter, "Why I Am So Clever," he expresses it as follows (and suggests that he only recently became able to revalue values):

> For the task of *revaluing values* more capacities were perhaps necessary than have ever dwelt together in one individual, above all contradictory capacities [. . .] an immense multiplicity which is nevertheless the opposite of chaos—this was the precondition, the long, secret labour and artistry of my instinct. Its *higher concern* was so pronounced that I never even suspected what was growing within me—that all my abilities would one day suddenly *spring forth* ripe, in their ultimate perfection. (EH, Clever, 9)

There are a large number of further references and statements in the text of *Ecce homo* which show that it was written to be preparatory to the *Umwerthung aller Werthe*. To select just a few examples, he writes, "you can guess why I am publishing this book *beforehand*" (EH, Destiny, 1); he speaks of having a long future (EH, Clever, 9), and did not know that he was going to collapse, and thus had no reason to summarize his life for its own sake, but does this for the sake of the coming work; he refers to optimism, and claims that he will have occasion to discuss it in the future, that is, in the *Umwerthung aller Werthe* (EH, Destiny, 4); again referring to the future, he claims that he is "destined to fulfil great tasks" (EH, Clever, 10); twice he states that he will publish the *Umwerthung aller Werthe* in the near future, in 1890 (in the reviews of *Menschliches, Allzumenschliches* and *Der Fall Wagner*).[2] That Nietzsche wrote *Ecce homo* to explain how it has been possible for him to see and revalue what others have not seen and realized is visible also in the early draft of the title: *Ecce Homo: Or, Why I Know a Little More.*[3]

That *Ecce homo* was written as preparatory to the *Umwerthung aller Werthe* can be seen with perhaps even more clarity in his letters. On October 30, 1888, he writes to Peter Gast, "I did not only want to present myself with it [*Ecce homo*] *before* the whole incredible solitary act of the *Revaluation*," but also to test the German freedom of the press. A few days later (November 6, 1888), he writes to his publisher Naumann, that *Ecce homo*

> is a in the highest degree *preparatory* text, so that I after a period of a year or so can come forward with the first book of the *Revaluation*. [. . .] Thus I have *solved* an *extremely difficult* task—that is, to tell about myself, my books, my views, in snatches, so far as it for this was necessary, to tell *my life*—between 15 Oct. and 4 November.[4]

Later in the same letter he discusses the production of the book: "It is my intention to give this work the same form and appearance which that *magnum opus* [*Hauptwerk*] shall have, to which it in every sense constitutes a long preface." In another letter, to Georg Brandes, dated November 20, 1888, Nietzsche describes his *Ecce Homo* and continues: "the whole thing is a prelude to the *Revaluation of All Values*."[5] A month later he writes to Jean Bourdeau, on December 17, 1888, that he is "condemned to a great task" and that "now *Ecce Homo:* Or, How One Becomes What One Is will be published. Later the *Revaluation of All Values.*"

The revaluation project, both as a philosophical theme and as a literary project, reverberates in his notes from 1884 onward.[6] However, for the time when Nietzsche wrote *Ecce homo* and afterward there are so few extant philosophical notes that it is difficult to draw any clear conclusions about the project from these. What we can determine from the notes is that Nietzsche continued to make plans for the three last volumes of the *Umwerthung aller Werthe* at least until November 1888, and these final notes give some further indications about their planned content.

For a correct understanding of *Ecce homo*, an awareness of its relation to the revaluation project is necessary. Such an awareness has consequences for how we read and use the book.[7] Surprisingly, the close connection between *Ecce homo* and the revaluation of all values has not been recognized and discussed in the literature so far.

Ecce homo is a difficult book to use, at least for philosophers, for it does not contain much conventional philosophy. Reading it the way done in this study, I would argue, is both more correct and more fruitful, as well as closer to Nietzsche's intention, than the conventional reading of it as a sort of autobiography. We are not only able to better understand and use the book and the biographical information it contains but also gain information about the late Nietzsche's most important philosophical project, the revaluation of all values, as both a philosophical and literary project.

1.2 *Ecce Homo* as Misunderstood and Misread

Ecce homo is obviously different from Nietzsche's other later books (those published after *Also sprach Zarathustra*, after 1885). It contains a somewhat stylized presentation of himself and discussions of all his published books and is philosophically much less concentrated than his other works; in it Nietzsche's self-overestimation and self-affirmation (although often done with self-irony and hidden humor) reach a disturbing climax. Considering how explicit Nietzsche was in indicating that *Ecce homo* was written to prepare for the *Umwerthung aller Werthe*, as we have seen earlier, one would expect commentators to both show an interest in the *Umwerthung aller Werthe* and discuss the relation between it and *Ecce homo* thoroughly. This, however, has not been the case. Instead, it appears to me as if *Ecce homo* has been badly misunderstood and misused. Almost all users and commentators have regarded and used it as primarily an autobiography—as Nietzsche's review of his life and of all of his books just before his mental collapse. This is obviously, in part, correct—and probably a necessary and an inevitable interpretation. However, when Nietzsche presents and discusses his life and work, he does not do so from a general perspective, which is attempted in most ordinary autobiographies—but, instead, from a very specific one: why am I able to diagnose and revalue values (when others even fail to see the problem). He does not really present his life, but, instead, attempts to answer the much more limited question: why and how am I different so that I can revalue values. Furthermore, the truth is that Nietzsche was *not* primarily looking back and summarizing his life at all, even from this perspective, but, instead, wrote *Ecce homo* while looking *forward*, as preparatory to his planned coming *Hauptwerk*, the *Umwerthung aller Werthe*, in four volumes. It was preparatory in the sense of giving an impression of what the revaluation can mean, and for the purpose of attracting attention to this coming work. Although the *Umwerthung aller Werthe* was never written and published (except the first volume, *Der Antichrist*), this different perspective and purpose of *Ecce homo* profoundly affects its contents and how we must read, interpret, and use the work.

Let us begin by examining how *Ecce homo* has been used and interpreted so far. One would expect biographers to show an extra interest in Nietzsche's "autobiography," but surprisingly this has not generally been the case.[8] Seemingly without exception, *Ecce homo* has been given merely superficial treatment, in spite of the fact that it has generally been regarded as an autobiography. This means that it has both received insufficient attention (and often all but ignored) and been interpreted from a false perspective. Frequently, the relatively uninteresting question of the state of Nietzsche's mental health has received by far the most interest.[9]

The best and most authoritative Nietzsche biography in German, that of Curt Paul Janz, *Friedrich Nietzsche: Biographie*, 3 volumes (1978, second revised edition 1993), covering about 1500 pages, expends a mere three pages on *Ecce homo*, and much of that is in the form of quotations from the work. Janz presents no interpretation or analysis of it. This seems to have set the example for other biographers. He begins: "Thereafter Nietzsche attempts to give an account of himself [. . .] since at this time he met with much non-comprehension and misunderstanding" (part II, p. 657).[10] *Ecce homo* is thus presented as a backward-looking autobiography, and this is not later modified. Instead, he quotes Nietzsche's prologue: "And so I tell myself my life," which still further strengthens this interpretation. However, he also twice quotes Nietzsche's letters where Nietzsche states that it constitutes a preface to the *Umwerthung aller Werthe*, but this is not emphasized or elaborated upon by Janz. He, instead, discussed the much less important question of censorship, which Nietzsche had raised in one of these letters.

Probably the second most important modern biography of Nietzsche is Werner Ross' *Der ängsliche Adler* (1980), in which *Ecce homo* is treated as a work of insanity,[11] and with a remarkably critical attitude.[12] Although Ross spends many pages on this period of Nietzsche's life, he says little specifically about *Ecce homo*. He quotes the first sentence of the book, about Nietzsche's demand on humankind, and part of the sentence in the letter to Gast dated October 30, 1888, where Nietzsche states that he wants to present himself *before* the *Umwerthung aller Werthe*—but changes the meaning of this sentence so that its sense becomes merely that Nietzsche wants to test the risk of censorship. Ross regards *Ecce homo* as an autobiography: "that which he begins on the 15th of October, his birthday, is that which now alone he cares about: self-presentation, self-defence, self-explanation, war and victory" (p. 762).[13] Thus, if anything, he treats it as backward-looking, not forward-looking—and hence there is no discussion at all of the need to reinterpret the contents of *Ecce homo* in relation to the planned and in part executed *Umwerthung aller Werthe*.

Rüdiger Safranski, in his *Nietzsche: Biographie seines Denkens* (2000), a work which has also been translated into English and many other languages, treats

Nietzsche's writings from 1888 but scantily, mostly together, all at once, and he does so without enthusiasm. "The last works, which were quickly produced one after another, 'The Case of Wagner,' 'Twilight of the Idol,' 'Antichrist,' and 'Ecce Homo' develop no new thoughts any longer, but, instead, make the already known coarsened or exaggerated" (p. 318).[14] He claims that Nietzsche felt that he did not have much time left, although he later quotes Nietzsche's own statement from *Ecce homo* that "Even now, I look towards my future—a *distant* future!" (Why I am so Clever, 9). Safranski says little about *Ecce homo* specifically, but it is clear that he regards it as backward-looking: "'Ecce Homo' turns almost only around the question: who am I, so that I am granted and allowed to think as I think?" (p. 318).[15] He mentions the revaluation project, but he nowhere relates it to *Ecce homo* or how it affects how to use and interpret *Ecce homo*.

There is an ongoing project to write commentaries to all of Nietzsche's books, headed by Professor Andreas Urs Sommer, entitled *Historischer und kritischer Kommentar zu Friedrich Nietzsches Werken*, published by the Heidelberger Akademie der Wissenschaft and Walter de Gruyter. Volume 6/2 contains commentaries to *Der Antichrist, Ecce homo, Dionysos-Dithyramben* and *Nietzsche contra Wagner*, all written by Sommer (Berlin, Boston, 2013). The commentary to *Ecce homo* covers pages 322 to 640. These commentaries do not give overall interpretations of the books, but are highly helpful and contain much insight and useful information.

There is no standard biography of Nietzsche in English. The most influential ones are still probably R. J. Hollingdale's *Nietzsche: The Man and His Philosophy* (1965, reprinted with additions 1999), Ronald Hayman's *Nietzsche: A Critical Life* (1980), Curtis Cate's *Friedrich Nietzsche* (2002), and the best of them, Julian Young's *Friedrich Nietzsche: A Philosophical Biography* (2010). Hollingdale discusses *Ecce homo* in a chapter entitled "The Year 1888," pages 193 to 216. In it he has fairly detailed discussions of *Twilight of the Idols*, *The Antichrist*, and *The Case of Wagner*, but oddly enough *Ecce homo* is dealt with only on the last half page, and the treatment contains only discussions of its relation to Nietzsche's insanity, and praise of its literary style.

Hayman spends about five pages (328 to 332) on *Ecce homo*. He treats it as an autobiography, paraphrasing it fairly closely, and occasionally commenting on Nietzsche's biographical statements. He regards it as mostly inferior writing, but "the final section, 'Why I am Destiny,' looks impressively at the future" (p. 331), but he does not go on and discuss this chapter beyond a brief paraphrase and claims that Nietzsche possibly predicted "the wars of the twentieth century." He regards much of *Ecce homo*'s content as colored by Nietzsche's confused mental state. Hayman does not quote or discuss *Ecce homo* as forward-looking and related to the *Umwerthung aller Werthe* project at all.

Cate spends about seven pages on *Ecce homo*, generally staying very close to the text and accepting as truth even many of Nietzsche's obviously stylized comments about himself. He finds it to be "a charming book" (p. 538), but regards the last chapter—which Hayman valued as the best one—as containing "strident imperfections" (ibid). Almost half of his account consists of quotations, and most of the rest is paraphrase. He treats *Ecce homo* as an autobiography, as being backward-looking, referring to it as "this little book of pungent reminiscences" (p. 541). In the last paragraph of his discussion of *Ecce homo* he discusses Nietzsche's letter to Gast, where Nietzsche mentions censorship (which Cate then discusses) and thereafter paraphrases Nietzsche's claim that it was written to prepare for the *Umwerthung aller Werthe*: "as a 'long preface' to the major work (*The Anti-Christian* and the volumes that were to follow) which he wanted to have published some time later" (p. 543)—but this does not draw any comments from Cate, nor does it affect how he interprets the work.

Young begins his four-and-a-half-page discussion of *Ecce homo* with recognizing that the first sentence of the preface refers to the *Umwerthung aller Werthe*: "The reference, here, is to the immanent appearance of the masterwork (reduced, we shall see, in size [to only *Antichrist*]) and its urgent demand that we 'revalue all vales'" (p. 519). Unfortunately, he mostly ignores this thereafter and treats the book as "a self-presentation [. . .] a kind of autobiography" (p. 519), but, importantly, adds that what Nietzsche is doing is *not* presenting his life as much as "presenting his life as exemplary for the reader, fictionalizing, 'idealising', 'staging' one's life [. . .] is a legitimate, indeed essential, part of the project" (p. 519). He argues that this "idealizing" explains some of the oddity and inaccuracies of the work. In the later chapter 26, "The Rise and Fall of *The Will to Power*," he deals more extensively with the *Hauptwerk*, but then without relating it to *Ecce Homo*. Young concludes that "*Ecce Homo* is, then, a flawed work [. . .] Basically, the work does two things; first, it tells the reader how Nietzsche became 'what he is,' how *one* becomes what one is. And second, it tells us *what it is* that he has become" (p. 520). In the following and connected subchapter entitled "What Nietzsche Became," he mostly ignores what Nietzsche regarded as his "task," but does recognize and briefly discuss Nietzsche as someone who revalues values, and very briefly discusses this (pp. 522f.).

Sue Prideaux has written a pleasant and readable book about Nietzsche's life, *I Am Dynamite* (2018), but it does not contain much about his thought, nor about his books, and it is certainly not a philosophical or intellectual biography. She assumes and frequently refers to *Ecce homo* as Nietzsche's autobiography, but says nothing about its relation to his planned *Hauptwerk*, nor anything about why he decided to write *Ecce homo*.[16]

Strangely enough, many biographers dislike and all but ignore *Ecce homo*.[17]

Perhaps introductions, discussions, and commentaries to *Ecce homo* contain more explicit elaborations on its relation to *Umwerthung aller Werthe* and the consequences of this for the use and interpretation of the book?

Walter Kaufmann was for long the most influential Nietzsche scholar in the Anglo-Saxon world. His introduction to his translation of *Ecce homo* from 1966 (*Vintage Books*) is in many ways valuable and interesting, but he regards the work as backward-looking, and does not even mention Nietzsche's project of revaluation of all values, nor, of course, *Ecce homo*'s relation to it. On the contrary, he states that the book offers "Nietzsche's own interpretation of his development, his works, and his significance" (p. 201). I will argue later that it does none of these things in the general sense stated by Kaufmann, but only in a narrow and very specific sense.

R. J. Hollingdale's introduction to his own translation of *Ecce homo*, from 1977 (*Penguin Classics*), now unfortunately superseded by another introduction (see later), regards it as autobiographical and backward-looking, but clearly points out that Nietzsche "himself saw it as something quite different, that is as herald and path-preparer for something mightier —for something, indeed, for which he saw his whole life hitherto as no more than a preparation and precondition: the *revaluation of all values*" (p. 9). However, he argues that "not only did the revaluation fail to appear" (p. 9) but also, in contradiction to his first statement, that "it had probably already been abandoned by the date of *Ecce Homo*" (p. 9). Nonetheless, the *Umwerthung aller Werthe* receives a fair amount of discussion in the introduction (more than in any other introduction I have read).[18] Although in the end rejecting the *Umwerthung aller Werthe* project and claiming that Nietzsche abandoned it even before writing *Ecce homo*, Hollingdale nonetheless states: "But whatever one may think Nietzsche had concretely in mind when he spoke of a 'revaluation of all values', it must have been something a lot more comprehensive than the content of the *Anti-Christ*" (p. 11). However, since nothing as impressive as that came, Hollingdale, in the end, seems to have regarded *Ecce homo* as backward-looking. Certainly, there is no discussion of how regarding *Ecce homo* as preparing for the *Umwerthung aller Werthe* can or should affect our interpretation of the work.

Michael Tanner's new introduction to Hollingdale's translation, from 1991 and later (*Penguin Classics*), can hardly be called an improvement. Although he vaguely states that Nietzsche planned further books, he never even mentions the *Umwerthung aller Werthe* (much less discusses or draws consequences from how it relates to the latter): "Though Nietzsche had no idea that this was to be his last book, indeed was full of plans for further ones, he seems to have felt that a point had been reached in his life and his work where a retrospective celebration was in place" (p. viii).[19] All in all, his introduction regards *Ecce homo* as "partly pathological" and as "a retrospective celebration," with no words of its relation to the *Umwerthung aller Werthe* project.

A good exception among introductions to *Ecce homo* is Duncan Large's excellent introductory essay to his own translation for the *Oxford World's Classics* (2007). I find this translation to be the most accurate one, and it is the one used in this study. At a central point in his introduction Large quotes the first sentence of *Ecce homo*—quoted earlier: that Nietzsche will shortly confront humanity with the heaviest demand—and correctly concludes: "The most important context for the composition of *Ecce Homo*, then, is not the work he had already completed, but rather a work that was yet to come" (p. xiv). Large also makes the important point that *Ecce homo*, instead of being a description of Nietzsche's life, is a description of his ideal or sublimated life: "*Ecce Homo* instead promotes the process of self-becoming as an ethical ideal. [. . .] The ethics of self-becoming in Nietzsche is intimately connected to the strenuous ethic of self-overcoming [. . .] what is described here is what psycho-analysis would later call a projection, an 'ego ideal' [. . .] exemplary autobiography" (pp. xvii–xix).[20] However, Large does not argue his case against other biographers and commentators, and, more importantly, he does not discuss the consequences of this view for interpreting and using *Ecce homo*. Instead, he claims about *Ecce homo*: "Its task is not to break new philosophical ground, but—like the works which immediately preceded it, *Twilight of the Idols* and *The Antichrist*—to survey the ground already covered over the course of Nietzsche's career thus far" (p. xv). It is perhaps correct that *Ecce homo* is not meant to break new philosophical ground—but to bring attention to Nietzsche's philosophy, especially that part of it pertaining to the revaluation of all values, and to how it (especially the revaluation) was possible (and for that it was necessary to say something about who Nietzsche was). However, it seems to me as if *Der Antichrist* contains new ground, and certainly that Nietzsche regarded it as such—but, more importantly, that one needs to be aware of this intention regarding the future work *Umwerthung aller Werthe* while reading *Ecce homo*, which in this sense does significantly more than merely "survey the ground already covered by Nietzsche."

One of the best contemporary German language Nietzsche scholars, Hans Gerald Hödl, has, in his immensely rich Habilitationsschrift *Der letzte Jünger des Philosophen Dionysos: Studien zur systematischen Bedeutung von Nietzsches Selbstthematisierungen im Kontext seiner Religionskritik* (Berlin, New York, 2009), written partly in another context, that of Nietzsche's religious thought, a long final section on *Ecce homo* (pp. 464–593). He there recognizes that it was Nietzsche's intention that *Ecce homo* should prepare for the *Umwerthung aller Werthe*, and makes many interesting comments.[21]

In Richard Samuel's study "Friedrich Nietzsche's *Ecce Homo*: An Autobiography?," in *Deutung und Bedeutung*, edited by B. Schludermann et al (Mouton, 1973), (pp. 210–27), in spite of the question mark in the title (which seems to refer to the degree of sanity or insanity which can be found in the work, which remains undetermined according to Samuel), *Ecce homo* is treated as an backward-looking autobiography: "The intention here is to present *Ecce homo* first and foremost as an autobiography. It was written as such" (p. 210). He then states that "if one analyses the autobiographical contents of *Ecce homo* the result is meagre" (p. 215) and further (in part correct, but much better formulated by Duncan Large, who refers to it as an "exemplary autobiography," discussed earlier): "*Ecce homo* is, rather, an analysis of Nietzsche's self and a self-interpretation of his works" (p. 222). Only once does Samuel briefly touch upon *Ecce homo*'s relation to the *Umwerthung aller Werthe*—Nietzsche "points out that it is meant to be the preface to the just completed *Antichrist*" (p. 225). This is far too little to be useful for applying this perspective when analyzing the book—and Samuel actually regards Nietzsche's own choice as a distortion: "The self-interpretations of his writings are an indispensible starting point for their final evaluation, even if much in them is distorted [*sic*] in order to fit an overall pattern designed at the time of writing [*sic*]" (p. 226). Samuel can write this because he regards and treats *Ecce homo* completely as an autobiography, and fails to realize that Nietzsche (also) had other purposes with it. Samuel's just quoted statement would have been correct if the subclause was radically changed to "if one takes into consideration Nietzsche's intention of writing *Ecce homo* as preparatory to the *Umwerthung aller Werthe.*" That is not Samuel's view, and he gives us no aid for such an undertaking.

To examine a few more recent examples of treatments of *Ecce homo* for the purpose of seeing whether the view of *Ecce homo* as a backward-looking autobiography remains common and generally unchallenged and unchanged, we can examine Josef Rattner's *Nietzsche: Leben—Werk—Wirkung* (2000). Rattner expends four pages on *Ecce homo*, mostly by quoting and paraphrasing, with little discussion and analysis. He assumes *Ecce homo* to be a backward-looking autobiography[22] and completely ignores the relevance of the *Umwerthung aller Werthe* for *Ecce homo*. Looking up Nietzsche's *Ecce homo* in Wikipedia (July 2020) one is given the previously quoted statement by Kaufmann, and a backward-looking autobiographical interpretation is assumed: "One of the main purposes of *Ecce Homo* was to offer Nietzsche's own perspective on his work as a philosopher and human being." The planned *Umwerthung aller Werthe* is not mentioned at all, and it follows that there is no discussion of the relationship between it and *Ecce homo*.

Lesley Chamberlain's book *Nietzsche in Turin: The End of the Future* (1996) contains a chapter entitled "9. Ecce Homo" (pp. 158–81), where the work again is treated as an autobiography and analyzed mainly psychologically from that point of view: "*Ecce Homo* contains not only an autobiography, but what it means to be an autobiographer" (158). The author then mentions Nietzsche's preoccupation with revaluation, but he interprets it as a very different revaluation: "The transvaluation in his case is a rising from the dead, an account of the idealized dead father as he is imagined to have lived in the son, and thus a rendering of most important things at a great rhetorical distance. It is auto-obituary" (158).

An interesting case is the recent full book-length discussion of *Ecce homo* by Nicholas More, *Nietzsche's Last Laugh: Ecce Homo as Satire* (Cambridge, 2016), which emphasizes the literary value of the work. He rightly and skillfully brings forth an important aspect of the work as having many characteristics of satire, and its humor, but fails to recognize the close relation between the work and the project of revaluation. More's brief discussion of revaluation of all values as anti-moral, in his section on Nietzsche's discussion of "Dawn" in *Ecce homo* is interesting and valuable, but More says nothing at all about the relation between *Ecce homo* and Nietzsche's planned four-volume literary project. In many ways More's study argues the opposite of my work, which claims that a better reading of *Ecce homo* can lead to a better understanding of, and for taking seriously, the late Nietzsche's philosophy, and that there are good reasons for taking it seriously.

We have found no biography, with the possible exception of Young's brief treatment, which recognizes and discusses the pivotal role of the *Umwerthung aller Werthe* for the writing of *Ecce homo*, and with two exceptions, no commentary or academic text that does this either. And yet, such recognition is just a first step to extract from this book what Nietzsche put into it. A second step is to examine how this affects our reading of *Ecce homo*. A third step would be to see what we can learn about the revaluation of all values from this work, which is so closely intertwined with it.

1.3 How Has Such a Misreading Been Possible?

The short answer to how this misreading of *Ecce homo* has succeeded in becoming the paradigmatic way of interpreting the book since at least the 1970s is, I believe, twofold. For one thing, the *Umwerthung aller Werthe* never appeared (*Der Antichrist* was regarded as insufficient by almost all commentators) and this meant that the forward-looking aspect of *Ecce homo* could appear as irrelevant and simply vanish. What remained was the backward-looking interpretation. Furthermore, the selection of late notes which Elisabeth Förster-Nietzsche, together with Peter Gast, put together under the title *Der Wille zur Macht* (1904, 1911), which many understood to constitute Nietzsche's planned but never finished four-volume *magnum opus*, became more and more questioned and controversial. With the valuable work done by Mazzino Montinari, it was shown to contain forgeries, mere excerpts from books Nietzsche had read, many falsely deciphered words of his handwriting and worse, it was tendentious.[23] His severe critique of this compilation was accompanied by a critical and skeptical view of Nietzsche's whole project of a *Hauptwerk*. Discussions or considerations of a *magnum opus* came to be regarded as hypothetical and old-fashioned (as based on the situation *before* the critical edition of Nietzsche's works), as being influenced by Elisabeth Förster-Nietzsche's work and thus out of fashion.

The most detailed and most authoritative text written about Nietzsche's plans for a *Hauptwerk* and its relation to his late notes is Montinari's in many ways excellent essay "Nietzsches Nachlaß von 1885 bis 1888 oder Textkritik und Wille zur Macht" published in *Nietzsche lesen* (Berlin, New York, 1982).[24] As a very acute and perceptive scholar, and as the editor of the critical edition of Nietzsche's works, his views and arguments must certainly be taken very seriously. He was very skeptical and critical toward the idea of a *Hauptwerk* by Nietzsche, and he claims that "*Nietzsche's collapse in Turin came when he literally was finished with everything.*"[25] The same claim is made by the best and most influential Nietzsche biographer, Curt Paul Janz: "with it [*Der Antichrist*] and by 30 September 1888 his philosophy has come to an end!"[26] To me this claim seems both psychologically improbable and, in regard to Nietzsche's intention to write a *Hauptwerk*, simply wrong.

Montinari and almost all commentators have, regarding this question, "interpreted backwards," that is, from the fact that no *Hauptwerk* was finished. Strengthened by the interpretation that Nietzsche possibly gave up the idea of a *Hauptwerk* during the last weeks of his active life, they have concluded that Nietzsche's final position was that he had said all he wanted to say. In the debate over the status of the compilation *Der Wille zur Macht*, the claim that Nietzsche at the end had no intention to write such a work was an effective argument. Thus, no important work came after *Ecce homo* and it became natural, and perhaps inevitable, to read it as backward-looking, even if it was not written as a primarily summarizing or "objective" text. Furthermore, the greatest authorities argued against the notion that Nietzsche had relevant plans for a *magnum opus* at the end of 1888, and thus this view fell out of fashion. The result has been that *Ecce homo* has been treated and used as a summarizing autobiography.

The situation was perhaps further aggravated by the fact that it took a long time before *Ecce homo* was published. It was finally published in 1908, long after all his other books and manuscripts, and thus also long after *Der Antichrist* in spite of the fact that Nietzsche had intended it to be published before that work. *Ecce homo* has also in almost all published complete works of Nietzsche, including in the Colli–Montinari critical edition, KSA, been published last of his real books, after *Der Antichrist*.

Even if Nietzsche perhaps gave up the idea of writing a *Hauptwerk* during the last weeks or days before the mental collapse (and it seems reasonable to regard this, if, indeed, he did give up the idea of a four-volume *Hauptwerk*, in large part, as due to his mental state).[27] It seems more interesting and relevant to take into consideration his feelings and intention during the last five years when most of his life was directed toward writing a *Hauptwerk*. This includes the time of writing, and most of the revising, of *Ecce homo*.

It seems psychologically unlikely that Nietzsche was finished with everything when he collapsed at the age of forty-four. The evidence also seems to show that this was not the case. One of the titles he considered for *Ecce homo* was "*In media vita*"—"*In the middle of life*," suggesting that he regarded himself as having much more to do. In all of his later books, from *Jenseits von Gut und Böse* to *Ecce homo*, he referred to philosophical discussions which he would deal with in the *Umwerthung aller Werthe*. In these books he also more generally speaks of future plans and tasks. For many years he had planned and worked hard to write a major work beyond what we have today, and as late as November and December 1888 he still planned to write and publish the three remaining volumes of his *Hauptwerk*. A good way to resolve, or at least further develop, the question of the role, nature, and status of Nietzsche's philosophical revaluation project, and his intention to write a *Hauptwerk*, is to examine its place in his last original book, *Ecce homo*. Such an investigation is attempted in this study.[28]

What is necessary is not merely realizing that Nietzsche wrote *Ecce homo* in large part as preparatory to the coming *Umwerthung aller Werthe*—but further, to draw two consequences from this realization. One is to examine how this affects how we can and should interpret and use *Ecce homo* (and how not to use it—it cannot be used as a straightforward autobiography). I have seen no such examination and discussion. The second is to determine the degree to which *Ecce homo* can be used to gain information about the nature and content of Nietzsche's planned *Umwerthung aller Werthe*—both as a philosophical project and as a literary work. After having discussed the pros and cons of regarding *Ecce homo* as an autobiography, I will discuss the first of these questions in Chapters 3 and 4, and the second question in the last chapter.

1.4 Is *Ecce Homo* an Autobiography?

With very few exceptions, if any, *Ecce homo* has been treated as a summarizing autobiography. Most commentators have taken it for granted, although it has been regarded as an unusual one and called things like "perhaps the strangest autobiography ever written" (R. Samuel) and "the most bizarre example of that genre ever penned" (M. Tanner). Much of this seems, however, to be in response to Nietzsche's excessive self-importance. What else could *Ecce homo* be? The question is especially pertinent considering that no important work was published after *Ecce homo*.

Before returning to this question, let us examine Nietzsche's relation to autobiography. I will do this by examining five themes, of which the first three are by far the most important, and thereafter summarizing the arguments for and against (and perhaps beyond) regarding *Ecce homo* as an autobiography.

1. Nietzsche's whole philosophy emphasizes the close relation between life and thought. In *Jenseits von Gut und Böse*, for example, he says: "It has gradually become clear to me what every great philosophy has hitherto been: a confession on the part of its author and a kind of involuntary and unconscious memoir; moreover, that the moral (or immoral) intentions in every philosophy have every time constituted the real germ of life out of which the entire plant has grown."[29] Similar statements can also be found in earlier works: "However far a man may extend himself with knowledge, however objective he may appear to himself—ultimately he carries away with him nothing but his own biography."[30] It is Nietzsche's belief that "assuming that one is a person, one necessarily also has the philosophy that belongs to that person."[31] Nietzsche also emphasizes

this connection between books and life, not only for other thinkers but also for himself: "I have at all time written my work with my whole body and my whole life. I don't know any purely intellectual problems."[32] Most biographers also seem to accept this view. Nietzsche also believes that our thoughts and values are all connected and constitute a whole, a character, which forms a sort of 'system,' though not necessarily a conscious one:

> For this alone is fitting for a philosopher. We have no right to *isolated* acts of any kind: we may not make isolated errors or hit upon isolated truths. Rather do our ideas, our values, our yeas and nays, our ifs and buts, grow out of us with the necessity with which a tree bears fruit —related and each with an affinity to each, and evidence of *one* will, *one* health, *one* soil, *one* sun.[33]

We thus see that Nietzsche's whole approach to philosophy (and life) is biographical, both as a writer and as a thinker, also when analyzing and discussing others.[34]

2. Let us turn to Nietzsche's explicit autobiographical writing. If *Ecce homo* is to be regarded as an autobiography, we should be aware that it is not Nietzsche's only one, and it is neither his best nor his most reliable. Nietzsche was immensely fond of self-analysis and autobiography. We probably possess over twenty explicit autobiographies by him, most of them from his early life and the time before he went to Basel. In fact, Nietzsche's first impressive writing is a thirty-two-page autobiography from 1858, written at the age of thirteen.[35] Comparing it with other texts from this time, one may conclude that he showed exceptional aptitude for autobiographical writing. Thereafter there are a large number of shorter autobiographical texts, many of them written for specific purposes such as schoolwork, university graduation, presentation of himself for Basel, self-presentation for a philosophical journal,[36] as well as others that were written more for his own sake.[37]

Even ignoring these relatively early autobiographical writings, *Ecce homo* is not his only autobiography. In fact, if we search autobiographical information and Nietzsche's views of himself and his writings, there are other and better sources than *Ecce homo*.[38] Most obviously this is true for the many prefaces he wrote for his books in 1886 and 1887 (for *Die Geburt der Tragödie*, *Menschliches, Allzumenschliches*, two volumes, and thus two prefaces, *Morgenröthe*, *Die fröhliche Wissenschaft*, and the prefaces of the later published books, *Jenseits von Gut und Böse*, *Zur Genealogie der Moral*, *Der Fall Wagner*, *Götzen-Dämmerung*, *Der Antichrist*, *Nietzsche contra Wagner*, and *Ecce homo*). In these he often takes an autobiographical approach, and the texts are more reliable than *Ecce homo* (since less determined by an ulterior motive—to prepare for the coming *Umwerthung aller Werthe*, although these prefaces, too, are all influenced by that project which had begun already in 1884). Furthermore, Nietzsche writes a fairly large number of autobiographical descriptions of himself in letters to people he wanted to, or hoped would, review his books, such as Georg Brandes, Karl Knortz, J. V. Widmann, *et al.* But the letters are also important in other ways, obviously autobiographical in general (and most biographies of Nietzsche are in large measure based on his letters); but of especial interest and relevance are his discussions of his books in them. These ought to be used and compared with the reviews of them in *Ecce homo*. Again, often the information is more relevant and reliable in the letters. Finally, his notebooks also contain many explicitly autobiographical reflections, some of which are of great value.

We can conclude that *Ecce homo* is not Nietzsche's only autobiography.

3. Nietzsche also wrote much that was implicitly autobiographical. He is perhaps more obviously using himself and his own experiences to create his philosophy than any other great thinker. We can mention four scattered examples. While many of Nietzsche's observations and conclusions are based on himself, for some it is obvious while for others, less so. For example, when he in *Menschliches, Allzumenschliches*, section 272, entitled "Annual rings of individual culture," makes a general statement, it is in fact based wholly on his own life and development:

> Men at present begin by entering the realm of culture as children affected religiously, and these sensations are at their liveliest in perhaps their tenth year, then pass over into feebler forms (pantheism) while at the same time drawing closer to science; they put God, immortality and the like quite behind them but fall prey to the charms of a metaphysical philosophy. At last they find this, too, unbelievable; art, on the other hand, seems to promise them more and more, so that for a time metaphysics continues just to survive transformed into art or as a mood of artistic transfiguration. But the scientific sense grows more and more imperious and leads the man away to natural science and history and especially to the most rigorous methods of acquiring knowledge, while art is accorded an ever gentler and more modest significance. All this nowadays usually takes place within a man's first thirty years. It is the recapitulation of a curriculum at which mankind has been labouring for perhaps thirty thousand years.

Those who do not see this can be aided by examining Nietzsche's early draft of the note.[39] Nietzsche goes further than this, and regards whole books as portraits of him. This is especially true for the fourth book of *Die fröhliche Wissenschaft*.[40]

We also see this implicit autobiographical writing in the whole of *Also sprach Zarathustra*. This may even be one of the reasons why he holds it in such high esteem. Not only are many sections of it based on Nietzsche's life,[41] but Nietzsche also calls Zarathustra his son, and claims that his own name can be used instead of Zarathustra's. Other more general use of himself can be seen in the chapters "We Scholars" and "Our Virtues" in *Jenseits von Gut und Böse*, and even more obviously, the poem which ends the book, "From High Mountains." In some sense it is not completely erroneous to call all of Nietzsche's writings autobiographical.

4. In concordance with the view we have just sketched of Nietzsche, he not only wrote out of himself but he was also very fond of reading autobiographical and biographical texts. In spite of his frequent critical discussions of Rousseau and Carlyle, it seems as if the only thing he read by Rousseau (other than his *Emile*) was his *Confessions*, and as far as we know, nothing by Carlyle but a biography of him.[42] Nietzsche read and used a whole string of biographies and autobiographies, such as, for example, those of Jung-Stilling, Humboldt, St. Augustine, many German authors in the series *Modern Klassiker*, and many books similar to biographies, by among others, Strauss, Schenkel, Bahnsen, Plutarch, *et al.* Perhaps even more pronounced is Nietzsche's liking of *Memoirs* and *Collections of Correspondence*, of which he read many, and many attentively with much fondness.

5. Most people, when annotating books, do not clearly involve themselves. Examining Nietzsche's annotations, one finds a not inconsiderable number of annotations and longer comments that directly relate to his feelings and thoughts while reading the book in question. For example, while reading Emerson's *Essays*, Nietzsche writes in the margin of the book: "What have I learnt until today, 15 Oct. 1881." Other similar examples could be added.

We are now better able to compare the arguments for and against regarding *Ecce homo* primarily as an autobiography.

There are some obvious arguments for regarding and treating it as an autobiography. The book contains an account of Nietzsche's life (though very incomplete), but a more complete account of his intellectual development. It contains discussions and reviews of all his books. The title "*Ecce Homo,*" "see the man" or "see me," certainly suggests that it is an autobiography. Nietzsche himself seems to say that it is an autobiography: in the preface, "it seems to me essential to say *who I am*" and "*listen to me! For I am such and such. Above all, don't mistake me!*" and in the prologue, "And so I tell myself my life." He also seems to say so in many letters, although he never calls it a biography or autobiography.

We have also seen earlier Nietzsche's intensive interest in biography and autobiography, and that much of his writing can reasonably be regarded as autobiographical. Surely there is a strong case for regarding *Ecce homo* as an autobiography.

However, the case for regarding *Ecce homo* as a written preliminary for preparing for the planned coming *Hauptwerk* is perhaps even stronger.[43] Many of these arguments were given in the introduction, and these will therefore only be very briefly reviewed here. Most important is the very first sentence of *Ecce homo*, quoted in the introduction, where Nietzsche states that he wrote *Ecce homo* for the purpose of preparing for and attracting attention to his coming *Umwerthung aller Werthe*. Many later statements in the book, such as "you can guess why I am publishing this book *beforehand*" confirm this purpose. This is stated even more explicitly in letters (many of them quoted earlier)—especially the letter to his editor, where he states that *Ecce homo* should be given "the same form and appearance which that *magnum opus* [*Hauptwerk*] shall have, to which it in every sense constitutes a long preface," and when he earlier in the same letter says that he has been telling his life "in snatches, so far as it for this was necessary."[44] "The Revaluation of All Values," both as a philosophical theme and as a book project, constitutes the *leitmotif* throughout the book. The work on the *Umwerthung aller Werthe*, which now was coming to fruition, was something Nietzsche had worked on for five years. In fact, *Ecce homo* is not the only one of Nietzsche's books in being at least in part forward-looking. This is true for *Die fröhliche Wissenschaft* (in which the last section foreshadows *Also sprach Zarathustra*),[45] but still more clearly for *Jenseits von Gut und Böse*, *Zur Genealogie der Moral*, and *Götzen-Dämmerung*, which all also foreshadow the *Umwerthung aller Werthe* (see the discussion in Chapter 2).

It is furthermore possible to negate many of the arguments for the premise that it should be regarded as primarily an autobiography. Although it gives some biographical information about Nietzsche, it is really too little and too selective for it to justify the term autobiography. His intellectual development and books are, indeed, discussed, but from a very specific, forward-looking perspective (as I will show later). The title of the work actually suits both perspectives equally well (as I will also show). Although Nietzsche, in the foreword, prologue, and the text itself, several times says things that suggest that it is an autobiography (although significantly, he never uses that term), he also says that he writes it for the purpose of the future work.

The main theme in the first two chapters of *Ecce homo* is to show that revaluation of values constitutes the purpose of Nietzsche's life. He not only on several occasions explicitly refers to the *Umwerthung aller Werthe*, but twice even states that it will be published soon. He also states that he will in the future elaborate on optimism, just as he in *Zur Genealogie der Moral* and *Der Fall Wagner* had claimed that he would discuss the problem of nihilism and the physiology of art in his coming *Hauptwerk*. Finally, the last chapter, "Why I Am a Destiny," is so closely related to the coming *Hauptwerk* that it can be regarded as part of it (see the discussion in Chapter 4).

Even if one ignores (or rejects) all of these aspects, one must ask why he did write an autobiography. The obvious answer is that which Nietzsche himself gave, that it was written for the purpose of preparing and attracting interest in his coming work. This means that Nietzsche's intentions were forward-looking rather than backward. This has consequences. What we are given in *Ecce homo* is not an account of his life, nor even his life in snatches, nor reviews of his books, but a particular selection suited to the theme and message of his planned future work.

Perhaps one can summarize it as follows. At the end of 1888 Nietzsche was much concerned and involved with his project of *Umwerthung aller Werthe*, of which he already had written the first volume. To Nietzsche, this work was of enormous importance, but his books had so far received extremely few readers and reviewers. "Ten years—and no one in Germany has had enough of a guilty conscience to defend my name against the absurd silence under which it lay buried" (EH, Books, "Wagner," 4). Thus before writing the additional volumes of the *Umwerthung aller Werthe* and publishing them, he decided that he needed to write *Ecce homo*, for primarily three purposes. (1) To prepare for the *Umwerthung aller Werthe* in the sense of showing the problem (the life-denying character of our present values, Christianity, Christian morality) and suggesting the solution by referring to the two symbols Dionysos and Zarathustra, as also to tragedy, *amor fati*, and the idea of eternal recurrence. (2) To stimulate curiosity and interest in the project. (3) To explain how and why precisely he is able to revalue values, to make his claims both more comprehensible and credible.

The first two of these purposes are directly related to his project of *Umwerthung aller Werthe*, while the third one can be regarded as in part autobiographical. But it is autobiographical in a contorted way, since it is an account of his life from a very specific perspective where *Umwerthung aller Werthe* is regarded as the goal and meaning of his whole life.

Since the *Umwerthung aller Werthe* never appeared (except *Der Antichrist*), the first two purposes have been largely ignored or forgotten, and it has been the autobiographical aspect of the work which has been emphasized (but that too in an unsatisfactory manner since one has not taken sufficiently into account the contorted manner of the autobiographical aspect of the text, and its close relation to the *Umwerthung aller Werthe*).

1.5 The Nature and Status of the *Ecce Homo* Manuscripts and the Final Text

There are two misconceptions about the *Ecce homo* text that I want to throw some light on, apart from giving a brief history of the *Ecce homo* text: first, that Nietzsche worked on *Ecce homo* from October 15 until January 2 (implying a rather continual work on the manuscript for almost two and a half months); and second, that there exists a "correct" edition of *Ecce homo*, and that this is the one published in the critical edition.

Although the state of the *Ecce homo* manuscripts is somewhat complex, we have extant the finished printer's copy [*Druckmanuskript*], cleanly written in Nietzsche's hand finished on or near November 13 (but containing a fairly large number of minor revisions, most of them made by Nietzsche himself when the manuscript was returned to him for a few days in early December). This manuscript is in the Goethe–Schiller archive in Weimar. It is the only printer's manuscript of any of Nietzsche's books that has been published in both facsimile and diplomatic style and is thus easily available and readable.[46] This is of great interest and use for the Nietzsche researcher.

Also extant are printed and proofread pages of *Ecce homo*, from the prologue to the middle of the third section in the second chapter ("Warum ich so klug bin") in two parts. The first part is signed by Nietzsche with the words: "druckfertig/N" [Ready to print/N(ietzsche)] and dated by him as "Turin, den 18. Dez. 1888," the second part was returned to the printer two weeks later.[47] We also have extant a fairly large number of notes and versions of the text which Nietzsche wrote while working on *Ecce homo*. This enables us to follow the writing and the development of the text. See the appendix for a summary of the chronology of the manuscript.

It is possible to distinguish at least seven stages in the development of the *Ecce homo* text, resulting in two published versions, from the earliest Ur-*Ecce homo*, written during the first half of October, to the seventh at the end of December 1888, but even after that Nietzsche continued to send some minor additions and changes to the manuscript, until January 2.[48]

However, this can give the wrong impression. Nietzsche did not work on the manuscript continually from October to December. By far the greatest part of it was written before the middle of November; thereafter the revisions are relatively minor. There are two stages which are much more important than the rest (ii and iii), but let us discuss the five most important ones.

(i) The earliest version, the Ur-*Ecce homo*, was written during the first half of October, before Nietzsche had decided to write *Ecce homo*. It is relatively short, seventeen printed pages,[49] whereof six were soon transformed into the chapter "What I Owe the Ancients" and added at the end of *Götzen-Dämmerung* while proofreading that work. The other eleven pages constitute the beginning of *Ecce homo*, and remain relatively unchanged.[50]

(ii) By far the most important is the October version, written between October 15 and November 4, which contains almost everything. While writing and after having written it, he tells in letters that *Ecce homo* has "progressed well."[51] However, it differs in some important ways, and lacks some of the final text (most noticeably the reviews of *Die fröhliche Wissenschaft*, *Also sprach Zarathustra*, and all the post-Zarathustra books). It does not contain the chapter divisions of *Ecce homo*; instead, it is divided into twenty-four sections (of which six will not be included in the final text).

(iii) Nietzsche soon revises and makes additions to this, and before the middle of November he writes out a complete printer's manuscript and sends it off to his publisher to be printed. Now the chapter titles and the final structure have been added, as well as reviews of all of his books. This is *Ecce homo*, the rest can be regarded as just minor revisions. This is the "Druckmanuskript" which has been published in facsimile (but it also contains some later revisions).

(iv) In early December Nietzsche asks for the manuscript to be returned to him, and he makes a number of smaller changes. The most important of these are the probable rewriting of much of the review of *Also sprach Zarathustra*, adding the first two sections of the last "Destiny" chapter, and adding or revising a few sections in the other chapters. Nietzsche then also adds two epilogues (and the table of contents), a "Declaration of War," and "The Hammer Speaks," of which the first is destroyed by Nietzsche's mother, but the second remains in the "Druckmanuskript" (see the discussion in Chapter 3).[52] He then returns this to Naumann on December 6 and says (for the second time) that it is ready to be published.

(v) Nietzsche thereafter, during the second half of December, makes a number of minor changes up to the end of December and beyond until his collapse.

> Some of these are likely to have been lost, others destroyed by Elisabeth Förster-Nietzsche and perhaps by others. The most important of the changes we still have extant (and which are used in the critical edition) are as follows: The complete third section of the first chapter ("Wise") has been exchanged. The later one has obviously been affected by his mental state. The fourth section of the second chapter ("Clever"), which is somewhat strange, as well as sections 6 and 7 have been added. Among the reviews, he has added the complete section 6 of *Menschliches, Allzumenschliches*, and has rewritten the last third of section 5 of the Zarathustra review. Sometime at the end of December, or even later, he also changed the references to "the first volume of *Umwerthung aller Werthe*" to simply "*Umwerthung aller Werthe*" in the prologue and in the review of *Götzen-Dämmerung*.

What we can conclude is that by far the greatest part of *Ecce homo* was written before c. November 13, 1888. Thereafter the revisions are relatively minor. This lion's share of the text is not seriously affected by Nietzsche's later mental collapse. When it comes to the final additions and revisions made at the end of December and in early January, no obvious conclusion or solution will satisfy everyone and every question. My own preference is to primarily use the version without the final changes, that is, primarily use the proofread early part of the manuscript, thereafter the revised manuscript which Nietzsche sent to his publisher on December 6 and said should be published (however, the later additions and revisions should certainly also be read and considered). This is basically the older published version. Its main advantage is that it makes more sense, it connects with his thought for several years, and does not contain texts which most likely should be regarded as the product of an unstable mind. However, there will never be only one correct version. We will have to accept and work with several versions, at least two (that means taking into account, or at least into consideration, both the earlier and the later versions when it comes to the late revisions), and thus accept a more dynamic and pluralistic concept of the final edition. This is far from impossible. It makes it slightly harder to work with and write about *Ecce homo*, but only slightly.

1.6 *Ecce Homo* and Nietzsche's Mental Health

Nietzsche wrote most of *Ecce homo* before mid-November 1888, but continued to make minor revisions until his mental collapse on January 3, 1889. Much effort has been spent by biographers and scholars on commenting on the degree to which *Ecce homo* is influenced or determined by Nietzsche's mental illness and collapse. This is a question one cannot completely avoid, since one needs to decide what to do with the later changes to the manuscript. Normally, it is, of course, the last version of an author's text that should be published, but what shall one do when the author is becoming mentally unsound? Therefore there exist two printed versions of the published text, as mentioned previously: an older one (used by all versions published before c. 1970, and a few thereafter) which is based on the proofread manuscript (and approved by Nietzsche in mid-December and at the end of the month) for the first fifth of the text, and the printer's manuscript (without the changes made at the end of December) for the rest of the manuscript. This has now usually been superseded by the newer one used by Colli and Montinari's critical edition, KGW and KSA (which began to be published in 1967, and the KGW version is still in progress) which includes all of Nietzsche's changes (of those that remain extant—almost certainly further later ones were destroyed by Elisabeth Förster-Nietzsche) including those made in January 1889.

Some of these later revisions (and additions) seem to me unsound, but the only important one is the third section of the first chapter. However, the bulk of *Ecce homo* was written before mid-November, and before that there is little evidence of mental instability in Nietzsche's writing. It is true that already before then he did show a strong tendency to self-importance, but in my amateur psychiatric judgment it cannot be regarded as having reached a pathological state before mid-November or early December. In many ways Nietzsche had a strongly developed sense of self-importance throughout his life, which gradually grows more pronounced. It is difficult to determine when it becomes an indicator of mental instability (especially since he was so original that some of his statements actually contain much truth), but toward the very end of 1888 it appears increasingly to resemble delusions of grandeur. If it is not obvious when we read *Ecce homo*, it seems doubtful to me if it can be regarded as determined by mental instability in any relevant sense. And this certainly seems to be the case for that written before early or mid-December. It is only for the very minimal revisions and additions Nietzsche made after mid-December 1888 (which I pointed out in the previous subchapter, and will refer to in the text and in the appendix) that we need to take his mental collapse into account.

2

The Presence of the *Revaluation of All Values* in Other Later Books and Letters

There are two principal ways to see the presence and importance for Nietzsche of his revaluation project. One approach is to discover and examine all his explicit and implicit statements to that effect. As I will show, *Ecce homo* is not the only book which ends with references to the coming *Umwerthung aller Werthe*; on the contrary, almost all of his later books abound with references to it, as well as his later letters and notebooks. The other way to see this is to examine Nietzsche's views of his own development, and his feeling that he was moving into a new stage of his intellectual development associated with the revaluation of all values project as his great "task," especially in 1887 and 1888. Let us start with this second way.

2.1 Nietzsche's "Task" and His Move into a New Phase of Life

Nietzsche spent much time and effort in (and surely derived pleasure from) analyzing his own life.[1] In so doing, he also commented on his own intellectual development and how it falls into different periods or stages. In a letter to his best friend, Franz Overbeck, dated February 10, 1883, Nietzsche describes his life and his view of it:

> My whole life has crumbled under my gaze: this whole eerie, deliberately secluded secret life, which takes a step every six years, and actually wants nothing else but the taking of this step, while everything else, all my human relationships, have to do with a mask of me and I must perpetually be the victim of living a completely hidden life.[2]

This is one of several of Nietzsche's own descriptions of his intellectual development, dividing it into six-year periods, and into that which later has been called the early Nietzsche (c. 1870–76), the middle Nietzsche (c. 1877–82), and the later Nietzsche (c. 1883–88). Nietzsche had had a strong feeling of leaving something old and moving into something new in c. 1876 (centered on *Menschliches, Allzumenschliches*)[3] and in 1881/82 (centered on the idea of eternal recurrence and *Also sprach Zarathustra*),[4] and it seems as if he felt something similar at this time 1887/88 (centered on the *Umwerthung aller Werthe*).

We can see this in another letter to Overbeck, almost five years later, dated November 12, 1887, in which he writes that he is coming to the end of an era and has a task ahead of him, that is, the revaluation of all values: "It seems to me that a sort of epoch is coming to an end for me; [. . .] thereto I have a task [. . .] (a task, a destiny or what one wants to call it). This task has made me ill, it will make me well again."[5] Nietzsche had been working on the *Umwerthung aller Werthe* since 1884, but it is now, in 1887/88, that he feels that this work is coming to fruition, and that he thereby is moving into a new phase of his life. A little earlier, in a letter to Gast, dated April 19, 1887, Nietzsche had said approximately the same thing: "I feel that there now has come a break in my life—and that I now have the whole great task ahead of me! Ahead of me, and yet more, *on* me!"[6] He writes to Carl Fuchs on December 14, 1887, that he is leaving the past behind and entering a new form:

> For I am, almost without willing it so, but in accordance with an inexorable necessity, right in the midst of settling my accounts with men and things and putting behind me my whole life hitherto. Almost everything that I do now is a "drawing-the-line under everything." The vehemence of my inner pulsations has been terrifying, all through these past years; now that I must make the transition to a new and more intense form, I need, above all, a new estrangement, a still more intense *depersonalization*.

At this stage, during the winter of 1887/88, Nietzsche was working intensively on the *Hauptwerk* project. A week later, in a letter to Carl von Gersdorff, dated December 20, 1887, he writes:

> In an important sense, my whole life just now stands as if in *full midday*: one door closes behind me, another is opening up. The only thing I have done in the last years has been a settling of accounts, closing down, adding the past together, I am almost finished with humans and things and have drawn a line here. *Who* and *what* will remain with me now when I must turn (have been *condemned to turn* . . .) to the true main task of my existence, that is now a capital question. For, said in confidence, the tension in which I live, the pressure of a great task and passion is too great, now to also allow new persons to come close to me.

He seems to be saying that his post-*Also sprach Zarathustra* books, *Jenseits von Gut und Böse*, the fifth book of the *Die fröhliche Wissenschaft*, the many new prefaces he wrote in 1886/87, and *Zur Genealogie der Moral*, have primarily been looking backward, while he now wants or needs to look ahead toward a new stage of his development and to the writing of his *Hauptwerk*. He repeated a similar statement also in early January 1888, in a letter to his old friend Paul Deussen, dated January 3, 1888:

> Fundamentally, at present everything in me ushers in a new era, my whole past falls away from me; and if I summarize what I have done in the past 2 years, it seems to me now always as one and the same work, to isolate me from my past, to cut the umbilical cord between me and it. I have experienced, wanted and, perhaps, *achieved* so much, that a form of violence is necessary to again become free and far away from it. The strength of the inner changes of moods has been enormous. [. . .] I now only demand one thing for a number of years: Peace and quiet, being forgotten, the pleasure of the sun and the autumn for something that wants to *mature*, for the belated sanction and justification of my whole existence (which otherwise, from hundreds of causes has been, an ever problematic existence!).

We can notice that Nietzsche associates this "break" or change of epoches of his life with the great "task" he feels that he has ahead of him. In fact, throughout most of his life Nietzsche felt a sense of facing a great task, but it became more apparent around 1884/85 when he conceives the plans for his *magnum opus*, and then intensified much more again in 1887 and especially in 1888, when those plans and all the work he had done on it seemed to come to fruition.[7]

2.2 Early Thoughts on the *Hauptwerk*

There can be no doubt that Nietzsche planned a *magnum opus* in the middle and late 1880s, although this has received little attention. There is ample evidence of it in his writings, as well as in his letters. One can summarize the situation as follows: By the summer of 1881 Nietzsche felt that he was ready to move into a new stage of his thought and philosophy. Shortly thereafter, in early August 1881, he discovered the idea of eternal recurrence, which together with other "discoveries" he made around this time (to these "discoveries" belong, apart from the idea of eternal recurrence, *amor fati*, the figure of Zarathustra, the will to power, the *Übermensch* or Overman, nihilism, *Décadence*, and the "death of God"),[8] confirmed that he had moved into a new phase. He thereafter felt a new sense of purpose, but decided nonetheless to write his next book, *Die fröhliche Wissenschaft*, mostly in the spirit of the middle phase (that is, he withheld most discussions of eternal recurrence and other aspects in the work). He already in 1881 or at least by 1882 knew that he was going to write *Also sprach Zarathustra* (1883–5). He would always be most satisfied with this work, but he also realized that he in that work had presented his new thoughts as literature, poetically and metaphorically rather than philosophically, and possibly that it constituted only the beginning of his new thinking. Both for the sake of being understood and for his own understanding, he needed to work through most of the content of that work more stringently and philosophically. At least from 1884 onward he was very aware of this, and stated in several letters that *Also sprach Zarathustra* represented only a *Vorhalle* or "entrance hall" to his philosophy, the "main building" which he was going to work through in the next five or six years.[9] From 1886 he begins to explicitly refer to that projected work as a *Hauptwerk*, while *Jenseits von Gut und Böse* (1886), which he wrote and compiled from earlier notes (1881–85/86), he regarded as a sort of commentary on the ideas that led to *Also sprach Zarathustra*, and thus essentially as a pre-*Also sprach Zarathustra* work.[10] There are a very large number of drafts of titles for this project in Nietzsche's notebooks, far more than for any other projected or realized book. Already this can illustrate the extent to which Nietzsche planned and worked on this *Hauptwerk* for many years. Nietzsche used the word *Hauptwerk* more than half a dozen times for referring to this project, but most frequently he referred to it by means of the different planned titles and other more indirect means, including as his "major task" and the "purpose" of his life. On the whole, there is significant consistency between the different drafts, and on several instances it is a previous subtitle that has become the main title. There are good reasons to regard these different titles as referring to essentially the same planned *Hauptwerk*.

The Evolution of the Planned Title of Nietzsche's *magnum opus*, from Autumn 1881 to December 1888

Autumn 1881–Summer 1885 →	Aug. 1885–Aug. 1888 →	Sept.–Dec. 1888
3–5 books (but mostly 4)	Consisting of 4 books	4 books
Many different titles	Consistent title	Consistent title (earlier subtitle)
Not called *Hauptwerk*, but, for example, "Haupt-Bau" (from 1884)	Called *Hauptwerk*	Called *Hauptwerk*

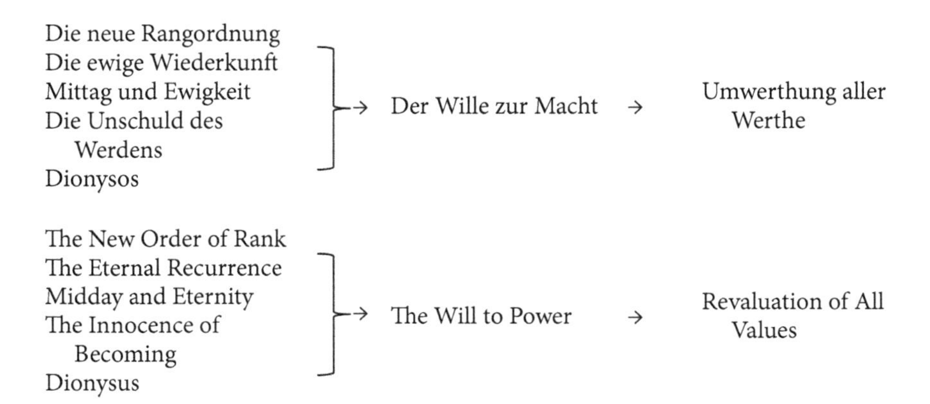

One of the early titles closely related to *Die ewige Wiederkunft* was "*Philosophie der ewigen Wiederkunft* / Ein Versuch der Umwerthung aller Werthe."[11] We can note that this subtitle later becomes a subtitle for *The Will to Power* and, eventually, the main title. We can also note that the very first title listed here, *The New Order of Rank*, also refers to a revaluation of all values.

The evidence for this intention to write a *Hauptwerk* can, apart from in the notebooks, be seen in his published works and in his letters. Let us examine the evidence that we can find in his books and letters in more detail.

2.3 The Presence of the Projected *Hauptwerk* in Nietzsche's Published Books

The intention of writing a *Hauptwerk* is visible in all of Nietzsche's works after *Also sprach Zarathustra*,[12] but this evident intention has been ignored or gone unnoticed by almost all commentators. The extent to which this forward-looking element, pointing to the coming *magnum opus*, has been ignored is remarkable.

Jenseits von Gut und Böse (1886) was to a large extent based on a selection of earlier notes, from and even before the Zarathustra period, and avoided much of the most interesting material that he saved for the *Hauptwerk*.[13] In fact, the book began as a rewriting of the pre-Zarathustra book, *Menschliches, Allzumenschliches*, which is still visible in the chapter divisions and their titles. It resembles *Die fröhliche Wissenschaft* in that in both works he avoids many of the themes he himself regarded as the most essential (most noticeably, the idea of eternal recurrence), only occasionally alluding to them except at the end of both works, where he becomes more explicit for the purpose of pointing forward to coming works (*Also sprach Zarathustra* and the *Umwerthung aller Werthe*, respectively). Hence the subtitle, "Prelude to a Philosophy of the Future," does not refer to a vague general hope but directly to the projected *Hauptwerk*, though this has rarely been understood. In fact, he even announced the *Hauptwerk* on the back cover of *Jenseits von Gut und Böse* as a work in progress: "Under preparation: *The Will to Power*. Attempt at a Revaluation of All Values. In Four Books."[14] The beginning and end of the book point to the revaluation project. In the preface Nietzsche emphasizes a dichotomy of values, the difference between dogmatic and experimental philosophy and the resulting tension which can lead us to a new task and "goal": "we *good Europeans* and free, *very* free spirits—we have it still, the whole need of the spirit and the whole tension of its bow! And perhaps also the arrow, the task, and, who knows? the *target* . . ."[15]—this is almost certainly a reference to the revaluation of all values. We have seen just a little earlier the importance and prominence of having a "task" for the later Nietzsche—and that when he refers to a task in his letters after 1884, it refers specifically to the work associated with his planned *magnum opus*. In the penultimate section, 295, Nietzsche calls himself "the last disciple and initiate of the god Dionysos" and he claims, since *Die Geburt der Tragödie*, to have "learned much, all too much more about the philosophy of this god" and states that "perhaps I might at last one day begin to give you, my friends, a little taste of this philosophy"—referring to the project *Umwerthung aller Werthe*, and specifically its fourth volume, which according to several notes was meant to be entitled *Dionysos philosophos*.[16] (See also my discussion in Chapter 5.)

The most important message of the penultimate section, 295, of *Jenseits von Gut und Böse* is not what it says, but what it promises—that it points forward to a coming work where Nietzsche has gone one step further in his philosophical development with the help of Dionysos, that is, to the *Umwerthung aller Werthe*, and especially to its fourth volume, *Dionysos philosophos*.[17]

None of all this—the allusion to a coming *magnum opus* in the subtitle, in the preface, in the announcement on the cover, and at the end—has led English-speaking commentators to discuss this theme and the role of the *Hauptwerk* for the writing of and for interpreting *Jenseits von Gut und Böse*.[18]

During 1886 and 1887 Nietzsche wrote prefaces to most of his earlier books, including adding a fifth book to *Die fröhliche Wissenschaft*, as well as the new preface and the final poems in that book. This added fifth book of *Die fröhliche Wissenschaft* (1887) begins, in the first section, and ends, in the penultimate section, by pointing at the revaluation project (although not completely visible).

The first section in the fifth book (343), which thus follows immediately upon the claim "the tragedy begins" in the last section of book four, starts with:

> The greatest recent event—that "God is dead," that the belief in the Christian god has become unbelievable—is already beginning to cast its first shadows over Europe. [. . .] and how much must collapse now that this faith has been undermined because it was built upon this faith, propped up by it, grown into it; for example, the whole of our European morality. [. . .] Indeed, we philosophers and "free spirits" feel, when we hear the news that "the old god is dead," as if a new dawn shone on us. (Kaufmann's translation)

Nietzsche is here pointing at the need for new values and a revaluation of values, without Christianity.

The penultimate section, 382 (the last section before the short epilogue which is there to introduce the final poems), contains a whole page of description of the search for new ideals and values:

> we Argonauts of the ideal [. . .] we now confronted an as yet undiscovered country whose boundaries nobody has surveyed yet, something beyond all the lands and nooks of the ideal so far, a world so overrich in what is beautiful, strange, questionable, terrible and divine that our curiosity as well as our craving to possess it has got beside itself—alas, now nothing will sate us any more! [. . .] Another ideal runs ahead of us, a strange, tempting, dangerous ideal [. . .] the ideal of a spirit who plays naively—that is, not deliberately but from overflowing power and abundance [. . .] the ideal of a human, superhuman well-being and benevolence [. . .] it is perhaps only with him that *great seriousness* really begins, that the real question mark is posed for the first time, that the destiny of the soul changes, the hand moves forward, the tragedy *begins.*

The beginning of tragedy, here, represents to Nietzsche both Zarathustra's "going under" and the beginning of a new tragic era, with revalued values, which Dionysos will proclaim. Nietzsche frequently refers to tragedy to symbolize the coming era, as, for example, at the end of his review of *Die Geburt der Tragödie* in *Ecce homo*, section 4, where he writes: "Let us glance ahead a century, and let us suppose that my attack on two millennia of perversity and defilement of the human has been successful. [. . .] I promise a *tragic* age."

The main purpose of *Zur Genealogie der Moral*, written during a few weeks in July 1887, seems to have been to elaborate on and clarify some themes which he had discussed in *Jenseits von Gut und Böse.*[19] It seems as if Nietzsche, when writing *Zur Genealogie der Moral*, like the case with *Jenseits von Gut und Böse*, avoided many notes and themes which he saved for the planned *Umwerthung aller Werthe*.

Already in the preface, there are some allusions to the planned *Umwerthung aller Werthe*. Like most of Nietzsche's prefaces, it is primarily backward-looking, discussing how he came to be interested in the problem of the origin of our moral values, and even giving specific references to where he had discussed it previously. In the first section, he speaks of himself and his equals as "seekers after knowledge" and as having a task, of wanting to "bring something home." It is at the end of the sixth and seventh sections of the preface that he alludes to the revaluation project.

> People have taken the *worth* of these "values" as something given, as self-evident, as beyond all dispute. Up until now people have also not had the least doubts about or wavered in setting up "the good man" as more valuable than "the evil man," of higher worth in the sense of the improvement, usefulness, and prosperity of mankind in general (along with the future of humanity). Now what about this? What if the truth were the other way around? What if in the "good" there lay a symptom of regression, something like a danger, a seduction, a poison, a narcotic, something which makes the present live *at the cost of the future*? Perhaps something more comfortable, less dangerous, but also on a smaller scale, something more demeaning? . . . So that this very morality would be guilty if the *highest possible power and magnificence* of the human type were never attained? So that this very morality might be the danger of all dangers? (GM, Preface, 6)

Nietzsche is here pointing not only to the revaluation of *moral* values generally, which was the intended theme of the third book of the *Umwerthung aller Werthe*, but also more specifically to the critique of "the good man," for which he wrote a fairly large number of notes. In a letter to Gast, dated September 15, 1887, Nietzsche is possibly alluding to this when he writes: "Regarding the main thing [this is probably an explicit reference to the *Umwerthung aller Werthe*, which he had also referred to earlier in the letter], it is *well*: the *tone* of these treatises will reveal to you that I have *more* to say than what is written in them."

At the end of the penultimate section of the preface, Nietzsche again refers to a revaluation of moral values and to Dionysos (the figure and symbol of the *Umwerthung aller Werthe*):

> But on the day when we say with full hearts: "Onwards! our old morality is part of the *comedy* too!" on that day we will have discovered a new plot and potential for the Dionysian drama of the "*Fate of the Soul*"—and one which

> that grand old eternal comic poet of our existence will exploit, on that you may depend! (GM, Preface, 7)

The eighth and last section was probably written later than the first seven, and is anyway different in tone, style, and content, being aimed at discussing how the book should be read. More than two months after having finished the text, on October 5, 1887, Nietzsche sent his publisher, Naumann, a shorter text that he wanted to have inserted into the preface, just before the last section (which then would become section 9). In this text Nietzsche emphasizes even more strongly the importance of morality and its connection to values, and then alludes to immoralism and thus to the revaluation project. Nietzsche here says that morality lies behind all philosophy, including epistemology, and also behind the origin of all great conceptions of value. However, there exist even more fundamental problems than those concerning morality, but these become visible only when one looks into the world and oneself as immoralist.[20] However, Nietzsche already later the same day wrote another postcard, withdrawing this addition.

Originally, *Zur Genealogie der Moral* consisted of the first two essays, the third essay being added later. The first essay ends with some mild references to the future and the themes of the *Umwerthung aller Werthe*. In the penultimate section, he writes:

> Let us conclude. For thousands of years, a fearful struggle has raged on earth between the two opposed value-judgements, "good and bad" and "good and evil"; and as certain as it is that the second value-judgement has long been in the ascendant [. . .] Which of these is in the ascendant at the moment, Rome or Judaea? But there is no room for doubt: consider before whom one bows today in Rome as before the epitome of all the highest values. (GM, I, 16, Douglas Smith's translation)

This is important background for the revaluation of values, and in the beginning of the last section, 17, he seems to hint that he will publish something which will change all of this, that is, the *Umwerthung aller Werthe*.

> —Was that the end of it? Was that greatest of all ideal oppositions then placed *ad acta* for all time? Or only postponed, indefinitely postponed? . . . Will the old flame not inevitably flare up again at some time in an even more fearful way, after much lengthier preparation? Moreover, is this not the very thing which we should desire with all our strength? Should even will? Should even promote? . . .

He also adds a note at the end of this essay and last section, which ends with the following words: "From now on, *all* disciplines have to prepare the future task of the philosopher: the task being understood as the solution of the *problem of value*, the determination of the *hierarchy of values.*—"

The second essay ends (in the 24th, the penultimate, section) with a very specific future reference to the first two volumes of the *Umwerthung aller Werthe* (and the critique of Christianity and nihilism he planned to discuss in them). It begins broadly, with the possibility that our ideals can become more natural, but ends with specific references to the title of one of these works (*Der Antichrist*), and with a reference to what was to be the central content of the other, nihilism:

> For too long man has looked at his natural inclinations with an "evil eye," so that finally in him they have become twinned with "bad conscience." An attempt to reverse this might, in itself, be possible, but who is strong enough for that, that is, to link with bad conscience the unnatural inclinations, all those aspirations for what lies beyond us, those things which go against our senses, against our instincts, against nature, against animals—in short, the earlier ideals, all the ideals which are hostile to life and which have vilified the world? To whom can we turn to today with such hopes and demands? . . . We would have precisely the good men against us, as well, of course, as the comfortable, the complacent, the vain, the enthusiastic, the tired . . . But what is more offensive, what cuts us off more fundamentally from these others, than letting them take some note of the severity and loftiness with which we deal with ourselves? And by contrast how obliging, how friendly all the world is in relation to us, as soon as we act as all the world does and "let ourselves go" just like everyone else! [. . .] But at some time or other, in a more powerful time than this mouldy, self-doubting present, he must nonetheless come to us, the redeeming man of great love and contempt, the creative spirit, constantly pushed away from the sidelines or from the beyond by his own driving power, whose isolation is misunderstood by people as if it were a flight from reality, whereas it is his immersion, burial, and absorption into nothing but reality, so that once he comes out of it into the light again, he brings back the redemption of this reality, its redemption from the curse which the previous ideal had laid upon it. This man of the future, who will release us from that earlier ideal and, in so doing, from those things which had to grow from it, from the great loathing, from the will to nothingness, from nihilism—that stroke of noon and of the great decision which makes the will free once again, who gives back to the earth its purpose and to human beings their hope, this anti-Christ and Anti-nihilist, this conqueror of God and of nothingness—*at some point he must come* . . . (GM, II, 24)

The first of the German words at the end, "Antichrist und Antinihilist" is, of course, the same as the title of the first volume of the *Umwerthung aller Werthe*,

Der Antichrist. Nietzsche played with giving all the first three volumes "anti-" titles,[21] and used that also for the third volume, the anti-moralist, that is, *The Immoralist*, but he never found a good term such as this for the second volume, meant to deal with truth and nihilism, which he therefore entitled *The Free Spirit*. The fourth volume was never intended to possess an anti-title, but, instead, the more affirmative *The Great Midday*, *The Eternal Recurrence*, or most frequently *Dionysos* or *Dionysos philosophos*.

In the brief last section, 25—originally intended to conclude the book—Nietzsche somewhat shifts his goal, and recommends his reader to turn to *Also sprach Zarathustra* (as the closest thing to his *magnum opus* so far), reflecting that he regarded *Also sprach Zarathustra* and the *Umwerthung aller Werthe* as two closely allied works, the former as more poetic and the latter as more philosophical, both centered on the idea of eternal recurrence.

However, Nietzsche thereafter adds a third essay on the meaning of ascetic ideals. He ends this third essay by pointing even more directly at the coming *Hauptwerk*, but before then, in section 8, he explicitly refers to his coming *magnum opus* while discussing the importance of sensuality for Schopenhauer's view of beauty, when he adds a comment in parentheses: "I shall return to this point on another occasion, in connection with the still more delicate problems of the *physiology of aesthetics*, which is practically untouched and unexplored so far.'" From Nietzsche's notes, as well as from references in *Götzen-Dämmerung* and *Der Fall Wagner* (see later), it is clear that this refers to the *Hauptwerk* and a theme he intended to discuss there.

In section 25, he again repeats that he intends to say more about art: "(*Art*, let me say in advance, for I will at some stage return to this idea at greater length—art, in which the *lie* is sanctified and the *will to deceive* has good conscience on its side, is much more fundamentally opposed to the ascetic ideal than science [. . .])."[22]

At the very end of *Zur Genealogie der Moral* he explicitly points forward and refers to his future intention: "I shall probe these things more thoroughly and severely in another connection (under the title 'On the History of European Nihilism'; it will be contained in a work in progress: *The Will to Power: Attempt at a Revaluation of All Values*)."[23] In an earlier version of this text, which was changed as late as in the proofreading stage, Nietzsche had written "my main work [*Hauptwerk*] which is under progress" instead of "a work in progress."[24] He thereafter ends this penultimate section with a reference to the theme of the third volume, *The Immoralist*, with the words: "There is no doubt that from now on morality will be *destroyed* through the coming to consciousness of the will to truth: this is the great drama in a hundred acts which is reserved for Europe over the next two thousand years, the most fearful, most questionable, and perhaps also most hopeful of all dramas . . . ." The last section, 28, ends with a reference to the main theme of the *Umwerthung aller Werthe*, the dichotomy between the affirmation of life contra "a rebellion against the most fundamental pre-conditions of life" (closely related to nihilism).

Nietzsche now felt that he was "*finished with* the effort to make 'comprehensible'" the books he had published so far, and that he had brought to conclusion his "preparatory activity"[25] (after having added material to *Die fröhliche Wissenschaft*, with new prefaces to most of his earlier books, and published *Zur Genealogie der Moral* as a sort of supplement to *Jenseits von Gut und Böse*, and both of these books were in turn meant to supplement *Also sprach Zarathustra*). He was now going to move on into a new stage of his life and work on the *Umwerthung aller Werthe*. As we will see later, in *Ecce homo*, Nietzsche characterizes *Zur Genealogie der Moral* as "three decisive preliminary works [*Vorarbeiten*] of a psychologist towards a revaluation of all values"; they are preparatory to, but not a part of the *Umwerthung aller Werthe*. Shortly after having finished writing the three essays of *Zur Genealogie der Moral*, he, as we saw earlier, writes to Gast, on September 15, 1887, that he has "*more* to say than what is written in them," with obvious reference to his forthcoming *Hauptwerk*.[26] After having finished *Zur Genealogie der Moral*, Nietzsche intended to work more or less exclusively on his *Hauptwerk* for a longer period of time—and this was also to a large extent what happened from the autumn of 1887 to the autumn of 1888. However, during the autumn of 1887, Nietzsche considered a continuation and second volume of *Zur Genealogie der Moral*, and that work too was meant to contain material which pointed forward to the *Umwerthung aller Werthe*, as can be seen by the last sentences of his summary of the planned contents: "The *task*. / **Entrance into the tragic era for Europe.**"[27] However, Nietzsche soon gave up this idea and most of the planned contents were incorporated into the work on the third volume of *Umwerthung aller Werthe* entitled *The Immoralist*.

In 1888 he twice paused from this work to write *Der Fall Wagner* and *Götzen-Dämmerung*, both of which he regarded as resting places in the midst of the greater and much more difficult task of writing his *Hauptwerk*.[28]

Although *Der Fall Wagner*, as limited to dealing with Wagner and modern art and music, is largely separate from the *Umwerthung aller Werthe*, and meant to have a different form, shape, and style, he once in it explicitly refers to the content of his coming *Hauptwerk*: "I shall have an opportunity (in a chapter of my main work [*meines Hauptwerks*], entitled "Toward a Physiology of Art") to show in more detail how this over-all change of art into histrionics is no less an expression of physiological degeneration [. . .]."[29] The epilogue, added to the manuscript later, although not explicitly referring to the *Umwerthung aller Werthe* project, contains in a concentrated form discussions of much that is relevant for this project.

Nietzsche's description of his next work, the short *Götzen-Dämmerung* (1888), is more ambivalent. He refers to it mostly, just as to *Der Fall Wagner*, as a "resting place," as completely separate from the *Umwerthung aller Werthe*, but sometimes he seems to regard it as closely related to that work, and much of its contents, unlike his last three books, are taken from notes originally intended for the *Umwerthung aller Werthe*.[30] That this work was written in the shadow of his projected *Hauptwerk* is visible in the title, preface, general contents, and the last sentence of the book. Until the very end, the proofreading stage of the manuscript, Nietzsche had a different and much less belligerent title for the work: *Müßiggang eines Psychologen* [*The Idle Hours of a Psychologist*], implying, as he also states in the preface, that he here takes a pause from the difficult task of writing his *Hauptwerk*—and, instead, produces some extracts from that work, for the purpose of tempting readers to the *Umwerthung aller Werthe*, and combines that with assorted timely reflections (which would not fit well into that more serious work). The subtitle to the new title, "Or How to Philosophize with the Hammer," is obscure and misleading and its primary meaning has not been understood by most commentators and readers. As one can see from Nietzsche's notebooks, "the hammer" is for him a symbol of eternal recurrence, and the title thus first and foremost means: how to philosophize from the perspective of eternal recurrence.[31]

In the preface to *Götzen-Dämmerung* Nietzsche explicitly says that he is working on his *Hauptwerk*, at this late stage entitled *Revaluation of All Values*:

> To stay cheerful when involved in a gloomy and exceedingly responsible business is no inconsiderable art: yet what could be more necessary than cheerfulness? Nothing succeeds in which high spirits play no part. Only excess of strength is proof of strength. —A *revaluation of all values*, this question-mark so black, so huge it casts a shadow over him who sets it up. (Hollingdale's translation)[32]

Furthermore, he ends the short preface by explicitly stating that he had just finished the first volume of the *Hauptwerk*, that is, *Der Antichrist*: "Turin, 30 September 1888, on the day the first book of the *Revaluation of All Values* was completed."

The content of *Götzen-Dämmerung* is highly interesting and (unlike the case for *Jenseits von Gut und Böse* and *Zur Genealogie der Moral*) he allowed himself to use material and notes which he had set aside for his *Hauptwerk*, but he nonetheless—intentionally—avoided many of the themes he planned to cover in his *Hauptwerk*, such as eternal recurrence and nihilism. Other topics, such as the physiology of aesthetics, higher human beings, the revaluation of all values, and *amor fati* were only alluded to. In fact, he states this explicitly in the title of the longest chapter (constituting the whole second half of the book when he wrote it), "Streifzüge eines Unzeitgemässen," which can be translated as "Expeditions of an Untimely Man," or "Reconnaissance Raids of an Untimely Man," or, in a less military and more intellectual sense, "Short Outlines of an Untimely Man['s Views]." We should thus not be surprised if several of the topics he planned to discuss in the *Umwerthung aller Werthe* are also touched upon here, such as the physiology of art. The penultimate sentence of the chapter also ends with the words: "my ambition is to say in ten sentences what everyone else says in a book—what everyone else does *not* say in a book . . . ." He claims this book contains his philosophy in a nutshell. Themes being mentioned here do not preclude them from being treated more fully in his coming work. The purpose of *Götzen-Dämmerung* was to tempt readers to his *Umwerthung aller Werthe*.

The last sentence of the book (with the exception of the quotation from *Also sprach Zarathustra* placed on separate pages at the end)—with references to revaluation of all values (the title of his *Hauptwerk*), Dionysos, and eternal recurrence—surely is meant to point ahead to his coming *Hauptwerk* (just as the end of *Die fröhliche Wissenschaft* promised *Also sprach Zarathustra*): "the *Birth of Tragedy* was my first revaluation of all values: with that I again plant myself in the soil out of which I draw all that I will and *can*—I, the last disciple of the philosopher Dionysos—I, the teacher of the eternal recurrence . . . ." This pointing forward to his coming *Hauptwerk* is still more obvious at the end of the penultimate chapter of the book, "Expeditions of an Untimely Man," which originally was meant to constitute the end of the book:[33] "I have given mankind the most profound book it possesses, my *Zarathustra*: I shall shortly give it the most independent [i.e., his *Hauptwerk*]."

That *Götzen-Dämmerung* did not constitute the end of Nietzsche's intention to philosophize (as Montinari and others after him have argued) is clear from letters in which Nietzsche speaks of the book as preparatory to and preparing the way for his *Hauptwerk*. In letters written immediately after having finished the manuscript, he states that "the book [*Götzen-Dämmerung*] can serve the purpose of *initiating* and *whetting the appetite* for my *Umwerthung der Werthe* (which first book is almost completed)."[34] Two days later he writes:

> My publisher already has another manuscript, which is a very stringent and subtle expression of my whole philosophical heterodoxy—hidden behind much gracefulness and mischief. It is called "Müssiggang eines Psychologen." In the last analysis, both these works [*Der Fall Wagner* and *Götzen-Dämmerung*] are only recuperations in the midst of an immeasurably difficult and decisive task which, *when it is understood*, will split humanity into two halves. Its aim and meaning is, in four words: the *revaluation of all values*.[35]

In December 1888, just weeks before his mental collapse, after having just received the printed book, he refers to it as being "in relation to that which it *prepares*, almost a piece of fate"[36] and in a postcard to Naumann, on December 20, 1888, he refers to it as "short and in the highest degree preparatory."[37] And that for which it was meant to be preparatory was his forthcoming *Hauptwerk*.

Der Antichrist, when written in September 1888, was certainly meant to be the first of four volumes of the *Umwerthung aller Werthe*.[38] In it, he, at least once, speaks explicitly of a theme he planned to discuss in one of the coming volumes: "A history of the 'higher feelings,' of the 'ideals of mankind'—and it is possible that I shall have to narrate it—would almost also constitute an explanation of *why* man is so depraved."[39] However, *Der Antichrist* was meant to be published after *Ecce homo*, and I will not discuss it further here.

Nietzsche's planned *Hauptwerk* is thus present in all his later published books, and affected how they were written and their contents. For example, Nietzsche avoided themes he was planning to discuss in his *Hauptwerk* when writing *Jenseits von Gut und Böse* and *Zur Genealogie der Moral*, and *Der Fall Wagner* and *Götzen-Dämmerung* were merely "resting places" while Nietzsche worked on his projected work, while *Ecce homo* (and perhaps also *Götzen-Dämmerung*) was written explicitly for the purpose of preparing the way for the *Hauptwerk*.

2.4 Signs of the Planned *Hauptwerk* in Nietzsche's Letters

Nietzsche's intention to write a *Hauptwerk* is still more prominent in his letters than in his published books. In them we also get some hints as to the nature of the *Hauptwerk*. He explicitly refers to such a work as his *Hauptwerk* in a number of letters between 1886 and 1888,[40] but the intention to write such a work is clear already from at least 1884 onward.

Nietzsche began to feel a new and intensive sense of purpose with his "discovery" of the idea of eternal recurrence (and other related "discoveries" made near that time) in early August 1881. He then began to refer to his "task," "life-task," "fundamental task," and "main task" (*Aufgabe*, *Lebensaufgabe*, *Hauptsache*, and *Hauptaufgabe*), and similar expressions, and that he will require several years to develop it. For example, in a letter to Elisabeth, dated August 18, 1881, he writes that he will regard anyone who disturbs the cultivation of his *task* and his working summer as an enemy.[41] Just a few days later, he writes to Overbeck, on August 20/21, 1881:

> Finally: it [*Morgenröthe*] is a start of my beginning—what is still ahead of me! On top of me! At some stage it will become necessary for me, for a couple of years, to completely disappear from the world [. . .] I am at the "height" of life, i.e. of my tasks, which life has gradually put before me, and must, wherever possible, dedicate the next four years, without all and every disturbance, precisely to these tasks, and on thinking about absolutely nothing else, help me with that, dearest of friends!

One could imagine that this refers to his specific work on the coming *Also sprach Zarathustra*, but it is probably more correct to see it as Nietzsche's general response to the idea of eternal recurrence and other ideas he had discovered at this time—which pushed him into a new philosophical phase. He continued to speak in a similar, but vague, manner in 1882:

> I am in Genoa! Bound here by a work that here, only here, can be completed, since it has a Genoese character—well, why should I not tell you? It is my "Dawn," planned with 10 chapters and not only 5 [Nietzsche refers to *Die fröhliche Wissenschaft*, which at first was planned as the second part of *Morgenröthe*, which consists of five books or chapters]; and very much of that which is in the first half [that is, *Dawn*], is merely the foundation and the preparation of something heavier, higher (yes! some "dreadful things" will also have to be said, dear Frau Professor! [most of these "dreadful things" would *not* be presented, or only hinted at in *Die fröhliche Wissenschaft*, but saved until later]). (Letter to Ida Overbeck, January 19, 1882)

Also in 1883 (when he wrote the first three parts of *Also sprach Zarathustra*, the third of which he finished in early 1884), he writes to Gast:

> Perhaps in the meantime I will work out something theoretical; my outlines for it now have the title *The Innocence of Becoming*: A Roadmap for the Salvation from Morality. (Letter to Gast, September 3, 1883)

The many drafts and notes for a projected work, "Philosophy of Eternal Recurrence," "Midday and Eternity," and "The Innocence of Becoming," can probably all be regarded as early versions of his *Hauptwerk*.

In early 1884, when he had finished *Also sprach Zarathustra* in three parts (he had no definite plans to continue it until late in 1884), he clearly had plans to write a greater work in which he planned to elaborate on his idea of eternal recurrence and on his critique of morality—he certainly wrote down a large number of titles for such a work in 1884 and 1885. This is hinted at in a letter to Overbeck, on February 12, 1884:

> —Ah, one should just well carry out one's task, that is the best for one. Now I have for the first time brought my main thoughts into a form—and, look here, I have probably thereby for the first time brought myself "in form." (Letter to Overbeck, February 12, 1884)[42]

The intention to write a *Hauptwerk* becomes explicit in four letters from spring 1884, in which Nietzsche speaks of *Also sprach Zarathustra* as merely an "entrance hall" to his philosophy, and that he was working on the main building. In the first of these letters, to Meysenbug, at the end of March 1884, he writes that he has finished his *Also sprach Zarathustra*[43] and thereafter calls that work "an entrance hall to my philosophy—built for me, to give me courage,"[44] and he hints that he is working on "the main building."[45]

In three further letters he refers to *Also sprach Zarathustra* as merely the "*Vorhalle*" to his philosophy, and to his strong sense of purpose and mission.[46] It seems clear that he had in mind a more philosophical (and less metaphorical) work than *Also sprach Zarathustra*, but which, in all likelihood, would elaborate on the same or similar fundamental ideas.

> If I get to Sils Maria in the summer, I mean to set about revising my *metaphysica* and epistemological views. I must now proceed step by step through a series of disciplines, for I have decided to spend the next five years on an elaboration of my "philosophy," the entrance hall of which I have built with my *Zarathustra*. (Letter to Overbeck, April 7, 1884)

A month later, he repeats the intention to work on a *Hauptwerk*, then referred to as "*Haupt-Bau*," i.e., "main building":

> Now, after that I have built for me this entrance hall to my philosophy, I will have to start again and not grow tired until the main building stands finished before me. (Letter to Meysenbug, early May 1884)

In fact, this was not only an intention, for during much of 1884 Nietzsche actually planned and worked on this *Hauptwerk* or "main building" of his philosophy.[47] At this early stage it seems most frequently to have been called "Philosophy of Eternal Recurrence" as title or subtitle, or occasionally "The Innocence of Becoming" ["Die Unschuld des Werdens"].[48] His notes, as well as numerous letters, show this:

> In the coming days I will leave from here, and since I for the next 3 months have determined to perform a revision of the most subtle things (the problems of epistemology), I ask forgiveness if I during this time remain completely silent and also do not want any letters from anyone. (Letter to Franziska, June 14, 1884)

In early autumn Nietzsche seems to confirm that he had fulfilled his plans:

> I have practically finished the main task which I set myself for this summer—the next 6 years will be for working out a scheme which I have sketched for my "philosophy." It has gone well and looks hopeful. (Letter to Gast, September 2, 1884)

It is probable that the scheme Nietzsche speaks of is the one he refers to in several notes from this time under the title "Eternal Recurrence."[49] During 1885 Nietzsche continued to plan and prepare for producing the *Hauptwerk*.

> I notice everywhere that it is over with what has so far been the case, and that I now must create, without every form of too great haste, *definitive* circumstances, which must last at least for 10 years, for the purpose of being able, with complete calm, to begin to tackle the work of my life. A surrounding which *suits* me, I mean my *work*! (Letter to Franziska, January 29, 1885)

From the autumn of 1886—after having finished *Jenseits von Gut und Böse*—Nietzsche began to refer to the projected major work explicitly as his *magnum opus*, his *Hauptwerk*, and he now had a better grasp of what it ought to contain after having drafted titles and contents in his notebooks for several years. He began to call it "The Will to Power" ["Der Wille zur Macht"] in August or September 1885, at first with a subtitle which connected it with the earlier projected titles: "Attempt at a New Interpretation of All Events" ["Versuch einer neuen Auslegung alles Geschehens"].[50] During the autumn of 1886 he then gave it the full title "The Will to Power: Attempt at a Revaluation of All Values" ["Der Wille zur Macht: Versuch einer Umwerthung aller Werthe"],[51] which it would continue to have for the next three years, and which he felt certain enough about to have it published on the back cover of *Jenseits von Gut und Böse* as a work in preparation.[52]

> For the coming 4 years the working out of a four-volume *magnum opus* [*Hauptwerk*] has been announced; already the title is enough to raise fears: "*The Will to Power*: Attempt at a Revaluation of All Values." For it I have need of *everything*, good health, solitude, good spirits, perhaps a wife. (Letter to Elisabeth and Bernhard Förster, September 2, 1886)

Nietzsche continued to work on this project during the following year, sometimes feeling that things were going well, at other times being more dejected and frustrated:

> Ah, everything in my life is so uncertain and shaky, and always this horrible ill health of mine! On the other hand, there is the hundredweight of this need pressing upon me—to create *a coherent structure of thought* during the next few years—and for this I need five or six preconditions, all of which seem to be missing now or to be unattainable. (Letter to Overbeck, March 24, 1887)

However, after having finished *Zur Genealogie der Moral*, he on the whole felt as determined and optimistic as he had done a year earlier after having finished *Jenseits von Gut und Böse*. His whole life continued to be determined by "the nowadays completely absorbing main task [*Hauptpensum*] of my life," that is, his work on the *Hauptwerk*:

> I hesitate, honestly, between Venice and—*Leipzig*: the latter for scholarly purposes, since I have in regard to the nowadays completely absorbing main task [*Hauptpensum*] of my life still much to learn, to question, to read. [. . .]—and furthermore, as you have guessed, I now need profound isolation still more urgent than to add to my knowledge or than to raise questions in regard to 5000 individual problems. For in the main thing [*Hauptsache*] things are going *well*: the *tone* of these treatises [*Zur Genealogie der Moral*] will reveal to you that I have *more* to say than what is written in them. (Letter to Gast, September 15, 1887)

During 1887 and most of 1888, Nietzsche was intensively engaged in this work on the *Hauptwerk*, which is frequently evident in his letters and notebooks. Here we can proceed to another question relating to his plans for a *Hauptwerk*.

There can be no question that when Nietzsche wrote *Götzen-Dämmerung* and *Der Antichrist* in September 1888, he planned to write a *Hauptwerk* in four volumes. He at that stage also mainly felt that his work on the *Hauptwerk* was going well and that he was on his way and close "to a great goal."[53] Also in October 1888, only two to three months before his mental collapse, Nietzsche frequently speaks of his coming *Hauptwerk* in four volumes:

> I am now the most grateful man in the world—autumnal in spirit in every good sense of that word: it is my great *harvest-time*. Everything becomes easy for me, everything goes well for me, in spite of the fact that it is unlikely that anyone before me has had such great things in their hands. That the *first* book of the *Revaluation of All Values* is finished; *ready to be printed*, I tell you with a feeling

> for which I have no words. It will become *four* books; they will be published as separate volumes. (Letter to Overbeck, October 18, 1888)[54]

When Nietzsche wrote *Ecce homo* he planned to have it published before the *Umwerthung aller Werthe*, which then still consisted of four books.

> The weather is so glorious that there is no difficulty in doing something *well*. On my birthday, I began again with something that seems to be going well and has already made considerable progress. It is called *Ecce Homo, or How One Becomes What One Is*. It concerns, with great audacity, myself and my writings. Not only did I want to present myself *before* the uncannily solitary act of the *Revaluation*—I would also just like to *test* what risks I can take with the German ideas of *freedom of speech*. My suspicion is that the *first* book of the *Revaluation* will be confiscated on the spot—legally and in all justice. With this "Ecce Homo" I want to make the *question* so intensely serious, and such an object of curiosity, that current and basically sensible ideas about what is *permissible* will here admit an exception for once. To be sure, I talk about myself with all possible psychological "cunning" and gay detachment—I do not want to present myself to people as a prophet, savage beast, or moral horror. In this sense, too, the book could be salutary—it will perhaps prevent people from confusing me with my *anti-self*. (Letter to Gast, October 30, 1888; I have slightly modified Middleton's translation.)

The last of Nietzsche's notes in which he refers to his *Hauptwerk*, and lists the titles of the three further volumes, are dated to October 1888.[55] Thereafter there exist no philosophical notes at all.[56] Furthermore, Nietzsche continued in late 1888, even in December, to feel and refer to his great sense of having a task and a mission as can be seen in several letters.[57]

It is often assumed, and Nietzsche encouraged such belief, that he read little, thought independently, and worked largely outside the cultural tradition. This is correct only in a limited sense. The truth is that Nietzsche read and even studied much, mostly philosophized in relation to the tradition and texts he read, and regarded himself as an heir to Greek thought. In particular, he read and studied intensively for the purpose of his *Hauptwerk*. For example, already in 1884, he spoke of his need "to undertake a revision of my *metaphysica* and epistemological views. I now need to get through, step by step, a whole row of disciplines,"[58] and in 1887 he emphasizes his need to read much and study for the purpose of his *Hauptwerk*.[59]

It is primarily with the aid of Nietzsche's notebooks that we can see and discuss the planned content of his *Hauptwerk*. However, already from the letters it is clear that it was planned as a four-volume work, which was meant to present and elaborate his thought in a more structured and theoretical manner than is done in any of his other books. Not only does Nietzsche refer to the planned work as a *Hauptwerk*, a "main building," "my lifework," "my main task," etc., suggesting not only that it was to be a *magnum opus* but also that it was going to be a more "complete," structured, and theoretical work than his other books. Already in 1883 he speaks of constructing something more "theoretical," thereafter he refers to his *Hauptwerk* as a "conceptio," as "*a coherent construction of thought*," "my conception as a whole," that he will perform a "working through of my 'philosophy,'" "work through a scheme, with which I have outlined my 'philosophy,'" "work through my complete system of thought," and in September 1888 he refers to its "very strict and earnest character."

It also seems clear that Nietzsche saw a close connection between his *Hauptwerk* and *Also sprach Zarathustra*. This is clearly visible in many of the letters from 1884, and in his discussions in *Ecce homo*.

In this chapter we have seen that *Ecce homo* is certainly not the only book in which Nietzsche points ahead, and in which there are references to the *Umwerthung aller Werthe*. In the next two chapters we will see how very present the *Umwerthung aller Werthe* is in *Ecce homo*, and how substantially it shaped that work.

3

Reading *Ecce Homo* as Preparatory to Nietzsche's *Revaluation of All Values*

3.1 Introduction: General Consequences and Observations

Reading *Ecce homo* as preparatory to Nietzsche's *Umwerthung aller Werthe* instead of reading it as a sort of autobiography leads to a rather different reading of the work, with different emphases that, in turn, lead to different results and conclusions. Let us start with some general observations.

Even if the view that Nietzsche changed his mind about the four-volume *Umwerthung aller Werthe* late in 1888, and that it came to nothing (i.e., only to *Der Antichrist*), discussed in chapter 4.4 below, is assumed to be correct, that happened *after* the writing of *Ecce homo*. I have found no discussion of how the incontrovertible fact that when Nietzsche wrote *Ecce homo* (as well as when he wrote *Der Antichrist*), he intended to publish a four-volume *magnum opus*, and how this affects the interpretation of *Ecce homo*. The revisions he made to *Ecce homo* after December 6, when he sent the manuscript to his publisher for the second time to have it printed and published, were minor.

Contrary to Montinari's claim that Nietzsche was finished with everything (discussed earlier in Chapter 1.3), we have no evidence that Nietzsche was aware that his work and productive life were at an end. On the contrary, our evidence points in the opposite direction. Nietzsche had been planning and working on this project for five years and in all of his later books, from *Jenseits von Gut und Böse* (1886) to *Ecce homo* (written from October 15 to mid-November, and revised in December 1888), he refers to themes he will elaborate on in the planned *Umwerthung aller Werthe*. In *Ecce homo* he also explicitly says that he has a long future ahead of him: "I look towards my future—a *distant* future" (EH, Clever, 9), and in the following section he speaks of being "destined to fulfill great tasks." One of the titles he considered for *Ecce homo*, at the age of forty-four, was also—so alien to us, who know that he collapsed immediately after having finished *Ecce homo*, that many commentators even fail to grasp its meaning—"*In media vita*"—"*In the middle of life.*" Nietzsche, during the last year and years, certainly had definite plans for the future—and these plans revolved around a revaluation of all values.

A consequence of my thesis is the realization that *Ecce homo* has perhaps been regarded as more paradoxical and self-praising than ought to have been the case. Interpreted as a "conventional" autobiography—as a text looking backward and summarizing Nietzsche's life—it is in many ways elliptic, paradoxical, absurd, and self-inflated. When interpreted as preparatory to an attempt at a revaluation of all values it becomes less so, and several of the seemingly absurd and contradictory statements are resolved or made less absurd. As summarizing his life, the self-overestimation serves no intelligible purpose at all and becomes merely irritating, disturbing, and unnecessary (and thus is often interpreted as due to his coming mental collapse), while if he was attempting to draw attention to what he regarded as an enormous event that will change our values, it is at least a little more comprehensible.

Although Nietzsche often speaks as if he was alone in revaluing values, this must not necessarily be taken at face value: he, for example, says in reference to the long period of blindness in regard to values: "The millennia [. . .] with the exception of five or six moments in history, with myself as a seventh" (EH, Destiny, 7), suggesting that at least he did not see himself as completely alone. He certainly assumes that at least once before a revaluation (in the opposite direction) has occurred, and this he attributes to different persons. Sometimes he speaks as if each of them alone was responsible; apart from the Jews and early Christianity, this includes the individuals Jesus, St. Paul, Socrates, and Plato. A second and reverse revaluation (in relation to the first one) has also been almost successfully performed once before, during the Renaissance ("my question is its question," *Der Antichrist*, 61) implying a number of persons contributing to the revaluation at that time. It is perhaps sufficient to assume that Nietzsche contributed in some important way to the questioning and examining of our values (and many would agree that this view is reasonable) for him to write *Ecce homo*, and to attempt to answer "how was this possible for me."

The question of how reliable *Ecce homo* is as an autobiography, discussed or remarked upon by large numbers of commentators, changes when we realize that *Ecce homo* is not a summation of his life, but written with a very specific forward-looking purpose in mind. In this case, it is obvious that he, for example, is going to be much more selective in both the amount and the nature of the information that he gives.

Ecce homo contains much humor, and a lot of word-, concept- and thought-play.[1] This too is easier to recognize when we read *Ecce homo* in its correct forward-looking perspective, but I will not regard it as necessary to point that out in this study. However, let me point out one example of how Nietzsche's humor has been missed, and, instead, misinterpreted as mental instability. One biographer writes:

> Nietzsche was also tending to confuse mental events with external events. Writing to Meta von Salis [November 14, 1888] he said: "Considering what I have written between 3 September and 4 November [i.e., *Der Antichrist* and *Ecce homo*], I fear there may soon be a small earthquake . . . two years ago, when I was in Nice, it happened, appropriately, there. Indeed, yesterday's report from the observatory mentioned a slight tremor." [. . .] He was becoming more solipsistic: cosmic and meteorological imagery reflect the tendency to think of himself as a world.[2]

What Nietzsche writes here is humor, not solipsism! Not only is it witty and obviously meant to be funny (and in Nietzsche's letter the quoted text about "a slight tremor" yesterday actually ends with an ellipsis (not included in Hayman's quotation), which here is surely equivalent to a smiley). It is also in line with Nietzsche's general sense of humor and with the letter itself, which begins: "as I continue to suffer from a small overdose of good humour and other happy symptoms, I hope you will forgive me for a completely meaningless letter." This is also understood by Meta von Salis, as shown by her response dated November 26, 1888. However, I do not wish to deny that one can find many examples where Nietzsche's degree of self-importance has become excessive, perhaps pathological, in his letters from late 1888.

There are far more frequent references to the planned *Umwerthung aller Werthe* than are explicit in the text of *Ecce homo* or that have been recognized in the conventional backward-looking interpretations. When Nietzsche speaks of the *Antichrist* or Christianity more generally, it is usually a reference to the first volume of the coming *Umwerthung aller Werthe* already written. References to philosophy and truth are frequently allusions to the planned second volume. Discussions of morality and moral good persons to the third volume. References to Dionysos and to the Noon-Day, as well as to eternal recurrence and tragedy, are often allusions to the fourth volume.[3]

To make the relation between *Ecce homo* and the planned *Umwerthung aller Werthe* more distinct, let us briefly look at Nietzsche's plans for the contents of these four volumes in 1888. Nietzsche had, as stated earlier, had plans for such a four-volume *magnum opus* since 1884, and had written a large number of notes and preliminary tables of contents for it. When Nietzsche in September 1888 wrote *Der Antichrist* as the first volume, this meant that he then decided to move all the material relating to religion and Christianity into the first book (which earlier had been distributed into several of the volumes), and this, of course, also affected the contents of the other books. For the period after this, we possess six or seven listings of the planned names of the volumes of the *Umwerthung aller Werthe*[4]—and these are all consistent with one another,[5] but they are less detailed than many of the earlier ones; in particular, they contain no listing of chapter titles. However, using the consistent divisions into four books after that *Der Antichrist* was decided upon, we can go back to the more detailed tables of contents from earlier in 1888 and classify these chapter titles according to these new book divisions. It turns out that this is relatively straightforward, using the three most detailed chapter divisions.[6] This information is presented in Table 3.1, and gives us a reasonably detailed view of Nietzsche's plans for the three remaining volumes of the *Umwerthung aller Werthe*.

It is important to realize that *Ecce homo* was written teleologically, not chronologically; that is, it was written with a goal, and that goal was the revaluation of all values and the main theme is Nietzsche's development to reach the capacity to revalue values. The whole text is written from this perspective. It determines the text, not only the first two chapters, but equally much his reviews of his books, and even more the last chapter. He selects and gives the biographical information which support and confirm this story. The main story of the first two chapters is Nietzsche's development toward what he had become at the end of 1888, someone able to revalue values. In the review of his *Unzeitgemäße Betrachtungen* he expresses it thus: "It is my kind of cleverness to have been many things and in many places, so as to be able to become one thing—to be able to come to one thing" (EH, Books, "The Untimelies," 3), that is, to be able to revalue values. At the end of "Why I Am So Clever" he expresses it as follows:

> For the task of *revaluing values* more capacities were perhaps necessary than have ever dwelt together in one individual, above all contradictory capacities [. . .] an immense multiplicity which is nevertheless the opposite of chaos—this was the precondition, the long, secret labour and artistry of my instinct. Its *higher concern* was so pronounced that I never even suspected what was growing within me—that all my abilities would one day suddenly *spring forth* ripe, in their ultimate perfection. (EH, Clever, 9)

On several occasions one discovers new aspects when reading *Ecce homo* as being forward-pointing. I will, for example, show, in the chapter where he reviews his books, that on at least three occasions, when it generally has been assumed that

Table 3.1 Chapter Titles for *Umwerthung aller Werthe* from Earlier in 1888, Here Classified according to the Six Book Divisions from September to November 1888

Umwerthung aller Werthe Sept.-Nov. 1888	**Table of contents from early 1888**	**Table of contents from May or June of 1888**	**Table of contents from August 26, 1888**
	KSA 13, 12[2]	KSA 13, 16[51]	KSA 13, 18[17]
Book 1 of *Umwerthung aller Werthe*	…………………………………	…………………………………	…………………………………
The Anti-Christ: Attempt at a Critique of Christianity			
	Critique of the Christian ideals	The *religious* man as a typical *décadent*	The homines religiosi
		The pagan in religion	Thoughts about Christianity
Book 2 of *Umwerthung aller Werthe*	……………………………	……………………………	……………………………
The Free Spirit: Critique of Philosophy as a Nihilistic Movement			
To prove that the nihilistic way of thinking is the result of the belief in morality and priest-values. KSA 13, 22[3]	*Nihilism, considered to its final conclusion*	The true and the apparent world	The psychology of errors
	The "will to truth"	The philosopher as a typical *décadent*	The value of truth and error
	Psychology of the "will to power" (pleasure, will, concept etc.)	Science against philosophy	The will to truth
	Culture, Civilization, the ambiguity of "the modern"	*Nihilism* [and its *opposite*]	The metaphysicians
			To the history of European nihilism

Continued

Table 3.1 Continued

Umwerthung aller Werthe Sept.-Nov. 1888	Table of contents from early 1888	Table of contents from May or June of 1888	Table of contents from August 26, 1888
Book 3 of *Umwerthung aller Werthe*	....	....	....
The Immoralist: Critique of Morality as the Most Dangerous Kind of Lack of Knowledge			
Morality, in regard to its origin, its methods, its purpose: the most immoral fact of history . . . its self-contradiction, since to be able to hold its values it must practice the opposite values (22[3]).	*The origin of ideals* *How virtue becomes victorious* *Herd instincts* *Morality as the Circe of the philosophers*	The *good* human being as a typical *décadent*	The good and the improvers
Book 4 of *Umwerthung aller Werthe*	....	....	....
Dionysos: The Philosophy of Eternal Recurrence			
Eternal recurrence	*Life-prescriptions for us*	The will to power as life: Peak of the historical *self-consciousness*	*The principle of life: "Order of rank"*
The type of the lawgiver	*The "eternal recurrence"* *The great politics*	The will to power: as discipline	*The two ways* *The eternal recurrence*

he speaks of his previously published books, he is actually discussing his planned coming *Umwerthung aller Werthe.*

Another important consequence concerns less the *Ecce homo* text directly, but the status and relevance of Nietzsche's late notes. If one assumes that Nietzsche gave up on the project of the *Umwerthung aller Werthe* and was "finished with everything," the notes may perhaps be treated mainly as discarded material, while if one views *Ecce homo* as forward-looking and that for many years he had been working on and been writing notes for this four-volume project, the later notes remain of much interest and value, since they are then likely to contain much thought and material for this project, even if it was never finalized.[7]

Finally, a number of Nietzsche's statements that appear confusing, self-contradictory, senseless, or incomprehensible, become, when we take the true purpose of *Ecce homo* into account—preparing for the revaluation of all values and his *Umwerthung aller Werthe*—much more comprehensible. I will in the following section emphasize several such cases.

Ecce homo consists of four chapters, all with provocative titles (the book is summarized in the appendix, and the table of contents is also given there). The first two, "Why I Am So Wise" and "Why I Am So Clever,"[8] present him and his development (or, rather, a somewhat idealized picture of himself and his development) to what he is now, as someone who can revalue values. The third chapter, "Why I Write Such Good Books," contains first a discussion of why he has so far been misunderstood (his experiences have been too unique) and thereafter he discusses or reviews all his books from the perspective of his present preoccupations, and especially the revaluation project. The final chapter, "Why I Am a Destiny," is clearly forward-looking and gives important information about Nietzsche's plans for his *Umwerthung aller Werthe* and is surely meant to raise interest in that planned future work.

3.2 Title and Subtitle

Titles and subtitles are necessarily brief and thus subject, perhaps, to all too free interpretations. However, there may here be place for a short interpretative comment, even if not obviously related to whether *Ecce homo* is regarded as backward- or forward-looking. *Ecce homo*, Pilatus' words when Christ was shown to the mob, meaning "behold the man," has in the Christian tradition become "behold the man who is more than man, the son of God." It will probably always retain a touch of that religious meaning. However, Nietzsche, educated as a philologist, seems to have used it primarily in the original sense of the words, "behold the man" or "see me," as he did in 1882 when he named poem sixty-two about himself in *Die fröhliche Wissenschaft* with these words, with no obvious allusion to Christ or Christianity.[9]

Nietzsche's main point with the title, it seems to me, was "see the man" and in particular "see me,"[10] which is also a leitmotif in the whole work with recurring phrases such as "have I been understood" and "do not confuse me with someone else." See me, so that you can see what I am doing—see me so that you can understand what I am doing, and why I am able to do it—revaluating values. Secondly, it is often assumed that Nietzsche selected the title in a blasphemous sense, but although he severely criticizes Christianity in the book (and he shows a disturbingly high degree of self-importance), his point seems to me to be to show that he is just a man (albeit an important one), with his insistence on the small human things and physiology, while showing distain for the "godlike" things (idealism, religion, morality).

The subtitle, "How to Become What You Are," is a variant of a phrase of Pindar, which Nietzsche was fond of throughout his life, and used in many slightly different versions. Often its logical paradoxical nature is discussed and emphasized, but considering the content of *Ecce homo*, its meaning seems much more straightforward to me (the way Machiavelli's *The Prince* is different from other medieval and Renaissance texts)—in its "realism," in its psychological and moral realism—to become what one (potentially) is, one needs to avoid non-questions (morality, religion, idealism) and false living (bad "physiology") and, instead, trust (even affirm) fate, one's own questions, and select the correct living conditions. The primary meaning of the title and subtitle then becomes: "See me (as I am) and how I have become what I am *today*—someone able to revalue values." This foreshadows and echoes the main story of *Ecce homo*: that it is written from the perspective of "today," that is, from the end of 1888, and Nietzsche's concern with *Umwerthung aller Werthe.*

The title and subtitle contain another ambivalence, but which is unlikely to have troubled Nietzsche, who probably meant to include both senses: How much does it refer to Nietzsche himself (i.e., "I") and how much to others, or generally (i.e., "you" or "one"), the latter, which is what is literally referred to in the title and subtitle? "See yourself (as you are): How to become what you (potentially) are"—with the same emphasis on the avoidance of non-questions (morality, religion, idealism) and false living (bad "physiology"). This second aspect also connects with Nietzsche's existentialism and with the end of the foreword, "find yourselves."

3.3 Foreword and Prologue

The overriding purpose of the foreword is simply and explicitly stated in its first sentence: "In view of the fact that I will shortly have to confront humanity with the heaviest demand ever made of it, it seems to me essential to say *who I am*." That this "heaviest demand" refers to Nietzsche's revaluation of values is obvious from the text of *Ecce homo* (see, for example, the first section of the first chapter and the penultimate section of the second chapter), as well as from letters referring to this work, as shown in the first two chapters of this study. Thereafter he briefly presents himself, says what he is, for example, "a disciple of the philosopher Dionysos" and what he is not, for example, "no bogeyman, no moral monster," and emphasizes his *Also sprach Zarathustra* (which he in several letters had referred to as an entrance hall to the *Umwerthung aller Werthe*).

Even in the brief prologue, "On this perfect day"—reflecting the beginning of Nietzsche's writing *Ecce homo* on this forty-fourth birthday—he states (unlike almost every commentator who treats the book as a retrospective task): "I looked backwards, I looked ahead, I never saw so much and such good things all at once." Obviously, he is referring to *both* past and future. The last sentence "And so I tell myself my life" certainly suggests an autobiography, but taking the previous quoted line about looking both backward and ahead, and the first sentence of the preface, it is obvious that it is a special sort of autobiography, in which the future (that will never come, or come true only partially, due to Nietzsche's collapse) plays a pivotal role.

When Nietzsche in the second sentence of the foreword says "People ought really to know already [who I am]: for I have not failed to 'bear witness' to myself," this can perhaps appear to refer to all of his earlier books (as he will suggest in his reviews of them in what follows), but is probably a more specific reference to the five prefaces he wrote and added to the new editions of his books in 1886 and 1887. In these prefaces Nietzsche discusses not only these works, but also his life, and taken together they are, in fact, rather similar to *Ecce homo*. Together, these new prefaces actually contain more biographical information, and generally they are somewhat more reliable than *Ecce homo* in regard to the biographical information. Although in these prefaces also the project of the *Umwerthung aller Werthe* played a significant role, it is, nonetheless, a much less determining factor than it was for *Ecce homo*. In fact, it is the strong focus on the *Umwerthung aller Werthe* in *Ecce homo* that makes it different from these prefaces and explains why he wrote the book.

In the second section Nietzsche sets up a dichotomy between satyr and saint, a dichotomy that exemplifies his revaluation and which runs as a red thread throughout *Ecce homo* (and the later Nietzsche's writings). The satyr, with his buffoonery and sensuality, stands for a life-affirming attitude and relation to life, while the saint stands for the opposite.[11] Nietzsche even goes so far as to say that the cheerful expression of this contrast "perhaps that was the only point of this work." In a letter to Ferdinand Avenarius, dated December 10, 1888, he expresses it perhaps even more succinctly:

> During these years, when an enormous task, the *revaluation of all values*, weights me down, and I, literally, have to carry the destiny of mankind, it belongs to my proof of power to be clown, *satyr*, or, if you prefer, "essayist" ["*Feuilletonist*"]—to be *able to be* it to the degree I was in "The Case of Wagner." That the most profound spirit also must be the most frivolous, that is almost the formula for my philosophy.

Nietzsche's reference to himself as a satyr, clown, and buffoon probably also serves as a warning to the reader: not to take everything too earnestly and as objectively true, connecting it with the existential ending of the foreword ("find yourselves"). When Nietzsche in this section says that he sets up no new ideals, this does not mean that he does not suggest new values (even if the reader is meant to use her/his own judgment), but primarily that the present ideals have been false and what Nietzsche sees himself doing is primarily criticizing these, to make room for a return to an earlier, healthier, and more natural state before and without such false ideals (idols). This will be discussed further in the last chapter.

In this second section Nietzsche also briefly summarizes a large number of themes that he had discussed or touched upon in *Götzen-Dämmerung*: his claim to the toppling of idols (ideals);[12] his critique of a metaphysical double worldview, created for the purpose of denigrating the world, arguing instead for the need to see and affirm reality; a critique of those who claim to 'improve' mankind; the need for cheerfulness; Dionysos; the importance of the future; the need for a revaluation of all values; and his concrete project of the *Umwerthung aller Werthe*.

In the third section Nietzsche refers to that which has been hidden and forbidden ("everything that has hitherto been excluded by morality") and says that his philosophy will triumph under the sign: "we strive for what is forbidden." This too is a reference to Nietzsche's project of a revaluation of all values, and can probably be regarded as a hint that the "new" revalued values are not necessarily completely new, but have existed yet been hidden and forbidden for two millennia. The themes of honesty, and of courage, of accepting and daring to see *reality* as it is, are also strongly emphasized, as they will be throughout the book.

In the fourth section Nietzsche continues to stress that he is different from moralists and founders of religions. He needs to state this, for he shares one important similarity with them —that of being concerned with values. What truly changes our relation to the world is not politics or war, but *values*—and he both quotes from *Also sprach Zarathustra* that "thoughts that come on dove's feet direct the world" (not the noisy affairs people usually assume) and ends with the existentialist claim that the reader needs to find himself/herself rather than following Zarathustra or Nietzsche.

(Nietzsche here and elsewhere in *Ecce homo* gives enormous importance and praise to *Also sprach Zarathustra*. The reason for this will be discussed in Chapter 5.)

3.4 The First Two Chapters: Why Nietzsche Was So Wise and So Sagacious

The first two chapters are closely related to one another, and in them Nietzsche presents himself and his psychology, and discusses how he has become the one he is today. The first chapter gives the causes of why he is so wise—he is more multifarious—and the second discusses how to flourish (and what he has done to flourish). However, the purpose of the first two chapters is only in part to present Nietzsche—and that is why the biographical information is so limited and disjointed. This is not primarily due to confusion in Nietzsche's mental state but a consequence of his attempts to—and his success in—answering one specific question: How is he able to revalue values when no one else seems to be even aware of the problem? It follows that we are not given a complete biographical survey—what Nietzsche offers is only a selection (somewhat idealized) of his life relevant for answering that question. This realization also explains the provocative chapter titles—they are actually relating to the same question: "Why I Am So Wise" and "Why I Am So Clever" (that I can revalue values)? In the first sentence of the second chapter he expresses it perhaps still more clearly: "—Why do I know a thing or two *more*?"[13] —again in the sense of "why does he know a little more?" so that he can revalue values. The answer he gives in the first chapter, in brief, is that he is more multifarious[14] than others: specifically, Nietzsche has experience of both decadence and anti-decadence—of both being ill and being healthy—of having experienced values and the world from both below and above. He claims to be free from reactive feelings such as resentment, revenge, and guilt (but nonetheless knows them), but to possess the more active aggressive pathos and also intellectual cleanliness.

In the second chapter, concerning how to reach one's maximum, he claims not to have wasted himself on non-questions (such as idealism, religion, and moralism) and, instead, emphasized the real "small things" such as nutrition, place, climate, physical activity, the importance of selecting good reading and music, and possessing egoism and style. This emphasis on his being more multifarious than others and on physiology makes Nietzsche's text according to his own measure more true and honest than that of others (in spite of its ideal and exemplary nature). These two chapters culminate in Nietzsche's development to being able to revalue values: "Seen from this angle my life is simply miraculous. For the task of *revaluing values* more capacities were perhaps necessary than have ever dwelt together in one individual, above all contradictory capacities [. . .] that all my abilities would one day suddenly *spring forth* ripe, in their ultimate perfection" (EH, Clever, 9). We can note that Nietzsche says that all of his abilities for revaluating values arrived *suddenly*, and it is suggested that this occurred recently.[15] This would contradict his discussion of his books, where he emphasizes the presence of revaluation in almost all of them, unless we assume, as is reasonable, that Nietzsche with full awareness reinterprets them and points at those aspects of the books which are now of greatest interest to him. The chapter thereafter ends with making explicit the theme of *amor fati*, which unites past, present, and future in affirmation, and which echoes throughout the text.

Having established why and how he is different, and that he has finally arrived at the point of being able to fulfill his potentiality and revalue values, he goes on to discuss all of his books from this perspective.

Before we turn to the next chapter and Nietzsche's discussions of his books, let us more broadly discuss some of the general themes touched upon in these two chapters, and thereafter list and classify some of the "revaluations" that are mentioned or hinted at in them.

Nietzsche begins the book and this first chapter, where he gives an idealized description of himself and his psychology, conventionally by briefly mentioning his parents and claims that "this twofold provenance" has formed his life—making him both decadent and anti-decadent (words he always uses in French). With decadence and anti-decadence Nietzsche refers to the experience and the ability to view events and values both from a feeling of being above and of strength, and from a feeling of being below and one of weakness. This has given him a multifarious experience and knowledge of values. He mentions two of his three main health problems, migraines, eye problems, and stomach troubles, but instead of complaining he states that his illnesses have helped him form his philosophy and increased his understanding of values and the world. In this section, as well as in the whole chapter and book, Nietzsche thus expresses gratefulness to his illness, and he treats the different health troubles as consequences or symptoms rather than as being fundamentally causal. He also treats his books as reflecting his state of health (which is something that he also does to others, and then is often regarded as highly provocative). The first section of the chapter ends by stating what can be regarded as the purpose of the whole first chapter:

> Do I need say, after all that, that in questions of *décadence* I am *experienced?* [. . .] Looking from the perspective of the sick towards *healthier* concepts and values, and conversely looking down from the fullness and self-assuredness of *rich* life into the secret workings of the *décadence* instinct—this is what I have practiced the longest, this was my true experience; if I became master of anything then it was this. I have my hand in now, I am handy at *inverting perspectives*: the foremost reason why for me alone perhaps a "revaluation of values" is even possible.

There are two versions of the third section, one earlier version and one added very late (the first one is from October and the later one exchanged for the earlier one in late December or early January). Each continues the theme from the first section with more about his parents and their families, and in both he incorrectly claims to be of Polish nobility (but it may well be the case that the Nietzsche family and Nietzsche genuinely believed this). However, neither of these versions add much of substance, and the latter version (now generally regarded as the final text) contains many obvious signs of mental instability. For example, contrary to the truth and to some of the other contents in the section, he incorrectly claims not to possess a drop of German blood, he speaks of "my divinity," he criticizes his mother and sister without inhibition, he claims that one is least related to one's parents (in contradiction to his discussion of them and their relevance for his own personality in the first section), states that Caesar or Alexander the Great could be his father, and claims that the postman just brought him a Dionysos head.[16] As I argue in Chapters 1.4 and 1.5, we need to take both these versions into account, but I would argue that the very late and partly "mad" version should be treated as less genuine in regard to Nietzsche's intentions for the book.

In most of the rest of the chapter he gives a somewhat idealized description of his psychology, as lacking resentment, and also other reactive feelings like revenge and even a belief in "free will." At the end of the second chapter he presents *amor fati* as the healthy counterposition to belief in "free will" and other reactive feelings. Instead, he claims to possess the much more *active* aggressive pathos. We can note that the distinction between the active and the passive had been strongly emphasized in his book from the previous year, *Zur Genealogie der Moral*, and it will be a theme throughout *Ecce homo*. He also claims that an instinct for cleanliness and extreme honesty are part of his psychology, and, of course, important for a revaluation of values. He ends the chapter by quoting from *Also sprach Zarathustra* how Zarathustra has overcome the disgust at these life-denying times and persons.

Nietzsche had already in the first chapter explained the causes of and reasons why he is able to revalue values—he is more multifarious than others. He seems to regard the causes of this as basically beyond being affected or manipulated, as being part of his fate or "nature," that which he in *Jenseits von Gut und Böse*, 230, called "that eternal basic text *homo natura*." He discusses this further in the same work, and foreshadows important aspects of *Ecce homo*:

> Learning transforms us, it does that which all nourishment does which does not merely "preserve"—as the physiologist knows. But at the bottom of us, "right down deep," there is, to be sure, something unteachable, a granite stratum of spiritual fate, of predetermined decision and answer to predetermined selected questions. [. . .] "convictions." Later—one sees them only as footsteps to self-knowledge, signposts to the problem which we *are*—more correctly, to the great stupidity which we are, to our spiritual fate, to the *unteachable* "right down deep." (*Jenseits von Gut und Böse*, 231)

Among the "necessary" things (those that Nietzsche could not affect) mentioned or discussed in the first chapter are birth, family, nationality, ancestors, and Nietzsche's propensity to physical maladies. In the second chapter he will discuss how one flourishes with what one has, that is, how one oneself can affect one's development (especially for those who feel that they have a great purpose). Nietzsche begins the second chapter, "Why I Am So Clever," by asking why he knows a thing or two *more*, why he is so clever (or so sagacious)—that he is able to revalue values (although this latter part is not stated explicitly). The answer he gives in this second chapter in its simplest form is that he has not wasted himself on unreal questions (religion, morality, and idealism) but, instead, emphasized the real "physiological" causes. The first section mentions a large number of such useless themes, especially those relating to religion, but to idealism as well. Instead, he emphasizes the more real and physiological questions—which his illnesses forced him to realize—of nutrition, place, climate, and choice of relaxation (reading and music). He draws some odd and other perhaps more likely conclusions from taking these aspects seriously. Often it is difficult to know whether he says it tongue in cheek or really is as serious and extreme in his conclusions as he seems to be. However, most of the things he mentions, he actually attempted to live by (see the letters quoted later). We should also be aware of the fact that Nietzsche's illnesses made him much more sensitive, at least to climate and food, than are most people.

When he in the second section speaks of "the *task* of my life," this is a reference to his project of revaluation, as can be seen not only from his treatment of the revaluation in *Ecce homo*, but also from a large number of letters in which he refers to this project as his "*task*" (discussed in the previous chapter, 2.4).

In sections 3 and 4 (as well as in the latter part of section 8), he discusses his reading, and in sections 5 to 7 (of which 6 and 7 were added to the manuscript in the middle of December), his relation to Wagner and music. Let us stop and examine what he says about his reading, and what consequences this has for our understanding of *Ecce homo* and Nietzsche.

Throughout *Ecce homo* one can easily get the impression that Nietzsche, and especially the later Nietzsche, read little. He criticizes reading as insufficiently life-affirming and Dionysian: "Early in the morning at the break of day, in all the freshness and dawn of one's strength, to read a *book*—I call that vicious!" (EH, Clever, 8). He also criticizes reading for making one reactive and forcing one to be concerned with the thoughts of others rather than with one's own:

> My eyes alone put an end to all bookwormishness, in plain terms philology: I was redeemed from the "book," for years I read nothing—the *greatest* favor I have ever done myself!—That deepest self, as it were buried and grown silent under a constant *compulsion to listen* to other selves (—and that is what reading means!) awoke slowly, timidly, doubtfully—but at length *it spoke again*. (EH, "Human, All Too Human," 4)[17]

This impression is strengthened by the fact that he mentions very few contemporary and minor authors and titles in his books. He also explicitly claims that he read little: "It does not perhaps lie in my nature to read much or many kinds of things: a reading room makes me ill. [. . .] Caution, even toward new books is rather part of my instinct" (EH, Clever, 3).[18] Concretely, he claims in *Ecce homo* that he could go months between reading books.

However, Nietzsche's claims are to a large extent false. He was, in fact, a rather substantial reader. This is true not only of his younger days but of his entire life, including even his last active years before his mental collapse in January 1889.

Nietzsche's own words about his reading are thus not to be fully trusted. He seems to have wanted to appear more Dionysian and original than he actually was. Contrary to his claim that a reading room makes him ill, he in fact praised Turin for its good libraries and he wrote to his sister: "one cannot even with ten horses draw me to a place where, if I am correctly informed, not even a good library is to be found."[19] Libraries were important for his reading and the quality of the libraries was an important determining factor in deciding his travels and places of residence. He even occasionally wrote to libraries to enquire if they were suitable for his purposes before deciding to visit a town.[20] During his last four active years he used at least the libraries in Nice, Leipzig, Chur, Venice, and Turin, and the Hotel Alpenrosen's library in Sils-Maria. He probably also used the library in Zürich and possibly in other towns, and he planned to visit Stuttgart for the sake of its library. Meta von Salis, who knew Nietzsche personally in the second half of the 1880s, claimed that he was an avid reader: "Nietzsche had 'le flair du livre' and read much in spite of his problem with the eyes."[21]

His claim not to have held a book in his hands for half a year (since Brochard) is far from true, even if we interpret "catch myself with a book in my hand" as meaning that he had read all or most of the book. We have evidence that he read at least eight books during this half year: Jacolliot, Spitteler, Stendhal, Nohl, Goncourts, Brandes, Féré, and Hehn.[22] There is, further, strong reason to assume that he read more than that, especially fiction, but we have no definite evidence of that.

After claiming that he read little, Nietzsche states: "I take flight almost always to the same books, really a small number, those books which have *proved* themselves precisely to me" (EH, Clever, 3). He goes on to identify the books: "It is really a small number of older Frenchmen to whom I return again and again," and he mentions Montaigne, Molière, Corneille, and Racine.[23] He then lists more recent French writers: Paul Bourget, Pierre Loti, Gyp, Meilhac, Anatole France, Jules Lemaitre, and Guy de Maupassant. He also names Taine, Stendhal, and Prosper Mérimée. In the next section, he mentions Heinrich Heine, Byron's *Manfred* and Shakespeare. This listing is not particularly informative or reliable. For example, no ancient authors are mentioned in spite of their importance to him, which can be seen in his claim that the "Graeco-Roman splendor, which was also a splendor of books [. . .] some books for whose possession one would nowadays exchange half of some national literatures."[24] A major reason for this is that Nietzsche moved the section dealing with antiquity—"What I Owe to the Ancients"—from the earliest version of *Ecce homo* to *Götzen-Dämmerung*. Another reason that it is uninformative is that the listing seems mainly to refer to fiction—reading as recreation and "mere literature." More scholarly and philosophical books are missing—and Nietzsche read a considerable number of such books, returning frequently to some of them, such as Lange, Spir, Rée, Schopenhauer, and Emerson. As a consequence, there is only a weak correlation between this list and a listing of the writers to whom Nietzsche most often, and most approvingly, referred in his published works, such as Goethe, Homer, Shakespeare, Voltaire, Sophocles, Aeschylus, Lessing, Heraclitus, Horace, Byron, and Montaigne.[25]

Surprisingly and interestingly, the first version of this text, exchanged for the text which now is regarded as belonging to *Ecce homo* in early December, is rather different and a little more informative.[26] It listed Montaigne, Stendhal, Emerson, Sterne (*Tristram Shandy*), Lichtenberg, Galiani, and Petronius. This listing, too, fails to mention many incontrovertible figures. The fact that only two names occur in both lists should make us a bit skeptical as to their reliability. In fact, an examination of Nietzsche's reading generally confirms that he often reread books, but it also shows that he read much more often—and at least to some extent more widely—than he suggests.[27]

Another reason for why this account of his reading is unreliable is that he suggests that he reads only as relaxation: "In my case all *reading* is a relaxation: hence it is one of those things that release me from myself, that let me stroll among alien sciences and souls—that I stop taking seriously. For reading is a release from *my* seriousness. When I am deep in work there are no books to be seen around me" (EH, Clever, 3). However, his claim is not fully correct and it ignores the more work-oriented reading—reading as a source of knowledge and information, inspiration and stimuli—which he, in fact, did (much of which is clearly visible in his notes and in all of his books, if one looks carefully). For example, *Beyond Good and Evil* (1886) contains more than 107 different names of persons, most of them authors whom he had read. *On the Genealogy of Morals* (1887) is to a large extent a response to Nietzsche's reading of, and about, "English psychologists," especially including Paul Rée, but to his reading of anthropology, cultural history and the history of law as well (his library contains ten books within this field and the majority of these he read carefully and annotated). *Twilight of the Idols* (1888), which Nietzsche called "my philosophy in a nutshell," contains two main parts. The first is a sort of selection of extracts from Nietzsche's philosophical notes, and the second (with chapters entitled "The 'Improvers' of Mankind," "Expeditions of an Untimely Man," and "What I Owe to the Ancients") is essentially a discussion of Nietzsche's reading. *Der Antichrist* (written shortly before *Ecce homo*) would have been a very different book had he not read Jacolliot, Strauss, Renan, Wellhausen, Tolstoy, Dostoyevsky, and many books about Buddhism, Christianity, St. Paul and Luther, as well as the Bible, shortly before and while writing it.

What we have seen from Nietzsche's account of his reading is that it contains much truth, but also that it is very far from giving the whole truth. Those who read *Ecce homo* as an autobiography and have accepted his statements as more or less the whole truth have gotten a very false view of Nietzsche as a reader.[28] What he does here—as elsewhere in *Ecce homo*—is to describe his view of how one should, and how he ideally would, read and relate to books as relaxation.

Sections 5 to 7 discuss the importance of music as relaxation and express Nietzsche's profound gratitude to Wagner as man and as artist, but at the same time voice a severe critique of him. It is here that we encounter Nietzsche's views and experiences of how personal relations (friendships) relate to how one can reach one's maximum. He describes Wagner as a decadent artist, and that it was only because Nietzsche himself also was decadent in the 1870s that he could appreciate, even need, the "hashish" which Wagnerian art constitutes. We can note that Nietzsche's earlier version of this text in *Ecce homo* emphasized the critique of Wagner still more.[29] All three of these sections are also strongly colored by harsh critiques of Germany (and Germans), while contrasting it with France and Paris, a city for which Nietzsche expresses great admiration as a cultural center, although he had never visited it.

In section 8 Nietzsche continues his critique of selflessness and reactive feelings from the first chapter. It is a sort of self-preservation and wisdom [*Klokheit*] to react as little and as rarely as possible. This is taste. It prevents one from becoming a mere reagent. One must learn to think out of oneself—not merely in reaction to reading or in response to others. This emphasis on the importance to actively think and create out of oneself is another theme that runs throughout the book. To mention just a few of the times it comes to surface: it is one of the things Dionysos represents, "the great poet creates only by drawing on his own reality" (EH, Clever, 4), and how Nietzsche because of his illness was forced to listen to himself, which he mentions on many occasions, for example: "That deepest self, as it were buried and grown silent under a constant *compulsion to listen* to other selves (—and that is what reading means!) awoke slowly, timidly, doubtfully—but at length *it spoke again*" (EH, "Human, All Too Human," 4).

In section 9 Nietzsche summarizes "*how to become what you are*," which has been the theme of these two chapters—at least for those who, like Nietzsche, feel that they have an important and difficult task or purpose. They must accept and use their egoism. The other theme of this section is anti-Socratic—not emphasizing the importance of knowing oneself and one's task—that would lead to dejection. Instead, one needs to trust fate. In the first third of the section Nietzsche has spoken generally; in the second third he speaks of himself—and that this difficult task for him is his work on the revaluation of values:

> For the task of *revaluing values* more capacities were perhaps necessary than have ever dwelt together in one individual, above all contradictory capacities [. . .] an immense multiplicity which is nevertheless the opposite of chaos—this was the precondition, the long, secret labour and artistry of my instinct. Its *higher concern* was so pronounced that I never even suspected what was growing within me that all my abilities would one day suddenly *spring forth* ripe, in their ultimate perfection. (EH, Clever, 9)

In the last third, he gives two biographical examples of how fate has led him on his way without his desiring it—becoming a classical philologist and becoming a professor.

When he proofread and revised the manuscript in early December, Nietzsche added a final tenth section which again summarizes this chapter, but in a different way. He again states that he (with his revaluation of all values) is "destined to fulfil great tasks" in the future —"an unprecedented overturning and rebuilding" and that he carries "a sense of responsibility for all the millennia after me." He exemplifies his revaluation and the dichotomy of values it presumes (healthy and unhealthy values) in three different ways:

1. The "petty" things discussed in this chapter are more important than the things considered important hitherto: "This is precisely where one must start *relearning*. What humanity has hitherto deemed important are not even realities, but merely illusions, more strictly speaking *lies* born of the bad instincts of sick natures that are in the most profound sense harmful."
2. The wrong sort of persons have been regarded as great, and thus we have had the wrong sort of individuals as exemplars. Nietzsche argues that he himself would suit much better as being regarded as great.
3. A third dichotomy which goes through this whole chapter, and the whole book, mentioned earlier, is that between being active and being reactive.

When he in this section speaks of having a great task and responsibility, he also continues a theme from the foreword and the first chapter (being a satyr and buffoon) by stating, "I know of no other way of dealing with great tasks than by *playing*: as a sign of greatness this is an important precondition."

In the course of this last tenth section, Nietzsche makes some claims about himself that cannot be regarded as correct. He, for example, states: "*Suffering* from solitude is an objection, too—I have only ever suffered from 'multitude,'" while, in fact, his suffering of loneliness is a frequent theme in his letters. He also claims that there is "not a jot of arrogance, of secret contempt" in him, but in the sixth section of the last chapter he claims that "*Disgust* at man is my danger," and elsewhere makes several similar statements.

He ends the chapter by proclaiming *amor fati* (love fate, or love your fate), his total affirmation and his antidote to reactive feelings and a twin concept to eternal recurrence (the idea of affirming your life so much that you are willing to relive it again and again in identically the same way)—which was planned to constitute the pinnacle of the *Umwerthung aller Werthe*: "My formula for human greatness is *amor fati*: not wanting anything to be different, not forwards, not backwards, not for all eternity" (EH, Clever, 10).[30]

Ecce homo gives a very stylized, idealized, and exemplary image of Nietzsche and his psychology. In this sense, *Ecce homo* is both reliable (giving an accurate picture of what he regards as a healthy psychology) and non-reliable (as a definite description of his own actual life and psychology).[31] This is perhaps an inevitable consequence of the twofold purpose of these chapters: both to give a picture of Nietzsche (from the revaluation perspective) and to more generally discuss how one becomes what one is or can be. There is an irreconcilable tension between these two purposes. For us to get a better view of his actual life and psychology—and a much better view of how he lived his life during the last years before the collapse—I will quote two letters. The first one is to his mother, written in Nice on March 20, 1888, in which we see much agreement between his minor claims and descriptions in *Ecce homo* and his life (and which gives a good representative picture of Nietzsche's life at this time).

> I would also mention that my digestion is better here than elsewhere; but above all, my mind feels more alert here, and carries its burden more easily—I mean the burden of a fate to which a *philosopher* is inevitably condemned. I walk for an hour every morning, in the afternoon for an average of three hours, and at a rapid pace—the same walk day after day—it is beautiful enough for that. After supper, I sit until nine o'clock in the dining room, in company mainly with Englishmen and English ladies [. . .]. I get up at six-thirty in the morning and make my own tea and also have a few biscuits. At twelve noon I have breakfast; at six, the main meal of the day. No wine, no beer, no spirits, no coffee—the greatest regularity in my mode of living and in my diet. Since last summer I have

> accustomed myself to drinking water—a good sign, a step forward. It happens that I have just been ill for three days; today everything is all right again.[32]

The other letter, to his sister eleven days later, on March 31, 1888, exemplifies some of the greater themes in *Ecce homo*—such as his view of his illness, his view of his own decadence and of his slow ascent out of decadence (which he apparently saw himself as still working on even as late as 1888), and his critical view of his earlier writings (unlike what is expressed in *Ecce homo*):

> I wish that I myself had "shone" a little more this winter: but there were gloomy weeks when I sat as a weary bear in a cave. Nonetheless, I believe that in the main thing ["*Hauptsache*"; i.e. the work on the *Umwerthung aller Werthe*] *progress* has been made and that I have taken a step further out of the many years of misery and *décadence*. I am also relieved that I have finished with my "literature" [probably a reference to having finished writing the prefaces, 1886–7]: I am even cultured enough, no longer to like them. One does not write masterpieces while in a state of *décadence*: that would be counter to natural history!—How ill I have really been no one truly knows. And it is good so. — [. . .] Now I need a kind of self-control and concentration without equal—for the purpose of the famous "life-task" [i.e., the *Umwerthung aller Werthe*], for which I fear, I *have* so far *not suited at all*.

3.5 Why Nietzsche Wrote Such Books

In the beginning of the first six sections of this chapter Nietzsche attempts to explain why he is not read and understood—because that which he writes about is too new and original—and in the last three sections of these, four to six, he continues to present himself, his style, and his psychology.

When Nietzsche as the first sentence of "Why I Write Such Good Books" says: "I am one thing, my books are another,"[33] he may seem to be wanting to separate his writings from his life,[34] in contradiction to his usual emphasis on their belonging together. However, that is not the purpose of the sentence—rather the opposite. In fact, in the earlier version of the third section of this chapter, Nietzsche had emphasized the close relation between his life and his writings: "Finally, I only speak of what I have experienced, not merely of 'thoughts'; the opposition between thinking and life is lacking in me. My 'theory' grows out of my 'praxis.'"[35] Already in the third section of the foreword, Nietzsche had emphasized this close relation between his life and his thought: "Philosophy, as I have understood and lived it so far." This emphasis reverberates throughout *Ecce homo* and all of Nietzsche's writings.

The first sentence of this chapter is, in fact, in line with the whole theme of *Ecce homo*, and is a direct consequence and culmination of the previous two chapters, ending with Nietzsche's statement that the purpose of his life is to revalue values, and that he has now reached it, quoted at the end of the previous section. He therefore downplays the importance of his earlier published books—as minor and partial events of his life, as merely preparatory and/or resting places, in contrast to the planned (and in part written) *Umwerthung aller Werthe*, for which he now regards his whole life to have been a preparation. A way to rephrase that first sentence would be "I am now the revaluation of all values"—he will even later in the second section of the chapter state: "I am [. . .] the *Antichrist*"—"my books so far (with the possible exception of *Also sprach Zarathustra*) are merely stepping-stones on the road to where I am now—they are not me today." On the other hand, he increases their importance by interpreting into them many of his present views and values (relating to the revaluation), not present or only very weakly present in the books themselves (as I will show later). Both these strategies aim at emphasizing and increasing the importance of his coming *Umwerthung aller Werthe*. The whole final chapter will be a sort of pre-publication review or preview, where life and writing are united, of his *Umwerthung aller Werthe*.

To the reader of the present text, it may seem as if Nietzsche is merely complaining about the responses to, and the lack of understanding of, his books. However, this is not at all the case. After having claimed that he is not yet timely, that he and his truths belong to the future —"some are born posthumously"[36]— he attempts to explain why he is *not* understood—and the reason is not ill will, nor lack of ability or intelligence. His real point is that even those most capable and most favorable toward him fail to understand him because what he writes is so new, original, and counter to common views and assumptions that it is simply not understood, or often not even seen at all. This message does not come through completely in the present text—for Nietzsche deleted his first positive introduction of Widmann and Spitteler (who are both present in the first section), which is needed to make this point clear. In fact, Nietzsche knew and appreciated both Widmann and Spitteler, and more importantly, they were both younger admirers of him. He had not only corresponded with them, but also read works by them (he had even attempted to find a publisher for Spitteler, who, much later, in 1919, received the Nobel Prize for literature).[37] Nietzsche's main point is made much clearer in the original version of section one (these few lines of text were unfortunately exchanged for the present text during the second half of December): "Not that it in the one or the other case [i.e., in regard to Widmann and Spitteler] lacked in 'good will'; even less in intelligence. I even regard Herr Spitteler as one of the most welcome and best among those who write critiques these days; his work on French drama—not yet published—is perhaps of first rank." The original text then continues with the present text: "All the more reason to attempt an explanation."

What Nietzsche does in these preliminary six sections of this chapter is to show what is needed to read and understand him—this is true for all his books—but especially *Also sprach Zarathustra* (stated explicitly) and for the planned *Umwerthung aller Werthe* (not stated explicitly). The sixth section ends with a reference to the *Umwerthung aller Werthe* (in the form of a quotation from the penultimate section of *Jenseits von Gut und Böse*): the claim that "the touch of the genius of the heart," that is, that of Dionysos/Nietzsche, makes us richer, newer, opened up, "full of hopes that still remain nameless, full of new willing and streaming, full of new not-willing and back-streaming . . . ." The full section 295 in *Jenseits von Gut und Böse* ends with Dionysos wanting to make man "stronger, more evil and more profound, also more beautiful."

I believe there is a reason why Nietzsche quotes the end of *Jenseits von Gut und Böse* here. Already at the time of writing that book in 1885/86 he was working on his future *Umwerthung aller Werthe*, and *Jenseits von Gut und Böse* was given the subtitle "Prelude to a Philosophy of the Future" and the four-volume *magnum opus* was announced as a work in progress (at that time under the title *Der Wille zur Macht*, with the later title as subtitle) on the cover of the book, as we saw in the previous chapter. The last section of *Jenseits von Gut und Böse*, 296, constitutes a sort of anticlimax when reading the book, for he there refers to the content of the book almost as old truths, "on the verge of withering and losing its fragrance!" and as being "only weary and mellow things"—newer truths will be presented in the coming *magnum opus*. That is also the sense, but more full of hope and promise, of the penultimate section where Dionysos' teachings are touched upon. In a draft of it, Nietzsche spelled it out even more clearly: "and perhaps there will come a day with so much stillness and halcyon happiness [. . .] that I will tell you, my friends, the philosophy of Dionysos."[38] This is obviously a reference to the future *Umwerthung aller Werthe*, and especially to its last volume with the planned title *Dionysos philosophos*.

I am not sure that this sixth section of *Ecce homo* works well as presenting Nietzsche "as psychologist" as he claims, but what he also does is to connect to the promise he had made to expound on Dionysos' philosophy at the end of

Jenseits von Gut und Böse, a theme he will return to again in the last chapter and the last section of *Ecce homo* (I will discuss this further in Chapter 5 on the roles of Zarathustra and Dionysos in *Ecce homo*).

I would like to suggest that the fact that the reviews of *Die Geburt der Tragödie*, the *Unzeitgemäße Betrachtungen*, and *Menschliches, Allzumenschliches* are longer than the later reviews (with the obvious exception of *Also sprach Zarathustra*) is due to the fact that these early works are biographically relevant (Nietzsche wants to show that already then he had an inkling of what was to come), but from *Morgenröthe* onward, they are (or, rather, will soon be) superseded by the work Nietzsche feels certain will soon be published. The exception is the review of *Der Fall Wagner*, which is therefore placed last and out of order—but that text does not really constitute a review of the book, but, rather, a general critique of the Germans.

3.6 Nietzsche's Contorted Reviews of His Books

The Birth of Tragedy

It is obvious that Nietzsche is not attempting to describe how he regarded *Die Geburt der Tragödie* (and the other books reviewed) when he wrote it (and them), but stating what it (and they) meant to him now, when writing *Ecce homo* and planning the major work *Umwerthung aller Werthe* in 1888. For example, here he discusses Dionysos and the Dionysian extensively (but ignores the Apollonian), while in 1872 they were two equal principles or *phenomena*.[39] He refers to the book's "profound, hostile silence about Christianity," and this may well be regarded as correct in regard to the silence (but there is little or no evidence that it, at this time, was due to hostility), and his comment in *Ecce homo* that his references to "spiteful kinds of dwarves" and "subterraneans"[40] referred to Christian priests are far from certain or obvious in the 1872 text (and it can be doubted that that was his intention at that time).[41]

The fact that the review of *Die Geburt der Tragödie* was written for the purpose of emphasizing that it was preparatory to the *Umwerthung aller Werthe* is visible in the claim that the book was anti-Christian, in his reference to his discovery that morality is merely a symptom of decadence (which he really made much later than *Die Geburt der Tragödie*, but which was to be a major theme in the third book of the *Umwerthung aller Werthe*) and in the stress on the Dionysian and eternal recurrence, a thought he discovered in August 1881 (both themes of the planned fourth volume).

At the beginning of the second section of the *Die Geburt der Tragödie* review, Nietzsche states: "This beginning is utterly remarkable. I had *discovered* the only analogy for and counterpart to my innermost experience [i.e., *amor fati*] that history has to offer—I was precisely therewith the first to understand the marvelous phenomenon of the Dionysian." This assertion may be true for Nietzsche in 1888, with *amor fati* and a different concept of Dionysos, but it was in no way true in 1872. Again we see that *Ecce homo* was written from the 1888 perspective, and looking forward to the *Umwerthung aller Werthe*, not a backward-looking perspective.

He begins the last section of the review by pointing forward a century and to his *Umwerthung aller Werthe* and to what will happen if "my attack on two millennia of perversion and defilement of the human has been successful," and to the consequences of what he planned to treat as a major theme in the last volume of the *Umwerthung aller Werthe*: "I promise a *tragic* age: the highest art of saying 'yes' to life, tragedy, will be reborn."

The four *Untimely Meditations*

Regarding the four *Untimely Meditations*, he now (since a couple of years) reinterprets the latter two to be more about himself than about Schopenhauer and Wagner, obviously in contradiction to his views when he wrote them. Furthermore, in the discussion of them, he again emphasizes the critique of Christianity, in agreement with his present views and with the coming *Umwerthung aller Werthe* (especially *Der Antichrist*), although it became a major theme only in *Morgenröthe* (1881) and thereafter.[42] Nietzsche ends the discussion by echoing a theme from the end of the second chapter, that to become able to revalue values he needed many experiences—and here he expresses gratefulness for the period when he was a scholar: "It is my kind of cleverness to have been many things and in many places, so as to be able to become one thing—to be able to come to one thing [i.e., the revaluation]. I *had* to be a scholar, too, for a while" (3).

Human, All Too Human

His discussion of the three volumes of *Menschliches, Allzumenschliches* consists to a large degree of an accurate account of his life between 1876 and 1879 (but containing a few minor inaccuracies such as his claim that he read nothing, although it is true that he read less than normally, and that his book and

Wagner's *Parsifal* crossed at the same time, while actually several months passed between the two). However, he describes these years here in a simpler manner, as another positive step (away from ten years of idealism), pointing toward his present and future philosophy. Earlier, and especially in the prefaces to the two parts of *Menschliches, Allzumenschliches* (from 1886), Nietzsche emphasizes the errors and exaggerations of this step, as being overscientific, and the view he then suggested was more complex and Hegelian, as thesis, antithesis, and his mature philosophy as a sort of synthesis.

Nietzsche correctly emphasizes the relevance of Voltaire, the "*grandseigneur* of the spirit"—then as an Enlightenment thinker, while now it is primarily his role as a critic of Christianity. Nietzsche quotes his "*Écrasez l'infâme*" at the end of *Ecce homo*—which connects it still more to his present project. In the last, the sixth, section, added in late December 1888 (and thus possibly influenced by the impending collapse), he interprets section 37 of *Menschliches, Allzumenschliches* as foreshadowing his present views (a bit odd since he is actually speaking of and quoting Paul Rée's words):

> The passage [from Nietzsche's Preface to *Zur Genealogie der Moral*] reads: "but what is the main principle that has been arrived at by one of the boldest and coolest thinkers, the author of the book *On the Origin of Moral Sensations* (*lisez*: Nietzsche, the first *immoralist*), by means of his incisive and penetrating analyses of human behavior?" "The moral individual is no closer to the intelligible world than to the physical one—*for* there is no intelligible world . . ." This principle, hardened and sharpened under the hammer blows of historical knowledge (*lisez*: *revaluation of all values*), may perhaps at some future point —1890! — serve as the axe which will be applied to the roots of humanity's "metaphysical need"—whether more as a blessing or curse on humanity, who can say? But in any event as a principle with the most significant consequences, at once fruitful and fearful, and looking into the world with the *double vision* that all great insights have."[43]

He seems to be saying that we can read it as Nietzsche's words (in parallel to how he reinterprets himself in his description of Schopenhauer and Wagner earlier).[44] This anti-metaphysical and anti-idealistic principle—through the *Umwerthung aller Werthe*—will perhaps in 1890 (with the publication of the *Umwerthung aller Werthe*) serve as the axe to humanity's "metaphysical need." (The claim that the *Umwerthung aller Werthe* will perhaps be published, within one or two years, in 1890, is repeated in his review of *Der Fall Wagner*.)

Dawn

In his review of *Morgenröthe*, he now, possibly unconsciously, refers not to its correct subtitle, "Thoughts on the Prejudices of Morality," but to the more radical "Thoughts on Morality as Prejudice" in line with his present immoralism and intention to revalue all moral values.[45] His first sentence, "With this book my campaign against *morality* begins," is a correct description of its role when first written in 1881 and also suits the present aim of preparing for the *Umwerthung aller Werthe*. Referring to the motto of the book, "There are so many days that have not yet broken," he emphasizes that it looks forward to new mornings and new days—and now explicitly claims that this refers to the revaluation, obviously part of his argument in 1888.[46]

> —this *Indian* motto is inscribed on the door to this book. *Where* does its originator *seek* that new morning, that still undiscovered delicate blush with which another day—ah, a whole series, a whole world of new days!—sets in? In a *revaluation of all values*, in freeing himself from all moral values, in saying "yes" to and placing trust in everything that has hitherto been forbidden.

The end of the first section had originally, in the October version, a different ending, which emphasizes *Morgenröthe*, *Die fröhliche Wissenschaft*, and *Also sprach Zarathustra* as yes-saying books: "Morality is not attacked, it is simply no longer heard . . . Beyond good and evil!—*Morgenröthe*, the *gaya scienza* (1882), my *Zarathustra* (1883) are, before all else, *yes-saying acts*—the immoralist speaks in every sentence. The denial in it, however, is simply a *conclusion*, it follows, it is not emphasized."[47]

I do not believe that it has been pointed out before, but the whole second and last section is *not* about *Morgenröthe* at all, but about the future *Umwerthung aller Werthe* (*Der Antichrist* and the further planned volumes). The first long sentence of the second section begins,

> My task, that of preparing the way for a moment of highest self-contemplation on humanity's part, *a great noon-day* when it will look back and look ahead [. . .] and for the first time ask the question "why?" "what for?" *as a whole*—this task follows necessarily from the insight that humanity has *not* found the right way by itself, that it is definitely *not* divinely ruled but that precisely among its holiest conceptions of value the instinct of negation, of corruption, the *décadence* instinct has seductively held sway (EH, "M," 2).

Only in the last sentence of the second section does he again reconnect to *Morgenröthe*, and states that it was with this work that he began his critique of selflessness (which he planned to treat in the coming *Umwerthung aller Werthe*). This whole section is important, for it shows some of the planned content of the *Umwerthung aller Werthe*, including his intention to push it beyond *Der Antichrist*, and to contain a severe critique not only of Christianity (done in *Der Antichrist*) but also of morality and its preconditions (planned for the third volume of the *Umwerthung aller Werthe*). This section also hints at the problems of nihilism and philosophy, which he planned to deal with in the second volume, and to the problems of giving mankind as a whole a goal or a "why," meant to be discussed in the fourth volume, in several notes entitled "*Dionysos philosophos*," but in some as "The Great Noon-Day," which the first sentence of this section refers to (quoted earlier).

> This is why the question of the origin of moral values is for me a question of the *utmost* importance, because it determines the future of humanity [. . .] humanity has so far been in the *worst* hands, that it has been ruled by those who turned out badly, the cunningly vindictive, the so-called "saints," these world-slanderers and humanity-defilers. [. . .] Such a clash of values [. . .] What is the point of those mendacious concepts, morality's *ancillary* concepts "soul," "spirit," "free will," "God," if not to bring about humanity's physiological ruin? (EH, "M," 2)

The Gay Science

The review of *Die fröhliche Wissenschaft* is very brief: one page (in spite of the fact that he frequently referred to it as his most personal book and that it constitutes a sort of portrait of him, and it thus would be especially relevant to discuss in *Ecce homo*, if it were primarily to be an autobiography, and that it in some ways therefore was his favorite book). Apart from saying that it is a yes-saying book (like *Morgenröthe* and *Also sprach Zarathustra*), it is treated as *only preparatory*—preparatory to *Also sprach Zarathustra* and to the *Umwerthung aller Werthe* ("at the end of the third book, the granite sentences with which a destiny *for all time* is first formulated"—Nietzsche's first public formulation of the revaluation of all values was done here, in section 269: "*In what do you believe?* —In this, that the weights of all things must be determined anew").[48] He also suggests that the style of the book and especially the poems go "above and beyond morality."

This brief treatment is surely to undervalue *Die fröhliche Wissenschaft*, and very different from his treatment of it in the preface from the autumn of 1886.[49] Because Nietzsche so strongly overinflates his own importance (actually mostly the importance of *Also sprach Zarathustra* and the coming *Umwerthung aller*

Werthe), it has not been noticed that Nietzsche in almost all the reviews can be said to undervalue his other books.

Let me remind the reader that what we see is that Nietzsche is not giving an "objective" or general review of his books, but, instead, a very specific and limited one relating to the planned *Umwerthung aller Werthe*. Parts of the reviews are even, in fact, specifically discussing and referring to the *Umwerthung aller Werthe*—this is true for the reviews of *Morgenröthe* (section 2, as we have seen), *Jenseits von Gut und Böse*, and *Götzen-Dämmerung*.

Thus Spoke Zarathustra

The long review of *Also sprach Zarathustra* (written later than most of the other parts of *Ecce Homo*) is remarkably biographical and reliable, albeit at the same time excessively self-praising. In the fourth section, Nietzsche emphasizes the critique of Christianity contained in it, which is correct, but also again serves to connect it to his coming project. The text also contains two further allusions to what was to come in the planned fourth volume of the *Umwerthung aller Werthe*—the repeated references to Dionysos (or the Dionysian) and to the idea of eternal recurrence (especially in sections 1 and 6 to 8).[50]

Nietzsche's discussion of *Also sprach Zarathustra* in *Ecce homo* is further analyzed in some detail in Chapter 6.

Beyond Good and Evil

Most readers take the two sections of the next subchapter to be about *Jenseits von Gut und Böse*, as the title seems to announce. However, that is not the case (just as it was not so in the review of *Morgenröthe*). Originally Nietzsche wrote only the second section, and it stood alone. The first section was thereafter added and stood without being numbered, as a sort of introductory paragraph, not only to *Jenseits von Gut und Böse*, but also to the rest of this whole chapter about the post-Zarathustra books (and the second section was numbered as "1").[51] This first section thus refers to his main interest and preoccupation during the years following *Also sprach Zarathustra* (1885/86–88), that is, to "the no-saying [. . .] the revaluation of previous values," that is, to the first three volumes of the *Umwerthung aller Werthe*, "conjuring up of a day of decision," which probably refers to the fourth volume with the planned title *The Great Noon-Day* (as an alternative title to the more frequently used *Dionysos philosophos*). This is also the project on which Nietzsche spent most of his time during these three to four years, which finally had begun to come to fruition during the autumn of 1888 (with the writing of *Der Antichrist*).

He summarizes his books after *Also sprach Zarathustra*, that is, *Jenseits von Gut und Böse*, *Zur Genealogie der Moral*, *Der Fall Wagner*, and *Götzen-Dämmerung*, as "fishhooks" whose purpose it was to find those who could aid in this major undertaking of revaluation—but none were found. As we will see, these four books are therefore also reviewed from the perspective of *Ecce homo* as being preparatory to the *Umwerthung aller Werthe*—and thus they are simplified and undervalued in their own right (while we today, of course, read them for their own sake, not as preparatory, since the *Umwerthung aller Werthe* was never completed). This is obvious for *Jenseits von Gut und Böse*, *Zur Genealogie der Moral*, and *Götzen-Dämmerung*, which, apart from the content of the reviews, are all reviewed in less than a page each.

What Nietzsche says is that his main preoccupation during the period from 1885/86 to 1888 was working on the revaluation of previous values—that which would result in *Der Antichrist* and the other never finished volumes of the *Umwerthung aller Werthe*.[52] It does not follow that the books he wrote during this period were part of the revaluation project. They were not. *Zur Genealogie der Moral* is described in *Ecce homo* as a preliminary study for it (but not as part of it), perhaps *Götzen-Dämmerung* is related to it, but *Der Fall Wagner* (and *Götzen-Dämmerung*) are described as resting places from the work on the project,[53] and *Jenseits von Gut und Böse* as the result of recuperation after *Also sprach Zarathustra*.

That the review of *Jenseits von Gut und Böse* begins only with the second section is made clear in the first sentence: "This book (1886) is in all essentials a critique of *modernity*." The book—Nietzsche's most philosophical book—is here clearly undervalued (compare with its own preface), which emphasizes a dichotomy of values, the difference between dogmatic and non-dogmatic philosophy and the resulting tension which can lead us to a new task and "goal" —this is probably a reference to the revaluation of all values). *Jenseits von Gut und Böse* is in *Ecce homo* hardly discussed in its own right at all, but is, instead, primarily treated as a by-product of, and the result of, "recuperation" after *Also sprach Zarathustra*. Originally the review contained one further reference to Nietzsche's revaluation project, but this last sentence was later struck out: "What after all, [. . .] says my great teacher *Dionysos* at the end of this hard and all-too-serious book?"—alluding to the penultimate section, 295 (which Nietzsche had already quoted at length in section 6 of this chapter—and may be the reason he decided that he could not refer to it yet again), where Nietzsche has Dionysos say: "I often reflect how I might yet advance him [man] and make him stronger, more evil and more profound than he is."[54]

This treatment of *Jenseits von Gut und Böse* as primarily the result of recuperation after *Also sprach Zarathustra* is in some sense surprising. Assuming that Nietzsche wanted to look backward, the book summarizes his philosophic thought from 1881/82 to 1885, and assuming he wanted to look forward, there is much in *Jenseits von Gut und Böse* which fulfills such a desire: the subtitle "Prelude to a Philosophy of the Future" (given in the text of *Ecce homo* but not expanded upon), the end of the preface (tension leading to a new goal), and the end of the book (see the discussion earlier). On the other hand, Nietzsche lightly touches upon all of these themes. More importantly, it is perhaps the fact that—despite the subtitle of the work—Nietzsche regarded it as the result of a recuperation after *Also sprach Zarathustra* and that while working on *Jenseits von Gut und Böse*, he avoided and saved much material meant to be dealt with in his coming *magnum opus*.[55] In fact, most of the book is based on Nietzsche's earlier notes from the Zarathustra period, 1882–5.

On the Genealogy of Morals

The review of *Zur Genealogie der Moral* is equally brief, one page, and although basically correct, overemphasizes its critique of Christianity. In the review Nietzsche refers to Dionysos and three times to the revaluation of all values (although only once using that expression). The first essay of *Zur Genealogie der Moral* is essentially a description of Christianity as "a counter-movement, the great revolt against the dominance of *noble* values," and later in the review he refers to *Also sprach Zarathustra* as a counter-ideal to modern and Christian values. Most importantly, Nietzsche here is explicit about *Zur Genealogie der Moral* as being preparatory to his present project and ends the review with the claim: "Three decisive preliminary works [Vorarbeiten] of a psychologist towards a revaluation of all values."[56] While *Jenseits von Gut und Böse* is described as the result of recuperation after *Also sprach Zarathustra*, *Zur Genealogie der Moral* is depicted as a preliminary work for the *Umwerthung aller Werthe*.[57]

We can note that in both these reviews Nietzsche seems to suggest that *Also sprach Zarathustra*, in poetic and metaphorical language, contains many of the ideals associated with the revalued values. We will discuss the implications of this in Chapters 5 and 6.

Twilight of the Idols and the Revaluation of All Values (The Antichrist)

This subchapter (with the somewhat misleading title *Götzen-Dämmerung*) consists of three sections, of which the first one and a half review *Götzen-*

Dämmerung, and the rest of the second section discusses (or rather proclaims) Nietzsche's suitability for carrying out the revaluation of all values, and the third one discusses the writing of and the time of the first book of the *Umwerthung aller Werthe*, that is, *Der Antichrist*.[58] Fairly little is said about *Der Antichrist* (he does not even mention the title), apart from the important fact that it was already written, and that Nietzsche was most satisfied with it. He also says in this section that on the same day that he finished *Der Antichrist*, he wrote the foreword to *Götzen-Dämmerung*, and this ends with the words: "Turin, 30 September 1888, on the day the first book of the *Revaluation of All Values* was completed." We can note that originally there were only two sections; the third section was added later.

The role of *Götzen-Dämmerung* is not quite clear. In the preface to the book, from September 30, 1888 (and in letters from this time), Nietzsche refers to it as a resting place after working on the difficult task of the revaluation of all values (and thus its original title "The Idle Hours of a Psychologist").[59] Here, in *Ecce homo* (mostly written in October and November 1888) it is presented more as preparatory to (or even part of) the *Umwerthung aller Werthe*: "Anyone who wants to get a quick idea of how topsy-turvy everything was before I came along should make a start with this work. What the title page calls *idol* is quite simply what till now has been called 'truth.' *Twilight of the Idols*—in plain words: the old truth is coming to an end." Nietzsche emphasizes that *Götzen-Dämmerung* is brief (and written quickly) and contains "too many" truths—one trips over them, one tramples some to death—the point seems to be that *Götzen-Dämmerung* presents some of the content of the *Umwerthung aller Werthe* (which also seems correct when compared with the drafts Nietzsche made of volumes 2 to 4 of the *Umwerthung aller Werthe* after he had written *Der Antichrist*), but very briefly, very schematically, in a nutshell.[60]

The review of *Götzen-Dämmerung* points forward to the *Umwerthung aller Werthe*—at least I take it that when Nietzsche at the end of the second section says, "I am the first to have the yardstick for 'truths' in my hand, I am the first to *be able* to decide" and continues, "no one before me knew the right way, the way *upwards:* only after me are there hopes, tasks, paths to prescribe to culture once again—*I am their evangelist* . . . And that is why I am also a destiny"—that is a "teaser" or presentation of what will come in the next chapter entitled "Why I Am a Destiny" and in his planned future publication.[61] Originally *Der Fall Wagner* was reviewed before *Götzen-Dämmerung* (in its correct chronological place), and this whole chapter thus ended with these very words.[62]

The Case of Wagner

The discussion of *Der Fall Wagner* is significantly longer, and different in nature, from the other post-*Also sprach Zarathustra* books. It does not really contain a discussion of *Der Fall Wagner*, except the first few lines, but contains, instead, a severe critique of the Germans (and in that sense, it is not really well placed here).[63] However, the transition from discussing Wagner to discussing the Germans is perhaps not as abrupt as it may at first appear. Earlier in *Ecce homo* Nietzsche emphasized that it was when Wagner turned German (returned to Germany and became anti-Semitic and nationalistic) that Nietzsche distanced himself from him (EH, Books, "Human, All Too Human," 2). Nonetheless, throughout the review Nietzsche refers and alludes to the coming *magnum opus*. In the first section he refers to Dionysos and states: "Ultimately my task's purpose and path contains an attack on a more subtle 'unknown' [i.e., other than Wagner] not easily guessed by anyone else." In an earlier version, instead of "unknown," he used the term "counterfeiter," which he often used to signify those who created or supported false (modern) values. It is not clear to me whom or what Nietzsche here is alluding to—possibly himself (as earlier a supporter of Wagner, and with his later view that the fourth *Unzeitgemäße Betrachtungen* was less about Wagner and more about himself), Jesus, St. Paul, Schopenhauer, or perhaps Christianity or modern values, especially aesthetic values, or modern morality, personalized. In the second section he refers to "the noble, life-affirming, future-confirming values" and "the opposing values, the *values of decline*" and he ends it with the words: "Does anyone beside me know a *way* out of this blind alley?"—again an allusion to his planned *Umwerthung aller Werthe*. In the third section he refers to the Germans as "Counterfeiters" and in the fourth and last to *amor fati* and twice to the coming work: "And so, roughly two years before the shattering lightning bolt of the *Revaluation*, which will have the earth in convulsions, I sent *Der Fall Wagner* out into the world" (4) and he ends this whole chapter with claims that he is carrying an enormous responsibility to succeed in revaluating our values: "I bear an ineffable responsibility [. . .] For I am carrying the destiny of humanity on my shoulders—" (4).

This chapter, "Why I Write Such Good Books," clearly builds up to the last chapter of the book, which will deal more explicitly with the *Umwerthung aller Werthe*. Originally, Nietzsche dealt with all of his books in chronological order, and the chapter would have ended with the review of *Götzen-Dämmerung* (which as we have seen earlier actually ends with a discussion of the *Umwerthung aller Werthe*), which is also, then—according to my argument—the theme of the last chapter. However, in mid-November, Nietzsche exchanged the order between the last two reviews, so that the discussion of *Der Fall Wagner* came last. However, the final words of this review also constitute a transition to the final chapter and a discussion of his coming *Umwerthung aller Werthe*, as we have seen earlier.

In this section we have discussed what happens to the text of *Ecce homo* when it is read as primarily forward-looking, rather than in the usual backward-looking manner. Let us now turn to the final chapter, "Why I Am a Destiny," to which the rest of *Ecce homo* has been building up and which in my view not only foreshadows the *Umwerthung aller Werthe* but can perhaps even be regarded as part of it, or at least as an introduction or preface to it.

4

The Last Chapter, "Why I Am a Destiny," as Preparatory to the *Revaluation of All Values*

4.1 Introduction: History and Structure of the Chapter

For those who read *Ecce homo* primarily as an autobiography, the last chapter does not make much sense. Nietzsche had presented himself in the first two chapters, and reviewed all of his books in the third. What is the purpose of this last chapter? The risk is that it becomes viewed merely as self-aggrandizement (and that is how it generally has been read). Nietzsche had given at least some answers to the questions with which each of the first chapters was headed—why he was so wise, clever, and wrote such good books—but what is the answer as to why he was a destiny? Again, it is likely to be interpreted primarily as self-inflation.

For those who read *Ecce homo* as preparing for and attracting attention to his planned *Umwerthung aller Werthe* project, this final chapter is a natural and necessary conclusion of the book—containing a brief summary and some allusions to what was to come, and an emphasis on how important it was going to be. In fact, the chapter contains several "cliff-hangers" to lead the reader on to his future work (which, however, with the exception of *Der Antichrist* did not appear). Excessive self-inflation is certainly still there, also in this reading, but it is not the only thing present, and it is more the importance of his task, the revaluation of all values, than of himself that is being claimed.

The early history of the text of this chapter is somewhat complicated, but an awareness of it helps us in important ways to understand the content and purpose of it (see also the appendix). The last three sections of the original October version of the *Ecce homo* manuscript in twenty-four sections, sections 22 to 24, were between early and middle of November used by Nietzsche to write an early version of the preface to *Ecce homo*. These sections were originally rewritten from a text which originally was a draft to the preface of volume 3 of the *Umwerthung aller Werthe* —entitled *The Immoralist.*[1] However, by the middle of November this was transformed into the greater part of the last chapter (that which now comprises sections 3 to 8). All of this, sections 3 to 8, relates to volume 3 of the *Umwerthung aller Werthe*, while section 9, which consists of a single line of text, points forward to volume 4, *Dionysos philosophos*. Early in December, shortly before December 6, Nietzsche added sections 1 and 2, which are broader and discuss the whole revaluation project, although only very briefly and generally.[2] At that time he also added a "Declaration of War" and "The Hammer Speaks" as two epilogues to the text (as well as the table of contents at the beginning of the book—which includes references to these two epilogues). These epilogues are *not* included in the critical edition (see the discussion later in the next section).

4.2 The Content of the Last Chapter

This short last chapter is, like a good preface, immensely rich and reverberates with themes from *Ecce homo* (many of which were also planned to have been dealt with more extensively in the *Umwerthung aller Werthe*).

Among the many themes Nietzsche touches on in the first section is that of "destiny" and "fate." It runs through the whole text, already before the last chapter, from the first sentence in the first chapter: "The fortunate thing about my existence, perhaps its unique feature, is its fatefulness," through many forms to the last sentence before the last chapter: "For I am carrying the destiny of humanity on my shoulders." The question asked in the title of the last chapter "Why I Am a Destiny" is answered twice: the first time in the more affirmative way as pointing to an alternative: "no one before me knew the right way, the way *upwards:* only after me are there hopes, tasks, paths to prescribe to culture once again—*I am their evangelist*. . . . And that is why I am also a destiny" (EH, Books, "*Götzen-Dämmerung*," 2) and the second time, by showing what has been in error: where he claims that anyone who unmasks Christian morality "is a destiny" and at the same time that person also unmasks "the valuelessness of all values that are or have been believed in" (EH, Destiny, 8).

Nietzsche also separates himself from founders of religion—and needs to do so, since according to his own definition of religion, that which characterizes them is that they change or create values—just as Nietzsche does or hopes to do. What then makes him different? That he is skeptical of seeking followers and of the many—that he is an existentialist in the sense that everyone must and should decide for him/herself (as he had emphasized in the foreword). He picks up another theme closely connected with this from the foreword—that of being a satyr in preference to a saint—here he claims to rather be a buffoon than a saint.

Another theme he picks up from the foreword, and which recurs throughout the text itself, is that of the importance of truth and truthfulness—as opposed to the lies of millennia.

In the second section, Nietzsche explains why he, in spite of his affirmative nature (and his *amor fati*), questions and destroys so much—because destroying the old is a necessary and integral part of true creation.

In the third section, Nietzsche emphasizes that it is truthfulness (for which much bravery is necessary) which is necessary for the self-overcoming of morality and the moralist, into immoralism—and all this happened in him. Immoralism is, then, also the main theme and the *leitmotif* of all the remaining sections, especially 3 to 6.

All of section 4 is an enumeration of the planned content of volume 3 of the *Umwerthung aller Werthe*, with discussions of immoralism, "the good," optimism, etc.

In the next section, he enumerates a number of different dichotomies of values and thereby exemplifies his revaluation of values: good—evil; decadence—"the strong man assured of life"; the human herd animal—the exceptional man; hypocritical truth—the really truthful; "good men"—*Übermensch*; and being alienated from reality—conceiving reality as it is.

In the sixth section Nietzsche continues the immoralism theme and emphasizes the critique of Christian morality—and the psychological profundity necessary for understanding man and Christian morality.

When Nietzsche in this section says: "Who before me has climbed into the caves from which the poisonous fug of this kind of ideal—*world-denial*!—emanates? Who has dared even to suppose that they *are* caves?" it is probably both a general (metaphorical) statement, but also a direct reference to section 14 in the first essay of *Zur Genealogie der Moral*—where Nietzsche the previous year had in a humorous spirit described the "dark workshop" where "ideals are made on earth" —in which account several "revaluations" are exemplified.

> Weakness is to be transformed into a *merit* through lies, there is no doubt [. . .] And the impotent failure to retaliate is to be transformed into "goodness"; craven fear into "humility"; submission to those one hates into "obedience" [. . .] the inability to take revenge is called the refusal to take revenge, perhaps even forgiveness [. . .] This workshop where ideals are fabricated—it seems to me to stink of nothing but lies [. . .] these experts in black magic who turn every dark

shade into the white of milk and innocence [. . .] "we good men—*we are the just*." (GM, I, 14, translated by Douglas Smith)

Shortly thereafter, at the beginning of section 16, Nietzsche summarizes an important aspect (but not the whole) of the revaluation: "Let us conclude. For thousands of years, a fearful struggle has raged on earth between the two opposed value-judgements, "good and bad" and "good and evil" [. . .] the second value-judgement has long been in the ascendant" (GM, I, 16).

The seventh section begins with the question "Have I been understood?" (also used in section 3), which then echoes on in the next two sections—combined with the theme of having unmasked Christian morality.

Nietzsche also claims that a revaluation of all values has already occurred—his task is thus merely to turn the world right side up again. In fact, already in Nietzsche's very first use of the word "revaluation" in his published works, in *Jenseits von Gut und Böse*, 46, he says: "the paradoxical formula 'god on the cross' [. . .] promised a revaluation of all the values of antiquity." That a decadent revaluation of values has already happened is also the whole theme of the first essay of *Zur Genealogie der Moral*, where Nietzsche argues that the dichotomy good–bad is the older, and that a second, moralized, good–evil dichotomy was created only in reaction to it, out of weakness, and which reversed the former.

In the eighth and penultimate section he again emphasizes the close connection between *Also sprach Zarathustra* and *Ecce homo* (as well as the *Umwerthung aller Werthe*). He claims to have unmasked Christian morality, and is therefore a destiny. He speaks of the new truth versus the old "truth" (which is a harmful form of lie)—and here seems to use truth not so much in relation to facts, but in reference to ethics and values. The rest of the section mentions a number of consequences of the unmasking of Christian morality.

The last section, 9, sets up the opposition between Christian values and the new revalued ones: "*Dionysos against the crucified one.*"

In the critical edition of Nietzsche's works (KSA and KGW), *Ecce homo* ends with this section 9, and that was also how the "Druckmanuskript" from the middle of November ended. This is likely to be the best editorial decision—and this is thus the primary text for any analysis of the last chapter.

However, when Nietzsche asked to have the manuscript returned to him for a few days in early December, he added two epilogues as well as a table of contents (with references to both these epilogues—all of it in the form of new pages added to the manuscript). The first epilogue, the "Declaration of War," three pages long, has been destroyed by Nietzsche's mother and is thus no longer extant.[3] Some of its probable contents can be gained from notes Nietzsche wrote at this time,[4] where Nietzsche criticizes contemporary politics and nationalism (especially in Germany—thus the reason for the destruction of this epilogue by his mother—it was not only insulting but could possibly have led to trial and punishment for author and publisher) and instead of wars between nations or classes, proclaims a "war" between ascending and descending forms of life—a war in which physiology is placed at the center—for the purpose of cultivating a higher human being. Possibly he also declared a "war to the death" against sin, that is, anti-nature, which essentially means Christian values. At the end of December, Nietzsche wrote a "mad" "Last Consideration"[5]—which in an odd manner seems to have been pacifistic—which he wanted to add as a supplement to the "Declaration of War"; but in the end, on December 29, he decided against all of these epilogues.[6]

The second epilogue was a quotation from the last part of "Of Old and New Law—Tables," section 30, in the third book of *Also sprach Zarathustra*, and this text is still on both sides of a page among the "Druckmanuskript" (and numbered as the last pages, 48 and 49). The text is as follows:

> O my Will, my essential, *my* necessity, dispeller of need! Preserve me from all petty victories!
> O my soul's predestination, which I call destiny! In-me! Over-me! Preserve and spare me for a great destiny!
> And your last greatness, my Will, save for your last—that you may be inexorable *in* your victory! Ah, who has not succumbed to his own victory!
> Ah, whose eye has not dimmed in this intoxicated twilight! Ah, whose foot has not stumbled and in victory forgotten—how to stand!—
> —That I may one day be ready and ripe in the *great noontide*: ready and ripe like glowing ore, like cloud heavy with lightning and like swelling milk-udder:
> —ready for myself and my most secret Will: a bow eager for its arrow, an arrow eager for its star:
> —a star, ready and ripe in its noontide, glowing, transpierced, blissful through annihilating sun-arrows:
> —a sun itself and an inexorable sun-will, ready for annihilation in victory!
> O Will, my essential, *my* necessity, dispeller of need! Spare me for one great victory![7]—

Perhaps this epilogue does not add anything essentially new to the manuscript, which we miss by excluding it, but it is consistent with the whole *Ecce homo* text. In it Nietzsche refers to "my soul's predestination, which I call destiny! [. . .] Preserve and spare me for a great destiny!" which is much in line with *Ecce homo* (where Nietzsche argues that the revaluation of all values is his task and destiny) and this last chapter (including its title). Still more important and prominent is that the whole tenet of the quotation is to preserve and prepare Zarathustra / Nietzsche for one last great future battle and victory—that is, the *Umwerthung aller Werthe*—"Spare me for one great victory!"

Nietzsche's reference to "great noontide" [*grosse Mittag*][8] is also part of this argument, although that may not be obvious to every reader. Already in *Also sprach Zarathustra* Nietzsche refers to the "great noontide" as the time of great decisions when his teaching, including the idea of eternal recurrence, will be accepted. Later it continues as an important symbol for Nietzsche, and it even becomes a synonym of the *Umwerthung aller Werthe* (it is then also used as a possible title for the fourth volume).[9] The great midday, and its associated time of great decisions and self-contemplation, is a red thread through *Ecce Homo*, from the first sentence ("confront humanity with the heaviest demand ever made of it"), through the review of *Die Geburt der Tragödie* ("into that *great noon-day*, when the most select dedicate themselves to the greatest of all tasks"), the review of *Morgenröthe* ("My task, that of preparing the way for a moment of highest self-contemplation on humanity's part, *a great noon-day* when it will look back and look ahead [. . .] and for the first time ask the question 'why?' 'what for?' *as a whole*"), to the first section of this last chapter, where the time of great decisions and self-contemplation is equated with the revaluation of all values ("*Revaluation of all values*: that is my formula for the highest act of self-reflection on the part of humanity"), to this epilogue ("that I may one day be ready and ripe in the *great noontide*"). The "great midday" (with or without the epilogue) thus connects *Also sprach Zarathustra* and *Ecce homo*, and points forward to the *Umwerthung aller Werthe.*

4.3 The Relation of the Last Chapter to the Planned Four-Volume *Umwerthung aller Werthe*

As we have seen earlier, the first two sections of the last chapter begin, not by predicting the terrible wars of the twentieth century, as it so often has been understood, but by predicting the consequences of the revaluation of all values. With the revaluation we can again look forward to new life-affirming hopes and goals, Nietzsche claims, but, since it stands "in opposition to the hypocrisy of millennia" and questions everything which has so far been hallowed—"the most profound collision of conscience, a decision conjured up *against* everything hitherto believed, demanded, hallowed" (EH, Destiny, 1)—there will be disasters and "the notion of politics will then completely dissolve into a spiritual war [*Geisterkrieg*]." In section 2 Nietzsche continues to point out that creating and destroying belong together.

This general introduction or presentation can be further supplemented by his explicit discussions of the *Umwerthung aller Werthe* in the reviews of *Die Geburt der Tragödie*, *Morgenröthe*, *Jenseits von Gut und Böse*, and *Götzen-Dämmerung*.[10] I would recommend that the reader return to and read especially the whole second section (except the last sentence) of the review of *Morgenröthe*, which consists of a general discussion of the *Umwerthung aller Werthe* project especially relating to religion and morality. Nietzsche there claims that mankind as a whole has been on the wrong road, in the worst hands, that of moralists and priests—who deny reality and want the end. Absolute value is bestowed on what is unegoistic, and hostility everywhere against egoism. "Selflessness" has been called morality till now.

Sections 3 to 8 discuss and present exclusively themes planned for volume 3 of the *Umwerthung aller Werthe*, with the title *The Immoralist*, which is the volume Nietzsche had been working on the most during the late autumn. Section 3 introduces the concept of immoralism and immoralist, and states that to be able to overcome morality one needs to possess the virtues of truthfulness and courage. What Nietzsche and Zarathustra represent is "the self-overcoming of morality out of truthfulness." Section 4 begins by stating that the word "immoralist" incorporates two denials: the "type of human being, who has hitherto been considered the highest type—the *good*," and decadent and Christian morality. Thereafter it contains a brief summary of much of the planned content of volume 3 (as does much of section 8). Sections 5 to 8 continue to argue for life-affirming values and against the false anti-natural decadence values, and touches upon many of the themes he planned to discuss in volume 3 of the *Umwerthung aller Werthe*.

The last short section, 9, with its "*Dionysos against the crucified one*," obviously points both toward volume 1, *Der Antichrist*, where the teaching of "the crucified one" is analyzed and criticized, and even more toward volume 4: *Dionysos philosophos*, where the philosophy of Dionysos was to be discussed. It may be regarded as a cliff-hanger. Nietzsche mentions and discusses this opposition in several notes from this time.[11] Especially in the first of these, the longest note, he points out that what makes Dionysos and the crucified different as symbols is not martyrdom—they are both killed—but, instead, the attitude toward life and suffering that this reflects. The suffering of Christ is interpreted as a condemnation of life, while the death of Dionysos is viewed as yet another temptation to life—and to an eternal rebirth—which Nietzsche associates with his own idea of eternal recurrence.

There are a few other vague allusions to volume 4 in the last chapter. Apart from references to Dionysos (sections 2 and 9), there are a few general statements of the type: "I am an *evangelist* the like of which there has never been; I know tasks so lofty that there has not yet been a concept for them; I am the first to give rise to new hopes." Again this is a sort of cliff-hanger. Two further, specific themes are also briefly mentioned. "*Great politics*," a theme closely related to the revaluation of all values,[12] which the later Nietzsche referred to occasionally, and may have been intended for elaboration in the *Umwerthung aller Werthe*. Somewhat greater space is given to the human ideal associated with the revalued values (in sections 5, 7, and 8), but hardly enough to say much about what that affirmative ideal would be like. This theme is discussed further in the last chapter of this study.

Almost all of Nietzsche's notes from October 1888 (thereafter there are essentially no philosophical notes) concern volume 3 of the *Umwerthung aller Werthe* and contain discussions of problems relating to the value and effect of the "good" human being,[13] but these notes also include a two-page preface to the volume, which is somewhat broader.[14] These notes, including the preface, seem never to have been translated into English.[15] Much of the content of these notes has been incorporated into this last chapter of *Ecce homo*.

The fact that volume 2 of the *Umwerthung aller Werthe*, with the working title of *The Free Spirit*, is only very vaguely present in the final chapter, and in *Ecce homo* at all, should not be interpreted to mean that Nietzsche had given up on it—its title is all along listed beside volumes 3 and 4 among his notes[16]—it is probably merely the effect of not working on these questions at this time. He had worked rather intensively on them, that is, on nihilism, pessimism, and truth the previous year. The concept of truth—the centerpiece of volume 2—is referred to in several of the sections of this chapter (1, 3, 4, 5, and 8), but mostly it is used merely to criticize the present concept of truth and suggests that there will be another in the future, but little is said about its nature here. About Nietzsche's view of nihilism, much further information (not included in his published books) can be gained by studying his notes from 1887. There are strong reasons for believing that much of this material was meant to be included in volume 2, as shown by several notes.[17]

The first volume, *Der Antichrist*, already written, is absent to a surprising degree in this last chapter. Some of the general statements certainly include it,[18] but there is little discussion of religion and Christianity, and surprisingly, there is no specific reference to this finished manuscript at all (if one does not count the last sentence with its "*Dionysos against the crucified*"). This, if anything, shows that what this chapter prepares for goes beyond *Der Antichrist* to the complete four-volume *Umwerthung aller Werthe.*

What we thus observe is that this chapter does, indeed, present the *Umwerthung aller Werthe* project, but only in part and incompletely. In the draft to a letter to Georg Brandes, quoted earlier, from late November or early December 1888,[19] Nietzsche writes: "Next to appear is the 'Ecce homo' about which I spoke [in my last letter], in which the last chapter gives a foretaste of *what will come*, and where I myself appear as a human fate." As we have seen, sections 1 and 2 (together with parts of the previous reviews of his books) present the whole revaluation project in general terms. The last section can be regarded as pointing toward the first and the fourth volume of the *Umwerthung aller Werthe.* However, most of the chapter, sections 3 to 8, essentially points forward only to volume 3 with the title *The Immoralist*, and this is done with a fair amount of detail. The main specific themes, related to volume 3, that Nietzsche discusses in this chapter are the following:

Most obvious is the theme of immoralism, which is not only a *leitmotif* in *Ecce homo* and this chapter (referred to in sections 2, 3, 4, and 6) but also expanded upon in some detail. I will discuss Nietzsche's concept of immoralism in what follows.

Otherwise, Nietzsche's references to questions which possibly were meant to be treated in volume 3 seem to fall into three to five groups.

1. General discussions and critique of morality—decadence and Christian morality—and the related theme of the question of the origin of moral values:[20] "the question of the origin of moral values is for me a question of the *utmost importance*, because it determines the future of humanity" (EH, "Daybreak," 2). During the autumn of 1887 Nietzsche had planned a second volume of *Zur Genealogie der Moral*, where he was to discuss herd morality, the history of how morality became anti-natural etc., but these themes seem later to have been incorporated into his plans for the *magnum opus.*[21]
2. An analysis and critique of the "good," the "benevolent." This is a distinct and explicit theme which Nietzsche obviously had intended to expand upon. It is not only the most prominent theme in Nietzsche's notes from October 1888, but was also a theme he had been working on and had regarded as an important part of his *magnum opus* at least since 1885.

Closely related to it, and probably meant to be dealt together with it, are other themes he also mentions in the "Destiny" chapter: the psychology of the good, optimism, and the desire to reform away from everything objectionable.

3. Related to the above mentioned themes, but nonetheless also separate, is the concept of the morality of unselfing oneself [*Entselbstungs-Moral*]. The expression is Nietzsche's own, and together with other related concepts and expressions,[22] we can see that it was important for him and that he worked on this question, especially in 1887 and 1888. Closely related to this theme, and mentioned in this chapter, are also the questions related to altruism (and egoism) and the herd animal mentality.
4. As for another theme mentioned in section 8, namely the "improving" or the "improvers" of humanity (and which is discussed briefly at the end of section 7),[23] Nietzsche had elaborated upon this in the short seventh chapter "The 'Improvers' of Mankind" in *Götzen-Dämmerung*, but from his notes it seems likely that he intended further elaboration on this theme in volume 3.[24]
5. A number of other concepts, which Nietzsche associates with our false and life-denying values, such as soul, spirit, immortal soul, sin, and free will are mentioned in the "Destiny" chapter. Nietzsche had mentioned or discussed all of them in *Götzen-Dämmerung* and *Der Antichrist*, but only very briefly in *Götzen-Dämmerung* and, in *Der Antichrist*, primarily their relation to religion. One needs to carefully examine his later notes to determine the likelihood that they would be dealt with further. It seems to me likely that they would again reappear in volumes 2 and 3, in relation to epistemological and ethical questions and consequences.

These themes mentioned in the final chapter of *Ecce homo* correspond closely to Nietzsche's notes for work on volume 3 of the *Umwerthung aller Werthe*, which is not surprising considering that we have seen that much of the content of this last chapter consists of rewritten notes that originally were explicitly written as part of the work on volume 3. In this sense, it is not unreasonable to regard this chapter not only as a presentation of, or as a preface to, the *Umwerthung aller Werthe*, but also as a part of it.[25]

Several of these themes are themes that the later Nietzsche had specifically worked on, and on which it appears that he had more to say than what is present in *Ecce homo* and his other published books. However, for a constructive discussion of this, one needs to go beyond *Ecce homo*. Let us here only briefly examine the most prominent one, immoralism.

Nietzsche has in this last chapter explained that the term "immoralism" means primarily three things: (1) the denial of "the good" as the highest type of man, (2) the denial of Christian (and decadent and modern) morality, and (3) the possession of enough intellectual conscience and psychological profundity to regard Christian morality as beneath oneself. What the reader of *Ecce homo* would not know is that it was also the planned title of the third volume of the *Umwerthung aller Werthe*, and that Nietzsche had been working on this theme for many years for this purpose. The word "immoralist" is not lacking in his other later published work, from *Jenseits von Gut und Böse* onward, but it is rarely used. It is really only two books in which its presence is of major interest to us. One of them is *Der Antichrist*, in which the term never occurs; the other is *Götzen-Dämmerung*, where the term is used frequently. Nietzsche there too, as in *Ecce homo*, calls himself an immoralist, but more frequently he refers to "we immoralists" (which, considering the fact that Nietzsche regarded himself as the first immoralist, is a reference to those—future ones—who have revalued values). However, at no place does he stop there and discuss immoralism and what it means and implies (not even to the extent he does it in *Ecce homo*).

One of the problems with modern morality for Nietzsche, who is concerned with human greatness and man's highest cultural achievements, is that it inhibits, commanding what we should *not* do without encouraging us to strive for excellence. Another is that it is, in its effect, life-denying. A third is that it is based on false assumptions about the natural and physical world. For these and other reasons, it needs to be done away with. However, Nietzsche's concept of immoralism is not only an a-moralism, not only a denial of modern morality, but one that also contains affirmative values. Its purpose is to illuminate moral thought and its preconditions (such as regarding moral values as absolute, objective, and true for all), with the aim, instead, to lead to a life-affirming morality. Immoralism is a relatively common theme in Nietzsche's writings from *Jenseits von Gut und Böse* (1886) onward. In his notes it becomes a major theme shortly before that time, and from the winter of 1885/86 it also becomes a frequent title—mostly as "We Immoralists" —of planned chapters and books,[26] later as the title of one of the volumes of the *Umwerthung aller Werthe*. Nietzsche suggests what such an ideal can look like in *Zur Genealogie der Moral*: "the *sovereign individual*, the individual who resembles no one but himself, who has once again broken away from the morality of custom, the autonomous supramoral [*übersittliche*] individual (since autonomous and 'moral' are mutually exclusive)."[27] In one of the notes for the third volume of the *Umwerthung aller Werthe*, Nietzsche writes: "What may against this, an *immoralist* demand of himself? What will *I* with this book regard as my task? Perhaps also to 'improve' mankind, only differently, only reversed: namely, *release* them from morality, above all from moralists [. . .] *Restoration of the egoism of mankind!*"[28]

4.4 Does *Ecce Homo*, Especially the Last Chapter, Point Toward Future Publications?

Another important conclusion can be drawn from this chapter (and related material). It is almost universally assumed that Nietzsche gave up the idea of publishing a four-volume *magnum opus*, but there are strong arguments against such a view.[29] We know that he referred to *Der Antichrist* as the first volume of the *Umwerthung aller Werthe* (and thus implying that further volumes would be coming) frequently until the middle of November as is shown by several of Nietzsche's letters,[30] at which point he had basically completed *Ecce homo*. In the "Druckmanuskript," from the middle of November, Nietzsche refers to *Der Antichrist* as the first volume of the *Umwerthung aller Werthe* in the prologue (this is the only time in the manuscript in which there is an unequivocal reference to *Der Antichrist*),[31] and this was not changed when he very carefully revised the manuscript—"weighing each word on a gold scale"—in early December, although he struck out the date on the note. Still more important is that he let this description remain, although he made a number of other changes in the prologue, when he returned the proofs of the first part of *Ecce homo* to his publisher Naumann with the words "ready to be printed/ N[ietzsche]," "druckfertig / N," and dated by Nietzsche as "Turin, den 18. Dez. 1888."[32] This makes the claim that *Der Antichrist* had become the complete *Revaluation of All Values* already a month earlier highly unlikely or incorrect. It is clearly stated here, and ready for publication, on December 18, 1888, that *Der Antichrist* is "the first book of the *Revaluation of All Values*."[33]

We still have one further piece of information that he actively continued to refer to *Der Antichrist* as "the first book of . . ." as late as in middle/late (before 22) December 1888. When he revised his *Nietzsche contra Wagner* in the latter part of December, a book which he had begun writing and compiling only on 12 December, he again refers to *Der Antichrist* as the "first book of the *Revaluation of Values*."[34]

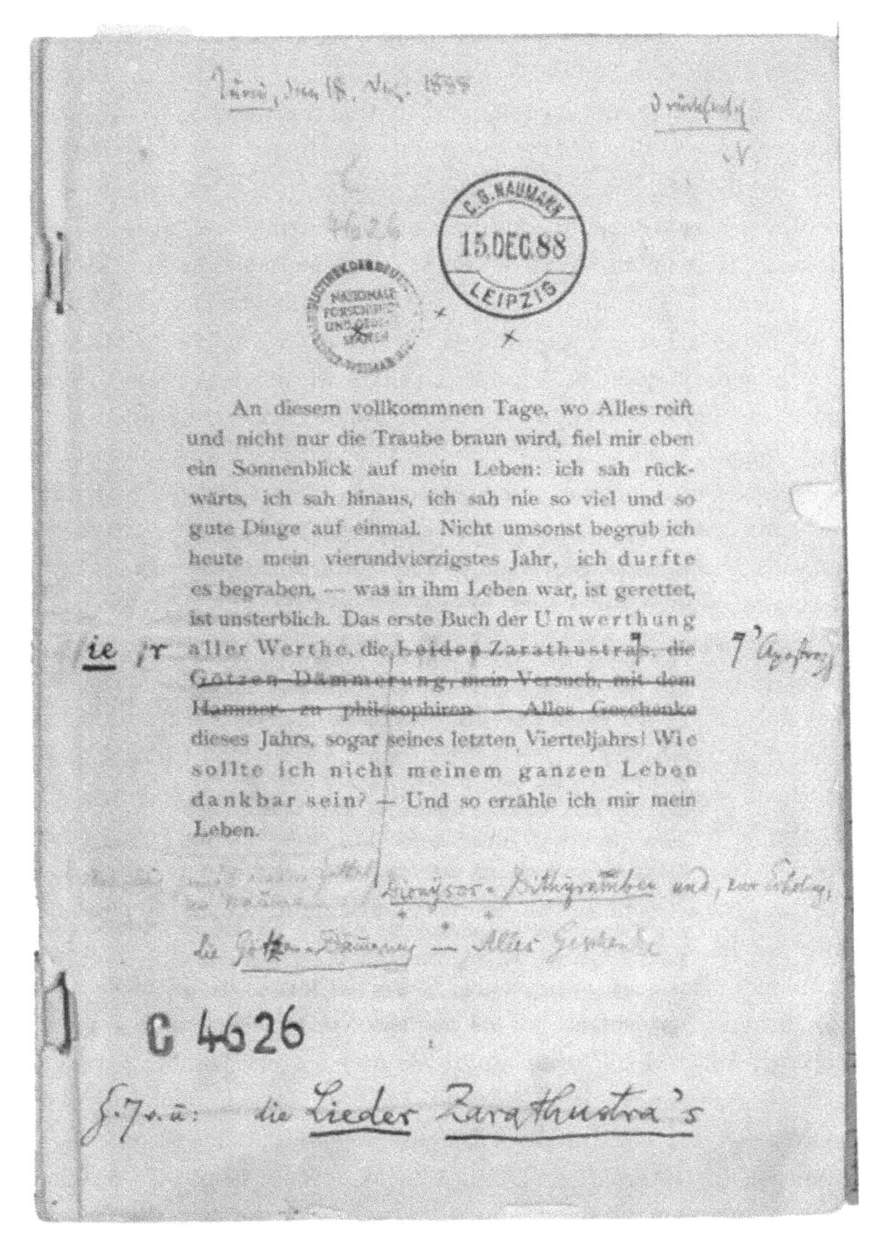

An diesem vollkommnen Tage, wo Alles reift und nicht nur die Traube braun wird, fiel mir eben ein Sonnenblick auf mein Leben: ich sah rückwärts, ich sah hinaus, ich sah nie so viel und so gute Dinge auf einmal. Nicht umsonst begrub ich heute mein vierundvierzigstes Jahr, ich durfte es begraben, — was in ihm Leben war, ist gerettet, ist unsterblich. Das erste Buch der Umwerthung aller Werthe, die beiden Zarathustra's, die Götzen-Dämmerung, mein Versuch, mit dem Hammer zu philosophiren — Alles Geschenke dieses Jahrs, sogar seines letzten Vierteljahrs! Wie sollte ich nicht meinem ganzen Leben dankbar sein? — Und so erzähle ich mir mein Leben.

Figure 4.1 First page of the *Ecce Homo* Korrektur: *Nietzsche*. *Source*: Digitale Faksimile Gesamtausgabe K-14, 1.

Only in a note found by Montinari in July 1969, in Peter Gast's *Nachlaß*, apparently a copy Gast had made of some revisions which Nietzsche had sent to the publisher Naumann on December 29 (the original is lost), which also included the new section 3 of the first chapter, said that several changes should be made in the prologue, among them the change from "Das erste Buch der Umwerthung aller Werthe" to "Umwerthung aller Werthe."[35]

However, it seems to me to be relatively unimportant whether Nietzsche changed his mind and came to regard *Der Antichrist* as the complete *Umwerthung aller Werthe* as late as sometime between November 14 and 26 (as Montinari argues), or at the very end of December, at a time when he was clearly mentally unstable (as I have shown and argued here), or did not change his mind at all.[36] What is important is Nietzsche's views and intentions while writing *Götzen-Dämmerung*, *Der Antichrist*, and *Ecce homo*—during which he undeniably planned the *Umwerthung aller Werthe* in four volumes (and referred to it as such), with *Der Antichrist* as the first! Furthermore, he had planned and worked on such a four-volume work for over four years! If Nietzsche had changed his mind in the last week (or even the last month) before his collapse, or not at all, does not really matter, not so much because of his mental instability, but because he was not writing or working on this project at all during that time. All the material we possess, published books and notes, was written while Nietzsche planned and worked on the *Umwerthung aller Werthe* in four volumes. From December 1888 (not to speak of the very end of December), we possess only a few pages of notes, and these are both clearly affected by his mental breakdown and anyway not relevant for the discussion of the content (and the number of volumes) of the *Umwerthung aller Werthe*.

Let us turn to the question of whether *Ecce homo* points to future publications. In fact, the very first sentences of the chapter seem to be best understood as a promise to publish the *Umwerthung aller Werthe* in the (near) future: "I know my lot. Some day my name will be linked to the memory of something monstrous, of a crisis as yet unprecedented on earth, the most profound collision of conscience, a decision conjured up *against* everything hitherto believed, demanded, hallowed. I am not a man, I am dynamite." Only a few lines below, he states that "you can guess why I am publishing this book *beforehand*"[37]—and thus makes it patently clear that he intended to publish the *Umwerthung aller Werthe* after *Ecce homo*. A few lines later, he refers to "*Umwerthung aller Werthe*" in a manner such that it is not completely clear whether he refers to it as the philosophical project and/or as the literary project—the most reasonable, as it seems to me, is that he includes both senses: "*Revaluation of All Values*: that is my formula for the highest act of self-reflection on the part of humanity, which has become flesh and genius in me."[38] The second section of this Destiny chapter seems to continue this line of thought by describing the *Umwerthung aller Werthe* as both destructive and creative and its author by explaining that he who wants to create values will by necessity also have to be a destroyer of values—he "is incapable of separating no-doing from yes-saying. I am the first *immoralist.*"[39]

That *Ecce homo* was written to prepare for the *Umwerthung aller Werthe* is also demonstrably clear from a large number of Nietzsche's letters. For example, in a letter to Georg Brandes, dated November 20, 1888, Nietzsche describes his *Ecce homo* and continues: "the whole thing is a prelude to the *Revaluation of All Values.*"[40]

Furthermore, when in the fourth section of this chapter he says that he will have occasion to discuss optimism in the future,[41] it is clearly a reference to either volume 2 or 3 of the *Umwerthung aller Werthe.*

As we have seen earlier, in the previous chapter, Nietzsche states twice in *Ecce homo* that he will soon publish a work, obviously the *Umwerthung aller Werthe,* that is, in 1890 or close to that year.[42]

Nietzsche had also in several earlier books, from *Zur Genealogie der Moral* to *Götzen-Dämmerung*, mentioned themes he planned to expand upon in his *Hauptwerk*, such as nihilism, the physiology of art, and eternal recurrence which can hardly be regarded as having been fully treated in *Der Antichrist;* in fact, they are not discussed or even mentioned at all there. Obviously, Nietzsche's intention was to publish more than *Der Antichrist*. Obviously he was not, at the age of forty-four, finished with everything.

Nietzsche's draft to a letter to Georg Brandes, in late November or early December 1888, quoted earlier, where Nietzsche states that "the last chapter gives a foretaste of *what will come*"—and since little in the chapter refers to *Der Antichrist*, it is obvious that he means the whole four-volume work.

More broadly, it is clear that the last chapter does not merely introduce *Der Antichrist,* which would be the case if he had given up the idea of publishing the rest of the *Umwerthung aller Werthe*. The general introduction, sections 1 and 2, is so general and vague that it is difficult to distinguish with certainty whether it refers to *Der Antichrist* or the complete *Umwerthung aller Werthe* project, but the rest of the chapter makes it clear that it refers to more than *Der Antichrist*.

As we have seen earlier, much of the chapter was created out of notes for the planned third volume of the *Umwerthung aller Werthe*, entitled *The Immoralist*, and large parts of the chapter point forward, to the revaluation of moral values.

That this is a theme outside of, or beyond *Der Antichrist*, can be seen from the simple fact that the term "immoralist" never even occurs in it.[43]

The idea of eternal recurrence is only vaguely alluded to in this chapter,[44] but it was a key theme throughout Nietzsche's work on a four-volume *magnum opus* (it even constituted the title of the complete work in one of the early drafts), and there can be little doubt that Nietzsche had intended to elaborate on it in the future volumes.[45] It is not mentioned at all in *Der Antichrist*, but was surely meant to be discussed in the later volumes, in particular in the last, the fourth, volume.[46]

Finally, the importance of Dionysos in the last section of this chapter, but also previously in *Ecce homo* (as well as in later notes, but also in other later books) makes it obvious that *Ecce homo* points beyond *Der Antichrist*, which does not contain a single reference to Dionysos.

Nietzsche's plans for, and work on, the *Umwerthung aller Werthe* project determined both the reason that Nietzsche wrote *Ecce homo* and most of its content. This *Umwerthung aller Werthe* project has attracted remarkably little attention, at least since the 1970s, but ought, to my mind, be examined thoroughly.

In the next chapter we will examine the role of Dionysos, and what he represents in Nietzsche's later writings and notes. We will thereby gain further insight into Nietzsche's later philosophy and the planned content of the *Umwerthung aller Werthe*. We will also discuss the question of Dionysos' relation to the other of Nietzsche's most important symbols, Zarathustra, in *Ecce homo* and in his later philosophy.

5

The Roles of Zarathustra and Dionysos in Nietzsche's *Ecce Homo* and Late Texts

5.1 Introduction: The Late Nietzsche's Two Most Important Symbols

Zarathustra and Dionysos are the two most important symbols in *Ecce homo*, and in all of Nietzsche's late writings.[1] *Ecce homo* begins and ends with references to Dionysos, and contains many further references in between: "I am a disciple of the philosopher Dionysos" (Foreword, 2), and ends with "Have I been understood —*Dionysos against the crucified one . . .* " (EH, Destiny, 9). This emphasis on Dionysos becomes even more pronounced when we know that the planned fourth volume of his *Umwerthung aller Werthe* was meant to be entitled *Dionysos philosophos*.

Nonetheless, it can be argued that Zarathustra is at least equally prominent and important. *Ecce homo* also begins and ends with references to Zarathustra (immediately after and before those to Dionysos): "Among my writings my *Zarathustra* stands alone. With it I have given humanity the greatest gift it has ever been given. This book, with a voice that stretches over millennia, is not only the most exalted book there is [. . .] it is also the *most profound* book" (Foreword, 4), and "I have not said a word just now that I might not have said five years ago through the mouth of Zarathustra" (EH, Destiny, 8). Between them are more than twice as many references to Zarathustra as to Dionysos, and these are almost without exception longer and more informative than those to Dionysos.[2] To that we can add the very large number of often long quotations from *Also sprach Zarathustra* (frequently without the source being given, though mostly it is obvious).

The usual interpretation of the fact that Zarathustra and *Also sprach Zarathustra* are so enormously pronounced in *Ecce homo* is that Nietzsche regarded *Also sprach Zarathustra* as by far his most important work. Most scholars today do not agree with this judgment, but admit that this seems to be how Nietzsche regarded it. My argument is that while it is true that Nietzsche regarded Zarathustra as by far the most important book among those he had written, he also planned and worked on another even greater work, for which *Ecce homo* was to be preparatory and about which he also makes many grand claims. Since most previous discussions of *Ecce homo* have failed to see this forward-looking role of *Ecce homo*, they have falsely understood almost all the congratulatory statements and grand claims to refer only to *Also sprach Zarathustra*—and thus exaggerating Nietzsche's already excessive comments about that book. Those who read *Ecce homo* backward (as an autobiography) have understood the focus of the book to be merely on *Also sprach Zarathustra* rather than on it together with the *Umwerthung aller Werthe* and Dionysos. This has probably been part of the reason why the book has a relatively low status among contemporary scholars; it is not in *Also sprach Zarathustra* and *Ecce homo* that most readers go to find "the new Nietzsche" or "the relevant Nietzsche" or Nietzsche's most profound and explicit critique of truth, science, values, history, and the self.

My claim is that Nietzsche did enormously emphasize *Also sprach Zarathustra* in *Ecce homo*—perhaps best seen in his statement in the penultimate section of the last chapter: "I have not said a word just now that I might not have said five years ago through the mouth of Zarathustra." Nietzsche had already in 1883 and 1884 claimed that *Also sprach Zarathustra* was his "*best* book,"[3] but he also felt that it only constituted a sort of "preface, entrance hall"[4] for something else, the revaluation of all values, which would require many years of preparation, which now in 1888 had come to fruition.[5] It was when writing *Also sprach Zarathustra* that Nietzsche began the literary revaluation project, while the philosophical revaluation project also intensified further at this time. In Nietzsche's eyes, *Also sprach Zarathustra* constituted a stepping stone (perhaps almost a necessary stepping stone), while all the other books are in comparison mere pebbles, to the momentous *Umwerthung aller Werthe*. Since no one read and understood *Also sprach Zarathustra*, it was natural that he emphasized *both* books in *Ecce homo*, *Also sprach Zarathustra*, and the coming *Umwerthung aller Werthe*, both Zarathustra and Dionysos.

Nietzsche seems to do all he can to bring attention to and raise knowledge of Zarathustra while Dionysos may seem to be a symbol of the future, just barely visible in the mist of dawn. That is not an unreasonable view, considering that the Dionysos book was yet to come while the Zarathustra work was already published, but little read. But what do these figures symbolize, apart from books? What is their relation to one another? Do they ever meet?

If we are able to answer these questions about their roles and meanings—and their relation to one another—we will gain further insight into the role and meaning of both *Ecce homo* and the never finished *Umwerthung aller Werthe* project, and perhaps also the philosophical position Nietzsche was moving toward before his collapse. In attempting to answer these questions I will examine Nietzsche's use of these two symbols in *Ecce homo*, as well as in other late books and in his late notebooks.

Perhaps an alternative way to rephrase these questions can be as follows: Was that which Nietzsche planned to treat in *Umwerthung aller Werthe* a more philosophical version of the contents of *Also sprach Zarathustra*, or was it meant to go beyond that? Was Nietzsche, as he sometimes suggests, moving into a new phase of his thought? However, this question cannot be completely answered without a very thorough and extensive examination of Nietzsche's late notebooks, and thus cannot be answered in this book. One should be aware that it is a question which almost certainly has no simple answer, and can at most be answered by identifying a tendency.[6]

Let us begin by reviewing Zarathustra's and Dionysos' roles in Nietzsche's writings generally. We can start with noting that on the whole they are fairly equal as symbols for Nietzsche when measured by how frequently he used them. Throughout his writings, there are approximately an equal number of references to them, though of course they differ in that Nietzsche's interest in Dionysos began early and was at its most intensive during the early 1870s, while he "discovered" Zarathustra only in 1881 and referred to the figure most frequently during the years 1882–85 and in late 1888. More relevant, at least for our interest here, is that the late Nietzsche's use of these symbols, that is, his use of them after 1885, is almost evenly distributed.

5.2 Zarathustra as Symbol

Nietzsche found and picked up the figure of Zarathustra as his spokesman while reading the cultural historian and anthropologist Friedrich von Hellwald's *Culturgeschichte in ihrer natürlichen Entstehung bis zur Gegenwart* (Augsburg, 1874) in August 1881. The introduction of *Also sprach Zarathustra* (and thus also the last section of the first edition of *Die fröhliche Wissenschaft*, 342) is almost a direct quotation from Hellwald, and this is even truer of Nietzsche's very first reference to Zarathustra in his notebook, where the introduction of the figure Zarathustra is set immediately under a draft title (presumably of a planned book), underlined several times, "Midday and Eternity" (both terms are closely associated with the idea of eternal recurrence) and a subtitle: "*Outlines for a new life.*"[7] The next two notes are on the same theme, and the second one, under the title "Zum 'Entwurf einer neuen Art zu leben'" ("For 'Draft for a New Way to Live'") is at the end dated with the words "Sils-Maria 26 August 1881"—that is, Nietzsche found the figure of Zarathustra already a few weeks after his discovery of the idea of eternal recurrence, which occurred early in August 1881.

We can thus not only see the origin of the figure of Zarathustra for Nietzsche here, but more importantly, also see the close connection between him and the idea of eternal recurrence, and the fact that he already then planned a work divided into four books, in which Prometheus for a brief period was going to play a role, and the fourth book was going to be 'dithyrambic' and present the idea of eternal recurrence.[8] This draft can perhaps be regarded as a very early draft for both *Also sprach Zarathustra* and the *Umwerthung aller Werthe*, before they had even become separate projects. Later in 1881, Nietzsche planned a work with the name Zarathustra in the title, and uses the expression "So sprach Zarathustra," which soon became "Also sprach Zarathustra."[9] By this time he had already written a number of very *Also sprach Zarathustra*-sounding notes. We should thus not be surprised that Nietzsche already in 1882, the year before he wrote the first book of *Also sprach Zarathustra*, knew that he was going to move into a new phase and would write this book (as he said on the cover of *Die fröhliche Wissenschaft*).

After 1885 and the intensive concern with Zarathustra in the years 1882–5, Nietzsche all but avoids Zarathustra as a symbol in his notes. However, Zarathustra (or references to the title or book *Also sprach Zarathustra*) does occur on a number of occasions. Most frequently these are in relation to a planned book of poems involving Zarathustra (which eventually was published as *Dionysos-Dithyramben*, but which appears already in the notes from 1885–6, or earlier, but most frequently from the summer of 1888 onward). Otherwise Zarathustra appears in general references to *Also sprach Zarathustra* (especially in drafts of prefaces to *Morgenröthe*, *Die fröhliche Wissenschaft*, and *Jenseits von Gut und Böse*), as part of titles of books and chapters, and in several notes in which he states that he should not have written *Also sprach Zarathustra* in German and that with it he has been throwing pearls before swine, and how difficult *Also sprach Zarathustra* is to understand (one must have suffered and enjoyed every word of it). In the notes from 1886–88 we thus see that Zarathustra and *Also sprach Zarathustra* were important, but we do not see signs of the great importance that he seems to attribute to them in *Ecce homo*.

Nietzsche began to use Zarathustra as a symbol and spokesperson in his published works already in *Die fröhliche Wissenschaft* (1882), but in the end he deleted all but the last reference to him in that work.[10] Instead, he wrote the four books of *Also sprach Zarathustra* between 1883 and early 1885. In a number of notes from 1885 he considered one or several further books about Zarathustra, in which he was going to die in the last one.[11] This project was not followed up and completed. Nietzsche's next book, *Jenseits von Gut und Böse*, was written to expand and elaborate on themes from *Also sprach Zarathustra*, or, perhaps more accurately, it was written to discuss ideas and themes which had occupied Nietzsche during the *Also sprach Zarathustra* period, many of which had not entered *Also sprach Zarathustra. Also sprach Zarathustra* is after all a sort of timeless book, while much of *Jenseits von Gut und Böse* is concerned with a critique of modernity, and thus discusses themes not always suitable for *Also sprach Zarathustra. Zur Genealogie der Moral* was written to elaborate on themes from *Jenseits von Gut und Böse* (as was stated on the cover of the book), especially from the last chapter. In fact, in both *Jenseits von Gut und Böse* and *Zur Genealogie der Moral* Nietzsche even avoided many themes, often closely akin to those in *Also sprach Zarathustra*, which he planned to treat later in *Umwerthung aller Werthe*. In *Jenseits von Gut und Böse*, Zarathustra is mentioned only once, in the long poem, *From High Mountains: Epode*, which ends the book, and where Nietzsche describes his life of increasing solitude from *Menschliches, Allzumenschliches* until Zarathustra became his new friend. He there describes how "one became two," that is, how he became Zarathustra and himself, or, better expressed, how Zarathustra was born out of Nietzsche.

In *Zur Genealogie der Moral* Zarathustra occurs in three places, in the last section of the preface and in the second and third essays. They all contain or suggest high praise of *Also sprach Zarathustra*, but with little actual content. In the last section of the preface Nietzsche emphasizes the strict requirements for understanding the book:

> For example, so far as my Zarathustra is concerned, I don't consider anyone knowledgeable about it who has not at some time or another been deeply wounded by and profoundly delighted with every word in it. For only then can he enjoy the privilege of sharing with reverence in the halcyon element out of which that work was born, in its sunny clarity, distance, breadth, and certainty.

After having called forth the anti-Christ and anti-nihilist of the future in the penultimate section of the second essay, Nietzsche in the short last one gives the honor to Zarathustra:

> But what am I talking about here? Enough, enough! At this stage there's only one thing appropriate for me to do: keep quiet. Otherwise, I'll make the mistake of arrogating to myself something which only someone younger is free to do, someone "with a greater future," someone more powerful than I—something which only Zarathustra is free to do, Zarathustra the Godless . . .

Thereafter he begins the third essay with a motto from *Also sprach Zarathustra*, but otherwise does not refer to him or it in the essay. We thus see a relatively modest role for Zarathustra in *Jenseits von Gut und Böse* and in *Zur Genealogie der Moral*, but nonetheless signs and claims that Zarathustra is of utmost importance.

Both the figure of Zarathustra and the book *Also sprach Zarathustra* are given extremely prominent roles in *Ecce homo*, much more so than in other books written during his last active year, 1888. However, even in the other late books, although Zarathustra is not always referred to frequently, he is still identified as a paramount symbol. In *Der Fall Wagner* Zarathustra is mentioned only once, in the preface, where it is stated that to possess the far-seeing eye of Zarathustra makes one realize the corruption of our own time. In *Götzen-Dämmerung*, in the "Fabel" chapter, a brief history of how we have falsely viewed reality from Plato until the present, Zarathustra represents the last stage mentioned, when the error has been removed. Furthermore, *Also sprach Zarathustra* is referred to as "the most profound book"—and at the same time Nietzsche places the *Umwerthung aller Werthe* (and perhaps Dionysos) beside it[12]—and *Götzen-Dämmerung* ends with a long quotation from it. In the *Dionysos-Dithyramben* (which for a long time was intended to be called *Songs of Zarathustra*), Zarathustra is the main character in five of the nine poems, while Dionysos is present in only one of them. In *Der Antichrist*, which was meant to be published after *Ecce homo*, the role of Zarathustra is more limited. The first reference, in the preface, emphasizes Zarathustra as an important stepping stone or precondition: "This book belongs to the very few. Perhaps none of them is even living yet. Possibly they are the readers who understand my *Zarathustra*." The only two other occurrences are less significant; Nietzsche uses and quotes Zarathustra against notions that martyrdom proves anything about truth, and he points out that all great intellects, including Zarathustra, are skeptics.[13]

There are probably two reasons why Zarathustra's presence in *Der Antichrist* is more limited than in the other books from 1888. The first is that Zarathustra after all is a literary figure, the main character in the metaphorical work *Also sprach Zarathustra*, a work which Nietzsche called both a symphony and a poem. As such, he is very useful as a metaphor or simile or for poetic descriptions—

but less fitting in direct arguments and polemics which *Der Antichrist* consists of. The second is that it seems likely that Dionysos was meant to take over as Nietzsche's supreme symbol, at least in the fourth volume of the *Umwerthung aller Werthe*. Their respective roles in the first three volumes are perhaps an open question, but a certain decrease in the use of Zarathustra seems natural.

5.3 Zarathustra in *Ecce Homo*

Nietzsche's references to and claims about Zarathustra and *Also sprach Zarathustra* in *Ecce homo* are very frequent and enormously pronounced. However, the references to and quotations from *Also sprach Zarathustra* do not quite fill the book, as some readers may feel, but are primarily limited to the last section of the preface and to two chapters; the review of *Also sprach Zarathustra*; and the final chapter.[14]

We have at the beginning of this chapter seen how strongly Nietzsche emphasized *Also sprach Zarathustra* in the last section of the preface. However, the other message he puts across is almost the opposite one—the existential one that the reader should not believe in or follow Zarathustra, but, instead, find and follow himself.

In the first chapter of *Ecce homo*, Zarathustra is used in Nietzsche's argument against pity and compassion, with reference to the fourth book of *Also sprach Zarathustra* ("Wise," 4), and referred to as a dithyramb to solitude, that is to say, to intellectual cleanliness and how to avoid disgust for man ("Wise," 8).

In the second chapter, Nietzsche makes two more personal points in relation to *Also sprach Zarathustra*: The first is that its style is outstanding (which is a claim that also recurs later in the book), but more importantly how deeply touched he himself always is on reading it.[15] The second point, also in section 4, emphasizes how different it is in comparison to *Menschliches, Allzumenschliches* (presumably to all three volumes)—thus confirming that he felt that he had moved into a completely new phase since then.

Considering Nietzsche's claims that *Also sprach Zarathustra* is his best book, it is not surprising that its place is prominent in the chapter "Why I Write Such Good Books." Most of the references to Zarathustra in the first part of the chapter, before the reviews, are either Nietzsche's own high praise of the work or references to how it has been misunderstood by reviewers and friends, and he refers to *Also sprach Zarathustra* when he speaks of his knowledge of women. He here also calls Zarathustra "that *destroyer* of morality" and attempts to clarify the concept of the overman [*Übermensch*] by negative example and by distancing it from Darwinism and Carlyle-type heroism.

In his review of *Die Geburt der Tragödie*, eternal recurrence is referred to as Zarathustra's teaching, and he claims that Zarathustra constitutes an "immense act of purifying and consecrating humanity." Thereafter, almost the whole of *Die fröhliche Wissenschaft* is treated as merely a preparation for *Also sprach Zarathustra* (and perhaps also for the revaluation). The longest review, by far, is that of *Also sprach Zarathustra*, and in it we encounter a fairly detailed and reliable (but also enormously self-congratulatory) account of his writing of the first three books of *Also sprach Zarathustra* (the fourth book is not mentioned here), and his mental exhaustion thereafter. On several occasions he refers to the search for new ideals and the revaluation of values. The chapter culminates in the last three sections, 6 to 8, where the figures of Zarathustra and Dionysos are merged, and it, or they, are described as representing a total affirmation of reality (see more later in the section on their meeting).

Just as *Die fröhliche Wissenschaft* was largely regarded as preparatory to *Also sprach Zarathustra*, so too is *Jenseits von Gut und Böse* largely regarded as a necessary recuperation after *Also sprach Zarathustra*. In his discussion of *Zur Genealogie der Moral*, the importance of Zarathustra is emphasized, and not only as a critic of present values but also for suggesting the new revalued values: "Above all, there was no *counter-ideal—till Zarathustra*."

In the final chapter of *Ecce homo*, Zarathustra continues to be strongly emphasized. He is described as more truthful and braver than any other thinker, which enabled him to overcome morality and to become (the symbol of) the first immoralist. Zarathustra is then used and quoted to criticize the present human ideal, "the good men," including both optimists and pessimists. Zarathustra is used to suggest an alternative human ideal of "the exceptional man," "a relatively superhuman type" that "conceives reality *as it is*"—but who perhaps will be regarded as evil when measured by present values. The last reference to Zarathustra in *Ecce homo* is in the paramount claim, quoted earlier, that Nietzsche has said nothing in *Ecce homo* that he could not have said through the figure of Zarathustra five years before.

Zarathustra is the teacher of eternal recurrence, and as such enormously important to Nietzsche. On the other hand, I think one must say that both Zarathustra and Nietzsche failed as teachers. Neither in the book *Also sprach Zarathustra*, where Nietzsche and Zarathustra more suggest than expound on the idea of eternal recurrence, nor outside of the book, are people aware of this idea, nor are the few that have that knowledge persuaded by it. A poetic and metaphorical intimation of eternal recurrence was not sufficient. Nietzsche knew that he also needed to present it (and other aspects) as philosophy—as the philosophy of the god Dionysos—and that was one of the purposes of the *Umwerthung aller Werthe*.

However much Zarathustra and *Also sprach Zarathustra* are praised in late notes and in *Ecce homo*, Zarathustra always represents the present and the past, not the future.[16] In fact, if we examine the relatively few philosophical notes from after the summer of 1888 (but this is also true for all the notes already from after the summer of 1887), and which appear not to be early drafts of *Ecce homo* or of the *Dionysos-Dithyramben*,[17] Zarathustra does not occur in them at all.[18] On the other hand, in Nietzsche's late letters, Zarathustra (most often the book rather than the figure) is fairly frequently referred to, and in 1888 several of these references praised the book almost to extremes, in line with how he speaks of it in *Ecce homo*.

5.4 Dionysos as Symbol

Nietzsche's interest in Dionysos goes back to long before he became a professor and published *Die Geburt der Tragödie*, before even his university studies, back until the time he was a pupil at Schulpforta.[19] It reached a crescendo during the years between 1869 and 1872. However, this early concept of Dionysos is somewhat different from the later one, so we can for the moment leave that and notice that already immediately after 1872 Dionysos all but disappeared from Nietzsche's writings (including his notes and letters).

To understand the role of Dionysos in Nietzsche's late published books fully, one needs to be aware of the development of Dionysos as a symbol in Nietzsche's notes. During the period between 1873 and 1882 Dionysos is all but completely absent in Nietzsche's notebooks. However, during the Zarathustra period, especially from 1884 onward, Dionysos acquires a relatively prominent place. Already by the summer of 1883 Nietzsche seems to consider him as an important symbol.[20] By 1884 he plans to use Dionysos in the title of his next book.[21] At this time, during the second half of 1884, it seems as if Nietzsche also ordered Friedrich Creuzer's *Dionysus* (Heidelberg, 1809), although he probably never received it and it is not in his library,[22] but he also bought another work by Creuzer in November 1884, in which Dionysos is present, his *Symbolik und Mythologie der alten Völker, besonders der Griechen*, 4 volumes (1836–43).[23] By the spring of 1885, at the latest, Nietzsche had certainly begun making plans for a book on his philosophy, with Dionysos both in the title and as a major figure in it: "Dionysos: An Attempt to Philosophize in a Divine Manner.'"[24] Thereafter follow a string of notes in which Dionysos constitutes either the title of planned books or parts of books.[25] We should thus not be surprised when Nietzsche in *Jenseits von Gut und Böse* alludes to a future work involving Dionysos. In fact, in Nietzsche's plan for *Jenseits von Gut und Böse* in the winter of 1885–6, with, eleven chapters at that stage, the last chapter was summarized with the word "Dionysos," revealing the importance of the penultimate section, 295 (discussed later).[26] Already at this time, during the summer of 1885, Nietzsche pronounced that "the Christian teaching was the opposite to the Dionysian one,"[27] which we recognize from the end of *Ecce homo*. In his notes for working through the fifth book of *Die fröhliche Wissenschaft*, he summarizes fourteen themes, of which two—"Pessimism and Dionysianism" and "Against Romanticism"—were later combined in section 370 (discussed later).[28] We can again learn from the notes that Dionysos is more important than it may appear for those who have read only Nietzsche's published books. The Dionysian is frequently set against pessimism. One important note is called "My new road towards 'Yes,'" in which he briefly describes his new pessimism which does not lead to a rejection of life but to a Dionysian affirmation of the world.[29] As an important aesthetic symbol, the Dionysian is also often set against romanticism in the notes. At the time of writing *Zur Genealogie der Moral*, during the summer of 1887, the title "*Dionysos philosophos*" occurs for the first time,[30] and Nietzsche speaks of "my Dionysos-ideal . . . ," here in relation to the necessity for dissimulation and playacting.[31]

In many notes from early 1888, Nietzsche extensively discusses *Die Geburt der Tragödie*, and in so doing also defines the meaning of the Dionysian and the Apollonian. Although he implicitly claims to discuss his own views as expressed in the early 1870s (and *both* these artistic symbols are, indeed, discussed as more or less equally important, as he viewed them then, while in the late 1880s he tended to ignore the Apollonian), at least for the Dionysian, he seems to describe it more along the line of what it meant to him in 1888:

> The word "*Dionysian*" means: an urge to unity, a reaching out beyond personality, the everyday, society, reality, across the abyss of transitoriness; a passionate-painful overflowing into darker, fuller, more floating states; an ecstatic affirmation of the total character of life as that which remains the same, just as powerful, just as blissful, through all change; the great pantheistic sharing of joy and sorrow that sanctifies and calls good even the most terrible and questionable

> qualities of life; the eternal will to procreation, to fruitfulness, to recurrence; the feeling of the necessary unity of creation and destruction.[32]

This affirmative—and Dionysian—view of the world is referred to in a number of late notes: "A highest state of affirmation of existence will be created, in which even pain, every sort of pain, is ever included as a means to ascending: the *tragic-Dionysian* state."[33] Another theme in the later notes is that with which *Ecce homo* ends, Dionysos against the crucified one, against Christianity, discussed earlier in Chapter 4.

The last references to Dionysos in the notes, from September and October 1888, are as part of the listings of the titles of the coming work *Umwerthung aller Werthe*, specifically the fourth volume with Dionysos in the title,[34] and as an early draft of the discussion of Dionysos in the last chapter of *Götzen-Dämmerung*, discussed earlier.[35]

In the published works, Dionysos returns only after having been absent since *Die Geburt der Tragödie* (1872), in *Jenseits von Gut und Böse* (1886), that is, shortly after he had decided and begun work on his *magnum opus* in four volumes. Dionysos is present in only a single section,[36] the penultimate one, 295, but there he is presented precisely as Nietzsche's teacher and a symbol of the coming work. Nietzsche spends a full page on describing Dionysos (and a large part of this was also quoted in section 6 of "Why I Write Such Good Books" in *Ecce homo*). He thereafter continues:

> Meanwhile, I have learned much, all too much more about the philosophy of this god [. . .] I, the last disciple and initiate of the god Dionysos: and perhaps I might at last begin to give you, my friends, a little taste of this philosophy, in so far as I am permitted to? In a hushed voice, as is only proper: for it involves much that is secret, new, unfamiliar, strange, uncanny. The very fact that Dionysos is a philosopher, and that gods too therefore philosophize, seems a by no means harmless novelty and one calculated to excite suspicion precisely among philosophers [. . .] Certainly the above-named god went further, very much further, in conversations of this sort, and was always many steps ahead of me.[37]

The most important message of this penultimate section is not what it says, but what it promises—that it points forward to a coming work where Nietzsche has gone one step further in his philosophical development with the help of Dionysos, that is, to the *Umwerthung aller Werthe*, and especially to its fourth volume, *Dionysos philosophos*.[38] Also, the second edition of *Die fröhliche Wissenschaft* (1887), with the added fifth book, ends by pointing to the revaluation of all values project in the penultimate section, 382, with a whole-page description of the search for new ideals and values, and although Dionysos is not explicitly mentioned, he is indicated as the god of the theater and of tragedy in several ways, including in the very last words "the tragedy *begins*."[39] However, Dionysos occurs explicitly in only one section of the fifth book of *Die fröhliche Wissenschaft* (written and added at the end of 1886), in the pivotal section 370, where the Dionysian represents the creative suffering from the overfullness of life as opposed to romantic suffering and creation out of poverty, as Nietzsche's most important criteria for distinguishing higher and lower forms of art and music. Furthermore, the Dionysian is also used as a counterpart to pessimism, not as its opposite, optimism, but as a sort of tragic pessimism, which Nietzsche calls Dionysian pessimism. The use of Dionysos and the Dionysian in this section is important, but does not as explicitly point forward to his coming work *Umwerthung aller Werthe* as at the end of *Jenseits von Gut und Böse*, although his claims that the Dionysian pessimism will come some day may also indicate that it was one of the themes he planned to expand upon in the coming work. The next time Dionysos occurs in Nietzsche's published works is in a somewhat vague but important statement at the end of the penultimate section of the preface to *Zur Genealogie der Moral*:

> But on the day when we say with full hearts: "Onwards! our old morality is part of the *comedy* too!," on that day we will have discovered a new plot and potential for the Dionysian drama of the "*Fate of the Soul*"— and one which that grand old eternal comic poet of our existence will exploit, on that you may depend![40]

Thereafter Dionysos becomes a major figure and symbol in *Götzen-Dämmerung* and *Ecce homo*.[41]

In *Götzen-Dämmerung*, Dionysos has a similar role to that which he will have in *Ecce homo*, but not quite as pronounced; Nietzsche claims to have learned from Dionysos, and we are given some allusions to what he represents, especially aesthetically. Furthermore, in the whole of the last chapter, "What I Owe the Ancients," Dionysos is strongly emphasized and the teaching of eternal recurrence, as well as tragedy, are closely associated with him. We can note that Dionysos is more present than Zarathustra in *Götzen-Dämmerung*. In the last section of the book (except the final quotations from *Also sprach Zarathustra*) there is again a strong reference to Dionysos, and just as in *Jenseits von Gut und Böse* and *Ecce homo*, a promise of what was to come is given: "I, the last disciple of the philosopher Dionysos—I, the teacher of eternal recurrence . . . ."[42]

5.5 Dionysos in *Ecce Homo*

Nietzsche begins *Ecce homo* by emphasizing that he is a follower of the philosopher Dionysos (in line with what he had said in the final sections of *Jenseits von Gut und Böse* and *Götzen-Dämmerung*). His second reference gives an example of this—he claims that his knowledge and understanding of women comes from Dionysos. Not surprisingly, Dionysos figures prominently in Nietzsche's review of his first book, *Die Geburt der Tragödie*.[43] He claims that one of the two greatest new insights of the book is "its understanding of the *Dionysian* phenomenon among the Greeks—it provides the first psychology of it and sees it as the single root of all Greek art" ("GT," 1). He also clearly states its most important function: "in the Dionysian symbol the outermost limit of *affirmation* is reached."

In *Der Antichrist*, 13, Nietzsche declares, "Let us not undervalue this: *we ourselves*, we free spirits, are already a 'revaluation of all values,' an *incarnate* declaration of war and victory over all ancient conceptions of 'true' and 'untrue.'" The "we" is not clearly defined (and in *Götzen-Dämmerung* Nietzsche says: "I say we out of politeness"), but is likely to include those whom he refers to at the end of the second section: "Anyone who not only understands the word 'Dionysian' but understands *himself* in the word 'Dionysian' has no need for a refutation of Plato or Christianity or Schopenhauer—he can *smell the decay* . . . ." ("GT," 2).

Nietzsche continues to give more variants of his definition of the Dionysian, in quoting himself from the last chapter of *Götzen-Dämmerung*: "Saying yes to life even in its strangest and hardest problems; the will to life rejoicing in the *sacrifice* of its highest types to its own inexhaustibility—*this* is what I called Dionysian [. . .] *being oneself* the eternal joy of becoming, that joy which also encompasses the *joy of destruction* . . ." ("GT," 3). Nietzsche claims to be the first who transforms this essentially artistic psychology "into a philosophical pathos." This is an interesting reformulation of his task—of what he is attempting to achieve by the revaluation of all values and in the *Umwerthung aller Werthe*. This has not yet been done—he summarizes: "*tragic wisdom* is lacking." However, he gives some examples of what such philosophical pathos and tragic wisdom consists of by referring to some aspects of the philosophy of Heraclitus: eternal recurrence and "the affirmation of transience *and destruction*, the decisive feature of any Dionysian philosophy, saying 'yes' to opposition and war, *becoming*, with a radical rejection of even the concept of 'being'" ("GT," 3). If the revaluation of values succeeds, Nietzsche promises a tragic, Dionysian, and life-affirming era in which music also will again be Dionysian.

Nietzsche continues to describe Dionysos and the Dionysian in the last three sections of his review of *Also sprach Zarathustra*—and as we will see later, it is also here that Dionysos and Zarathustra meet and sometimes almost merge. He describes his own inspiration while writing *Also sprach Zarathustra*—an inspiration out of an incomparable surfeit of strength—and then describes and quotes several aspects of *Also sprach Zarathustra* with the words: "*But this is the concept of Dionysos himself*" ("Za," 6; see the discussion later).

In the review of his last books, those written after *Also sprach Zarathustra*, he again refers to Dionysian music, to Dionysos' close association with tragedy, and to Dionysos as the god of darkness, which connects him to that whole concept of the hidden and the forbidden which Nietzsche often refers to, and had referred to in the foreword of *Ecce homo*:

> Philosophy, as I have understood and lived it so far, is choosing to live in ice and high mountains—seeking out everything alien and questionable in existence, everything that has hitherto been excluded by morality. From the long experience which such a wandering *in the forbidden* gave me, I learnt to view the reasons people have moralized and idealized so far very different from what may be wished: the *hidden* history of philosophers, the psychology of their great names came to light for me—How much truth can a spirit *stand*, how much truth does it *dare*?—for me that became more and more the real measure of value. [. . .] *Nitimur in vetitum* ["We strive for what is forbidden"]: under this sign my philosophy will triumph one day, for the only thing that has been altogether forbidden so far is the truth (EH, Foreword, 3).

The last chapter, "Why I Am a Destiny," ends not only with a reference to Dionysos; before that he repeats the claim that he has stated several times earlier—that it is part of the Dionysian nature to be "incapable of separating no-doing from yes-saying"—creating and destroying belong together.

The very last words of *Ecce homo*, and possibly the very last words Nietzsche published[44]—"*Dionysos against the crucified one . . .*"—refer to the planned *Umwerthung aller Werthe*—both its first volume, *Der Antichrist*, in which he severely criticizes Christianity, and the fourth volume, in which he planned to expound upon Dionysian philosophy, including eternal recurrence. This is supplementary to most of the rest of the chapter, which, as we have seen earlier, points primarily at the third planned volume on the theme of immoralism.

At the very end of his active life, in January 1889, Nietzsche identified with Dionysos, as can be seen in his letters, but by then he was certainly affected by mental confusion and the collapse. On January 1, 1889, he signed one draft note with "Nietzsche Dionysos," but then used just "Dionysos" in the actual dedication meant to be sent with the *Dionysos-Dithyramben* to the author Catulle Mendès. Then, on January 3, in a note to Cosima Wagner, he wrote: "It is an advantage that I am a human being [. . .] I have among the people of India been Buddha, in Greece Dionysos [. . .] This time, however, I will come as the victorious Dionysos, that will make the earth into a festival."[45] Thereafter he signed seven letters with the crucified and seven with Dionysos.

After having seen what Dionysos represents to Nietzsche, we also become aware that Nietzsche alludes to him on many occasions even when he is not mentioned explicitly. In fact, many of the late Nietzsche's writings seem to abound with allusions to Dionysos. Further information about what Dionysos represents to Nietzsche, and to Nietzsche's affirmative philosophy, can hence be gained if the discussion is broadened to include themes such as the divine, tragedy and the tragic, the transhuman, and some of Nietzsche's references to religion and paganism.

Nietzsche also associates Dionysos with secrets and secret teachings, in keeping with Dionysos' classical role as a god of the mask, of the theater, and of darkness. Further, Nietzsche also associates him with the secret mysteries that formed part of ancient Greek religion. In a more modern sense, the secret nature of his teaching is due to its being so new, radical, and dangerous (going against all the present values and customs) that much of it has of necessity been kept secret.

After having examined the evidence we have of Nietzsche's explicit references to Dionysos, it is also important to be aware of the fact that the god is a vague promise of the future. To capture some of his meaning and what he represents one needs perhaps also to use a more synthetic and imaginative approach.

5.6 The Meeting of Zarathustra and Dionysos

Zarathustra and Dionysos hardly ever "meet," but a few times they do or at least are close to meeting. Almost all the occasions when they are spoken of in the same breath are in *Ecce homo*, and in the reviews of *Die Geburt der Tragödie* and *Also sprach Zarathustra*. However, the first time they occur next to one another is much earlier and very different. In the winter of 1884/85 Nietzsche lists all of his books, from *Die Geburt der Tragödie*, as number one, to *Also sprach Zarathustra*, as number seven. He adds as number eight "*Dionysos*, or: the Holy Orgies"—thus already then Zarathustra represented the past and present, while Dionysos represented the future.[46] The next time they occur together is also in a plan for a book, in the early summer of 1885, a book divided into four sections or books.[47] In it we see Nietzsche's plan to let Zarathustra die and Dionysos take over. It seems to be a sort of continuation of his *Also sprach Zarathustra* books: What would happen if everything Zarathustra preached were to come true? This is elaborated in the draft of the first two books (or parts); thereafter the third book is characterized as "III. The superhuman conception of the world. Dionysos," and the fourth was intended to relate Zarathustra's return to his cave and animals, his blessing the world, and then his dying. We thus see here an early version of how Nietzsche planned to let his interest shift from Zarathustra, without rejecting him and what he stands for, to Dionysos. However, in the end Nietzsche never wrote a continuation of *Also sprach Zarathustra*, and Zarathustra never died.

Nietzsche hints at another slightly different but related approach in two letters from 1888, at the time when he planned a public edition of the fourth book of *Also sprach Zarathustra*. He describes this book and its place, to Carl Fuchs, on July 29, 1888, with the words: "More precisely, it is an intermission between Zarathustra and that *which follows* ('I name no names . . .'). A more exact title, a more descriptive one, would be *The Temptation of Zarathustra*: An Intermission."[48] It is my hypothesis that the name that is not mentioned is Dionysos.[49]

The later accounts of their "meetings," all but one of them in *Ecce homo*, are more as between two equals, but they are also more vague and occur mostly through metaphors. For example, in the last section of Nietzsche's late preface to *Die Geburt der Tragödie*, he describes Zarathustra as "that Dionysian monster," and in *Ecce homo*, "Why I Write Such Good Books," 5, it is suggested that Nietzsche's (and possibly also Zarathustra's) understanding of women is part of their Dionysian dowry. The other sort of metaphorical meeting involves language and style. The dithyramb, or *dithyrambos*, was a form of choral lyric sung to the god Dionysos in Greek antiquity. Nietzsche on several occasions in *Ecce homo* refers to the whole or parts of *Also sprach Zarathustra* as a dithyramb, for example, "the whole of my *Zarathustra* is a dithyramb to solitude, or, if I have been understood, to *purity* . . ." (EH, Wise, 8). Later, he refers to the poem "The Seven Seals" in the third book of the same work as a dithyramb (Write, 4) and he says that Zarathustra uses "the language of the *dithyramb*" (in the review of *Also sprach Zarathustra*, 7).

The primary and most fundamental ground shared by Zarathustra and Dionysos, the idea of eternal recurrence, is referred to in the third section of the review of *Die Geburt der Tragödie*, but a real meeting between the two is avoided. The section begins by referring to a total affirmation of life as Dionysian, and that before Nietzsche "this transformation of the Dionysian into a philosophical pathos: *tragic wisdom*" was lacking. But looking for possible predecessors, he states that "the doctrine of the 'eternal recurrence,' in other words, of the unconditional and infinitely repeated circulation of all things—ultimately this doctrine of Zarathustra's *could* also have been taught already by Heraclitus" ("GT," 3). In the next section this kinship is repeated, but more vaguely, with references to the Greek spirit and to tragedy, and with several references to Zarathustra, but they do not actually come together.

They finally are brought completely together, in any real sense, for the first time in the last three sections of Nietzsche's review of *Also sprach Zarathustra*. Nietzsche says here that his "concept of 'Dionysian' became the *highest deed*" in *Also sprach Zarathustra*. He continues:

> Zarathustra feels himself to be the *highest of all species of being*; and when we hear how he defines it, we will dispense with searching for his like.
>
> —the soul that has the longest ladder and so reaches down deepest,
>
> the most comprehensive soul, that can run and stray and roam the farthest within itself,
>
> the most necessary soul, that with pleasure plunges itself into chance,
>
> the being soul, that *wills* to enter Becoming; the having soul, that *wills* to enter willing and longing—
>
> that flees from itself and retrieves itself in the widest circles,
>
> the wisest soul, which folly exhorts most sweetly,
>
> the soul that loves itself the most, in which all things have their streaming and counter-streaming and ebb and flood— —
>
> *But that is the concept of Dionysos himself.* [. . .] Zarathustra [. . .] the opposite of a no-saying spirit [. . .] Zarathustra is a dancer [. . .] who has the harshest, most terrible insight into reality, who has thought the "most abysmal thought," nevertheless finds in it no objection to existence, or even to the eternal recurrence of existence—but rather yet another reason *to be himself* the eternal "yes" to all things, "the enormous and unbounded Yes- and Amen-saying" . . . "Into all abysses I carry my blessing Yes-saying" . . . *But that is the concept of Dionysos once again.* ("Za," 6)

In section 7, Zarathustra is referred to as "such a Dionysos," and after a long quote from *Also sprach Zarathustra*, Nietzsche writes: "Nothing like this has ever been composed, ever been felt, ever been *suffered*: this is how a god suffers, a Dionysos." Zarathustra, at his best, becomes like Dionysos. Nietzsche ends the review of *Also sprach Zarathustra* by referring to Zarathustra's "imperative 'Become hard!,'" the deepest conviction *that all creators are hard*, is the true badge of a Dionysian nature." This is thus another trait and teaching which they share.

Throughout these three sections, Zarathustra and Dionysos "meet" as near equals and without tension. However, they are not quite the same or equal. Zarathustra needs to strive and overcome his disgust for man, while Dionysos likes man. Zarathustra is the teacher of eternal recurrence, but Dionysos is that thought and the total affirmation itself. Zarathustra at his best comes close to the god Dionysos.

What we thus see is that the meeting of these two symbols constitutes no great problem for Nietzsche. Although they are slightly different, Nietzsche makes them compatible, and transference of his allegiance from Zarathustra to Dionysos, which never actually occurs due to Nietzsche's mental collapse, but is prepared for, would not constitute a problem.

That Zarathustra is used so much as a symbol in *Ecce homo* probably reflects the simple fact that the transference to Dionysos and the affirmative aspect of the revaluation of all values had not yet been reached, neither by Nietzsche the author and philosopher, nor in the text of *Ecce homo*, which was to be published before the *Umwerthung aller Werthe*. Furthermore, a reading and understanding of *Also sprach Zarathustra* is the best way to prepare for the *Umwerthung aller Werthe*, according to Nietzsche.

This harmonious relationship between Zarathustra and Dionysos can also be seen in that Nietzsche for a long time hesitated about which the better symbol to use for the title of his late collection of poems was. For a long time he planned to call it "The Songs of Zarathustra," and Zarathustra is also the major figure in them, but in the end Nietzsche decided to give preference to the superior representation and symbol of the future, and entitled it *Dionysos-Dithyramben*.

We have seen that the number of references to Zarathustra and Dionysos after 1885 are almost evenly split, and highly in praise of both. However, the nature of the references differs in that Zarathustra is continually seen as Nietzsche's equal, and is sometimes identified with Nietzsche himself, while Dionysos is always referred to as a god or as his teacher, and thus as standing above and beyond Nietzsche. Furthermore, all the references to Zarathustra and *Also sprach Zarathustra* are to the present or past, while many of those to Dionysos are directed toward the future.

5.7 Conclusion

As we have seen earlier, Zarathustra was a symbol of many things for Nietzsche. More than anything else, he was the teacher of eternal recurrence; but he also represents the overcoming of morality, thus immoralism, as well as atheism, skepticism, and the like. He is a severe critic of present values and ideals, and he also suggests new "half-written tables of values." Zarathustra can easily be taken to constitute Nietzsche's most important symbol, and that impression seems confirmed by Nietzsche's claim that there were no counter-ideals before *Also sprach Zarathustra*, and that he has said nothing in *Ecce homo* that he could not have said already five years before, through the mouth of Zarathustra.

We have also seen that Dionysos in Nietzsche's writings came to represent many important *topoi*:, tragedy, life-affirmation, creativity (and destruction) and realism. He also represents darkness (and the forbidden—which Nietzsche had referred to at the end of *Jenseits von Gut und Böse*, the beginning of *Ecce homo*, and in many late notes—probably another allusion to what was to come in the planned *Umwerthung aller Werthe*): revaluation, the anti-Christ,[50] *extasis*, music, immoralism, and association with Ariadne (which eventually will lead Nietzsche to identify with Dionysos).

Dionysos is a symbol that connects the late Nietzsche with the early Nietzsche, at least with *Die Geburt der Tragödie* (which we also could notice in the review of that work in *Ecce homo* and in the last chapter of *Götzen-Dämmerung*). This was valuable for Nietzsche, and helped him develop his attempt at a revaluation of all values, for many of the revalued values have a close kinship with ancient Greek values (as we will see in the next chapter). But it has also led many modern commentators and readers astray in accepting Nietzsche's own exaggerated claims of the similarities between his early and late thought.

Although the picture of Dionysos is in many ways vague, he more than anything else is a symbol of total affirmation! And thus he is closely associated with tragedy, *amor fati*, and eternal recurrence. Most of the other things he symbolized in *Ecce homo* follow directly from this.

The best interpretation of the meaning of the symbols Zarathustra and Dionysos, and their relation to one another, seems to be that Zarathustra is more or less synonymous with Nietzsche himself (in a somewhat improved version).[51] Nietzsche frequently refers to him as "my son" and at least twice to himself as Zarathustra's father and also as his mother (in the sense of being pregnant with him),[52] and in *Ecce homo* he states that his own name and that of Zarathustra's are interchangeable.[53] Zarathustra thus becomes a symbol that follows Nietzsche's intellectual development, and is therefore associated with a human and with an ever moving "present." Dionysos, on the other hand, represents a god, the future, and Nietzsche's teacher—that is, that which draws and tempts Nietzsche onward—a state which can never be achieved, but always striven toward. This fits well and is compatible with the theme of this study that *Ecce homo* is both backward- and forward-looking, that both Zarathustra and Dionysos are emphasized in it.

This is true for Zarathustra and Dionysos as Nietzsche's symbols—Zarathustra as representing Nietzsche and his development—from this perspective it is not surprising that Zarathustra becomes such a dominant figure in *Ecce homo* (which is meant to present Nietzsche, or a somewhat idealized picture of Nietzsche)—while Dionysos represents his goal and future.

But they are not only Nietzsche's symbols, they are both also Nietzsche's creations. He answers, in *Ecce homo*, the question why he chose Zarathustra as one of his symbols: because he, as Zoroaster, as the founder of Zoroastrianism, as the one who first moralized the world, who performed "the translation of morality into the metaphysical" and regarded "the struggle of good and evil [as] the true driving-wheel" should also be the first to acknowledge the mistake and thereby become "the first immoralist" (EH, Destiny, 3).[54] But why did he choose Dionysos? He needed not just a prophet, but a god. For his purpose, to represent new values and ideals—and to replace the old God—a new god seems an apt symbol. In fact, it is difficult to imagine a more suitable one. And if it were to be a god, Dionysos is surely the perfect choice. Not only because of what he stands for according to Greek mythology (such as being a god of tragedy, *exstasis*, darkness, mystery, masks, and repetition), and that Nietzsche thus reconnects with his own early work and first book, but also because ancient Greek values constitute so much of both specific and of general stimulus for the new revalued values. Furthermore, this new god, in contrast to the old God, is not only non-metaphysical but also a conscious *symbol*, that is, not something one believes in, but something that reminds us of our values and ideals. In fact, if we examine Nietzsche's view of gods and how they are created, we get a sort of answer to why he selected Dionysos. At the end of the second essay of *Zur Genealogie der Moral* (on guilt, and other feelings) Nietzsche discusses what the conception of gods can mean:

> The fact that *conceiving* gods does not necessarily, in itself, lead to a degraded imagination—that's something we have to consider for a moment, the point that there are *more uplifting* ways to use the invention of the gods than for this human self-crucifixion and self-laceration of man, in which Europe in the last millennia

> has become an expert. Fortunately that something we can infer if we take a look at the *Greek gods*, these reflections of nobler men, more rulers of themselves, in whom the *animal* in man felt himself deified and did *not* tear himself apart, did *not* rage against himself! [. . .] In this way, the gods then served to justify men to a certain extent, even in bad things. They served as the origin of evil—at that time the gods took upon themselves, not punishment, but, what is *nobler*, the guilt . . . [GM, II, 23].

A year later, in the early summer of 1888, Nietzsche expresses it even more strongly in a long note entitled "Towards a History of the Concept of God," where he argues that the nature of a god or gods is merely the reflection of the creative will, or will to power, of a people.[55] In the last, the fifth, section of this note he writes:

> Almost two millennia and not a single new god! [. . .]—And how many new gods are still possible! As for myself, in whom the religious, that is to say god-*forming* instinct occasionally again wants to become active: how differently, how variously the divine has revealed itself to me each time! [. . .] I should not doubt that there are many kinds of gods. . . . There are some one cannot imagine without a certain halcyon and frivolous quality in their makeup. . . . Perhaps light feet are even an integral part of the concept "god." . . . Is it necessary to elaborate that a god prefers to stay beyond everything bourgeois and rational? and, between ourselves, also beyond good and evil? His prospect is *free*—in Goethe's words.

Nietzsche used the first four sections of this note, which are all critical of Christianity, for *Der Antichrist*, but not the fifth and last section. It seems to me likely that he saved this last section on purpose to be used in the last volume of the *Umwerthung aller Werthe*, with the more affirmative and constructive approach suitable for the title *Dionysos philosophos*.

In the last few lines after this, Nietzsche connects to Zarathustra: "And to call upon the inestimable authority of Zarathustra in this instance: Zarathustra goes so far as to confess: 'I would believe only in a god who could *dance*' . . . To repeat: how many new gods are still possible!—Zarathustra himself, to be sure, is merely an old atheist. One must understand him correctly! Zarathustra, it is true, says he *would*; but Zarathustra *will* not . . . ."[56]

This may be read as an example of the transference of allegiance from Zarathustra to Dionysos. Zarathustra is a fantastic symbol for fighting the old values and liberating oneself, and even for pointing forward (wanting a god who can dance), but he is nonetheless not able to represent these new values. Already in a letter from May 1885 (Nietzsche had by then began work on his future four-volume *magnum opus*) he writes: "Do not believe that my son Zarathustra speaks *my* opinions. He is one of my preparations and intermissions."[57] To represent the revalued values was to be the task of Dionysos.

The last words in the block-quotation above is an allusion to the last scene in *Faust*, but it is also relevant to relate it to the end of the chapter "Reconnaissance Raids of an Untimely Man" in *Götzen-Dämmerung* and the discussion of Goethe in the last three sections there, 49 to 51. Nietzsche praises Goethe enormously here, and one can see much of Nietzsche's affirmative or positive human ideals in that portrait:

> He bore its strongest instincts in himself [. . .] he did not divorce himself from life but immersed himself in it; he never lost heart, and took as much as possible upon himself, above himself, into himself. What he wanted was *totality*: he fought against the disjunction of reason, sensuality, feeling, will [. . .] he disciplined himself into a whole, he *created* himself.

After having thus described Goethe (and his human ideal), he connects him to Dionysos:

> Such a *liberated* spirit stands in the midst of the universe with a joyful and trusting fatalism, with *faith* in the fact that only what is individual is reprehensible, that everything is redeemed and affirmed in the whole—*he no longer denies* . . . . But such a faith is the highest of all possible faiths: I have baptized it with the name of *Dionysos*.

We again notice the enormous importance of Dionysos to Nietzsche, but also that he makes clear that Dionysos is just a symbol. What is primary is the total affirmation.

Immediately after this account of Goethe at the end of *Götzen-Dämmerung* he summarizes, in the last sentence of the last section, 51, what was intended to have been the end of the book: "I have given humanity the most profound book it possesses, my *Zarathustra*: I shall shortly give it the most independent one—," that is, he points to his planned four-volume *Hauptwerk*, and promises to publish it soon with the title *Revaluation of All Values* (see the foreword to *Götzen-Dämmerung*, where he states that he has just finished the first book of the *Umwerthung aller Werthe*), for which both this work and *Ecce homo* are preparatory.

For those who read *Ecce homo* primarily as an autobiography, the emphasis on Zarathustra in the text is at least in part comprehensible (although, apparently, irritating to many commentators), both as attempting to give attention to that work and as pointing out that it was his best work (although, according to most commentators, he unfortunately uses exaggerated language to get this message across). Thereto comes the fact that most modern readers, at least academic readers, do not share this view and, instead, prefer other books.[58]

However, for such readers Nietzsche's references to Dionysos make little sense. Why begin and end the book with references to Dionysos, not to speak of all the references in between? And why does *Jenseits von Gut und Böse, Zur Genealogie der Moral*, and *Götzen-Dämmerung* likewise end in a similar way? This becomes just a shot in the dark—or may perhaps be seen as a sort of nostalgia for his first book (but, then, why is that which Dionysos represents so different in these later books?).

For those who read *Ecce homo* as pointing forward, the references to Dionysos are obvious allusions and pointers to what was to come. As he writes to his publisher, *Ecce homo* "is a in the highest degree *preparatory* text."[59] Of that which was planned, only *Der Antichrist* was written (with no reference to Dionysos), but there are strong reasons to assume that he planned to write three further volumes, and that some of that planned content can be found in his late books and more in his late notes. Realizing this "forward" intention of *Ecce homo* means reading it in a different manner than how it usually has been done. Furthermore, we have in this chapter seen many of the things Dionysos represents, but we are, in fact, able to excavate more things about Dionysos' teachings, or expressed differently, more about what Nietzsche planned to discuss and express in the *Umwerthung aller Werthe*, as we will see in the next chapter.

6

What Can We Learn about the *Revaluation of All Values* from *Ecce Homo* and Late Texts?

6.1 Introduction

We have seen that the philosophical theme of revaluation has been prominent throughout *Ecce homo*, and that it is also pivotal in several of Nietzsche's other late books and notes. It is obviously an important trope in his late writings, but is it possible to go beyond the rhetorical level—with statements such as that it will divide human history in two, and that Nietzsche is carrying the fate of mankind on his shoulders—and learn more about what, for Nietzsche, it actually stood for? There are three obvious questions to inquire about (A, B, and C) for the purpose of clarifying the meaning of Nietzsche's revaluation of all values, and which we will attempt to answer in this chapter. However, we cannot expect complete answers, for *Ecce homo* was only conceived of as a preface to the *Umwerthung aller Werthe*, in which these questions and themes would be dealt with in much more detail.

A. What does Nietzsche say explicitly and generally about the revaluation in *Ecce homo* (and some other late texts)? How does he describe and characterize it?
B. Is it possible to distinguish specific "revaluations" and in particular pairs of traits, attitudes, or systems with "opposite" valuation—where one represents decadence (or Christian or modern) values and the other represents the other sort of (according to Nietzsche) healthier and more life-affirming (Dionysian) values? If this is possible, it would certainly help clarify much of the specific nature of the revalued values.
C. Are we able to say more about the general nature of this set of revalued values? Do these values share common characteristics and/or a common origin or development (for example, belonging to or showing similarity with those of any specific period or culture)?

6.2 General Characterization of the Revaluation in *Ecce Homo* and Other Late Texts

Let us begin with the first question (A): How does Nietzsche generally describe and characterize the revaluation in *Ecce homo*? At first sight it might appear as if Nietzsche's words about the revaluation are merely rhetorical, but on closer inspection and after collecting all his scattered references to it in *Ecce homo*,[1] one discovers that he actually gives a fairly detailed description of how he regarded such a "highest act of self-reflection on the part of humanity" (EH, Destiny, 1).

Of great importance for our understanding of the nature of Nietzsche's revaluation project are two connected premises which he mentions. Probably the most specific clue to how Nietzsche regarded the revaluation is the first one of these premises, his view that one revaluation has already occurred, and thus that the one he strove for to a large extent was a re-revaluation, back to older and more original values. Furthermore, as the second premise, Nietzsche regarded these older values and ideals as more natural and healthier. This, Nietzsche's emphasis that one revaluation has already occurred, has important consequences for how one must view his revaluation project. Furthermore, since Nietzsche regarded the "older" value-system as more natural (and healthier), his emphasis is on the critique and removal of the false values and ideals, rather than on pointing at or creating *ab initio* new ones. This explains why he claims not to set up any new ideals in the foreword—what he largely sees himself doing is exposing the present false ideals and thus giving room for the older, more natural ideals and values again. "The psychological problem about the type of Zarathustra is how one who to an unprecedented degree says 'no,' *does* 'no' to everything people previously said 'yes' to, can nevertheless be the opposite of a no-saying spirit [. . .] but, rather, yet another reason *to be himself* the eternal 'yes' to all things" (EH, "Za," 6).

Already in Nietzsche's very first published use of the word "revaluation" and the expression "revaluation of all values," in *Jenseits von Gut und Böse*, 46, he clearly sets up a dichotomy and claims that a revaluation has already occurred. The dichotomy is between freedom, pride, and self-confidence on the one side and enslavement, self-mockery, and self-mutilation on the other, where the latter is associated with Christianity. Thereafter he states:

> Modern men, with their obtruseness to all Christian nomenclature, no longer sense the gruesome superlative which lay for an antique taste in the paradoxical

> formula "god on the cross." Never and nowhere has there hitherto been a comparable boldness in inversion, anything so fearsome, questioning, and questionable, as this formula: it promised a revaluation of all the values of antiquity.

Nietzsche thus sees or constructs a dichotomy between ancient and Christian values. In this first occurrence, the revaluation referred to is thus the earlier and *negative* one from antiquity to Christianity.[2] Nietzsche repeats this view in his next book:

> On the other hand, could anyone, using the full subtlety of his mind, imagine a more dangerous bait? Something to match the enticing, intoxicating, narcotizing, corrupting power of that symbol of the "holy cross," that ghastly paradox of a "god on the cross," that mystery of an unimaginable and ultimate final cruelty and self-crucifixion of god for the salvation of mankind? At least it is certain that *sub hoc signo* [*under this sign*] Israel, with its vengeance and revaluation of the worth of all other previous values, has triumphed again and again over all other ideals, over all nobler ideals. (*Zur Genealogie der Moral*, I, 8)

That Nietzsche also, in *Ecce homo,* assumed that an earlier revaluation had already occurred is visible in section 7 of the last chapter: "Indeed, this is *my* insight: the teachers, the leaders of humanity, theologians all of them, were also, all of them, *décadents*: *hence* the revaluation of all values into hostility to life, *hence* morality" (EH, Destiny, 7). We also see it, and its close connection to Christianity (even if he often also includes classical philosophy from Socrates and Plato onward and Jewish religion), in that he emphasizes that what he is criticizing is the past 2,000 years: "my attack on two millennia of perversion and defilement of the human" (EH, Books, 'GT', 4),[3] and thus that a previous "décadent" revaluation already occurred about 2,000 years ago.

The fact that Nietzsche regarded the Christian value paradigm as anti-natural is a constant theme in the books from 1888. In *Ecce homo*, he, for example, writes:

> Christian morality—the most malignant form of the will to falsehood, the true Circe of humanity: the thing that *ruined* it. It is *not* the mistake as such that incenses me about this sight, *not* the millennia-old lack of "good will," of discipline, of decency, of bravery in spiritual matter that its victory betrays—it is the lack of nature, it is the utterly dreadful fact that *anti-nature* itself has been receiving the highest honors as morality and as law, as categorical imperative, has been hanging above humanity! [. . .] the sole morality that has hitherto been taught, the morality of unselfing oneself, betrays a will to the end; at the most fundamental level it *denies* life [. . .] avenging themselves *on life*. (EH, Destiny, 7)

In section 6 of the last chapter he refers to the ideals of Christianity as "*world-denial*!" and in section 8 he states: "The concept 'God' invented as a counter-concept to life—bringing together into one dreadful unity everything harmful, poisonous, slanderous, the whole mortal enmity against life! The concept of 'hereafter,' 'true world,' invented in order to devalue the *only* world there is—so as to leave no goal, no reason, no task for our earthly reality."

This is made even clearer in his notes. In an important note, in which Nietzsche summarizes many of his plans for the *Umwerthung aller Werthe* project, with the title "To Plans" he writes: "In place of *moral values* nothing but *natural* values. Naturalizing morality."[4] In another note, with reference to how the early Christians regarded the body, he writes that they "revalued the natural value."[5] The fact that Nietzsche believes that the critique and removal of the false ideals and values would be sufficient for the more natural and healthier values to flourish is expressed in a note from early 1888: "If the tyranny of present values is broken in this way, we will have abolished the 'real world,' then a *new order of values* must follow of its own accord."[6] Shortly thereafter Nietzsche states in a note: "Let us now purify the *opposite valuation* [i.e., the healthy valuation] of the infection and half-measures, from its *degeneration*, in which form it is known to us all. Theory of *anti-naturalization* and *restoration of nature*: **moraline-free**" (emphasis in original).[7]

Nietzsche thus views one of the systems of value as natural and the other as not. Nietzsche writes: "I contradict as has never been contradicted and am nonetheless the opposite of a no-saying spirit" (EH, Destiny, 1). The reason he can make this apparently paradoxical statement is that he contradicts within one "paradigm," while praising or pointing at another—or, alternatively expressed, he regards himself as a philosophical physician who is negating a negation, who is attacking a disease and thus, by negating, being curative.[8]

Nietzsche suggests that examples of the sort of values and attitudes that are more natural and existed before the first negative revaluation can be found among the early Greeks, in tragedy, and in what he calls the Dionysian.[9] We can, for example, see this at the end of his discussion of *Die Geburt der Tragödie*, where Nietzsche clearly refers to a revival of Greek values: "Everything in this essay [*Die Geburt der Tragödie*] is prophetic: the proximity of the return of the Greek spirit, the necessity for *counter-Alexanders* to *retie* the Gordian knot of Greek culture after it had been untied. . . . Listen to the world-historic accent with which the concept 'tragic disposition' is introduced."

Also, in the very last section of *Götzen-Dämmerung*, originally written as part of an early version of *Ecce homo* and entitled "What I Owe the Ancients,"

Nietzsche suggests that early Greek antiquity, tragedy, and the Dionysian constitute essential parts of the healthy value-system:

> Tragedy [. . .] affirmation of life [. . .] is what I called Dionysian [. . .] the eternal joy of becoming [. . .] And with that I again return to the place from which I set out—the *Birth of Tragedy* was my first revaluation of all values: with that I again plant myself in the soil out of which I draw all that I will and *can*—I, the last disciple of the philosopher Dionysos.—, the teacher of the eternal recurrence. . .

Nietzsche is now, in 1888, able to regard his attempt at understanding and affecting a revival of tragedy as his first re-revaluation! I will discuss this healthier ancient value-system, which existed before the first decadent revaluation, later in this chapter.

6.3 Examples of "Counter-Movements," Periods, and Persons

Nietzsche is not alone in attempting to restore more natural and healthier values and valuations, in attempting a re-revaluation. In the last chapter of *Ecce homo* he criticizes the long period in which the life-denying values have prevailed: "The millennia [. . .] with the exception of five or six moments in history, with myself as a seventh" (EH, Destiny, 7). It is not completely clear which those other moments in history are, as persons, periods, or movements, but two or three of them are explicitly mentioned in the second section of the review of *Der Fall Wagner* (and in several notes);[10] the Renaissance, emancipated science (and scholarship), and perhaps Napoleon.[11] In fact, Nietzsche frequently refers to the "counter-movement" in his late notes, depending on the context, sometimes referring to those or that which represents "new" values, and sometimes "old" and decadent ones.[12]

The two most obvious periods Nietzsche praises as not being ruled by life-denying values are the early ancient Greek period (which I will discuss in the latter part of this chapter) and the Renaissance. In *Ecce homo* Nietzsche emphasizes the importance of the Renaissance in regard to the revaluation of values in his review of *Der Fall Wagner*, 2:

> The Germans robbed Europe of the harvest, the meaning of the last *great* period, the Renaissance period, at the point when a higher order of values, when the noble, life-affirming future-confirming values had achieved a victory at the seat of the opposite values, the *values of decline* [. . .] Christianity, this *denial of the will to life* made into a religion!

In the penultimate section of *Der Antichrist*, Nietzsche had already discussed the Renaissance (although it was intended to be published *after Ecce homo*), and we are there presented with perhaps the clearest expression of what the revaluation of all values means and what sort of values it implies. Nietzsche claims that a re-revaluation already has been attempted, and for a time succeeded, but in the end it failed:

> [. . .] *what* the Renaissance was? The *revaluation of Christian values*, the attempt, undertaken with every expedient, with every instinct, with genius of every kind, to bring about the victory of the opposing values, the *noble* values. . . . Up till now *this* has been the only great war, there has been no more decisive questioning than that conducted by the Renaissance—*my* question is its question—: [. . .] to set the *noble* values on the throne, which is to say to set them *into* the instincts, the deepest needs and desires of him who sits thereon [. . .] Christianity would thereby have been *abolished*!—What happened? [. . .] Luther *restored the Church*: he attacked it. . . . The Renaissance—an event without meaning, a great *in vain*!—[13]

Notice that Nietzsche here, and earlier, refers to "*the* opposing values" and not "a set of opposing values" or just "opposing values," strongly implying that it is a question of only two fundamental alternatives, that is, a dichotomy of values, life-affirming and life-denying ones.

Nietzsche constantly praises the Renaissance highly. Like antiquity, but more rarely and on a lower level, it constitutes an example and model for him. He refers to it as the "last *great* age"[14] and claims that "in the modern time it is the Italian Renaissance which has brought man the highest."[15] He highly commends its sense of *virtù* (closely related to the ancient, Homeric concept of virtue, but very different from the Christian one), and he regards modern man as inferior to the man of the Renaissance, but "the man of the Renaissance is inferior to the man of antiquity."[16] The Renaissance is generally regarded as a rebirth of antiquity and was so viewed by Nietzsche too: "There was [. . .] in the Renaissance an uncanny and glittering reawakening of the classical ideal, of the noble mode of evaluating all things."[17] Thus when he claims that "*my* question is its question" (quoted earlier in the last block quotation), he refers to the Renaissance revaluation of Christian values into essentially ancient values.

Another "counter-movement" to Christianity and decadent values is, according to Nietzsche, science or emancipated science. Nietzsche was convinced that *Wissenschaft*—science and scholarship—has been under the influence of moral values and Christianity for the past 2,000 years or more. However, much less so than philosophy, to the extent that he regarded science as an ally in his critique of Christianity,[18] and perhaps of much of decadence in general. Science now needs to be liberated from this influence, and that is what he referred to when he spoke of the "emancipation of science."[19] In fact, from Nietzsche's late notes it is possible to see how he distinguished "old," pre-revaluation science from "new," post-revaluation science (for comparative purposes I also include some of the related characteristics of "old" or traditional philosophy in the first column Table 6.1).[20]

Table 6.1 Nietzsche's Views of Pre- and Post-Revaluation Science

"Old" Philosophy	**Science before the "Revaluation"**	**Science after the "Revaluation"**
In the service of morality and religion	Under the influence of morality and religion	Emancipated from morality and religion
Much of "old" philosophy is of bad quality	Much of "old" science is of bad quality. Sociology: governed by herd-values, belief in altruism. History: influenced by nationalism, religion, and egalitarian values	—
Assumes reality to be a priori and static	? [Reality as semi-dynamic and semi-complex?]	Reality is dynamic and complex
Moralistic	Anthropocentric (without awareness of it)	Anthropocentric (with awareness)
Hostile to reality and the senses	Alienated from reality	Close relation to reality The natural again restored
Two-world dichotomy: "true" and "apparent"	Accepts two-world dichotomy, but speaks only of the "apparent" world	Only *one* world (does not accept the dichotomy)
Concepts, knowledge, and truth as absolute	?	Concepts as relational; knowledge and truth as perspectival
Lacks intellectual honesty	Possesses intellectual honesty	Strong emphasis on intellectual honesty
Wants values to be unconditional	Values as conditional	Values as conditional The natural again restored
Lacks methods to deal with values	?	?
Regards conscious (rational) as better than unconscious	Regards conscious (rational) as better than unconscious	Regards unconscious (not rationalized) as better than conscious
Dogmatic	Partly experimental and hypothetical	Experimental, hypothetical, provisional, a process

Science, independent of whether of the "old" or the "new" kind (for the difference between the two forms is much smaller than for "old" and "new" philosophy) was for Nietzsche an important counter-movement against idealism, Christianity, and decadence.

Another counter-movement was Napoleon, who, for Nietzsche, stood for active and noble values and ideals. Nietzsche's great admiration for Napoleon, and his statements about him, for example, in the fifth book of *Die fröhliche Wissenschaft* (1887) and in *Zur Genealogie der Moral* (1887) clearly suggest that he regarded him as the only genuinely positive outcome of the French Revolution, and that he saw him as a possible predecessor and as a representative of the counter-movement against decadence and Christianity:

> He should receive credit some day for the fact that in Europe the *man* has again become master over the businessman and the philistine [. . .] Napoleon [. . .] as one of the greatest continuators of the Renaissance; he brought back again a whole slab of antiquity, perhaps even the decisive piece, the piece of granite. And who knows whether this slab of antiquity might not finally become master again over the national movement, and whether it must not become the heir and continuator of Napoleon in an *affirmative* sense; for what he wanted was one unified Europe, as is known—as *mistress of the earth.*— (*Die fröhliche Wissenschaft*, V, 362)[21]

6.4 Finding Life-Affirmative Values in History

That Nietzsche was not primarily concerned with *creating* completely new values and ways of valuation (as it has often been interpreted), but, instead, searched for them in history can be seen, for example, in the sixth section of his review of *Menschliches, Allzumenschliches* in *Ecce homo,* where he states that the revaluation is a consequence of historical knowledge and development: "This principle, hardened and sharpened under the hammer blows of historical knowledge (*liesz: Revaluation of All Values*)."[22] The importance of history for the revaluation, and more concretely, what in history, is expressed in a note from the first half of 1888: "I sought in history the beginning of the construction of reverse ideals (the concepts 'pagan,' 'classical,' 'noble' newly discovered and expounded—)."[23] For the importance of noble and aristocratic values for Nietzsche, see also the discussion at the end of this chapter.

Does Nietzsche mean that all values are to be revalued? In one sense, when speaking generally, this certainly seems to be the case, as when the whole manner of viewing truth, the world, and values changes (even if some specific traits and virtues will remain with the same value). However, when approaching the revaluation by examining the value of each trait or property, one after another—it seems unlikely that Nietzsche expected each and every one of them to change (compare the discussion in the next section of this chapter, of, for example, courage and honesty). When Nietzsche in *Zur Genealogie der Moral* speaks of two fundamental value-systems, related to master- and slave-values, he assumes that most of us possess within us both sets of values and thus not all values will have to change:[24]

> For thousands of years, a fearful struggle has raged on earth between the two opposed value-judgements, "good and bad" and "good and evil"; and as certain as it is that the second value-judgement has long been in the ascendant, there is even now no shortage of places where the outcome of the conflict remains undecided. It might even be said that the conflict has escalated in the interim and so become increasingly profound, more spiritual: so that today there is perhaps no more decisive mark of the "*higher nature*," of the more spiritual nature, than to be divided against oneself in this sense and to remain a battleground for these oppositions. (GM, I, 16: Douglas Smith's translation)

We have thus seen that beside and behind Nietzsche's highly rhetorical references and statements about the revaluation in *Ecce homo,* it is in fact possible to find a fairly detailed description of how he regarded the revaluation.

6.5 Further Sources for Information about Nietzsche's Revaluation

For further sources and information about what Nietzsche meant with his revaluation of all values, and for further concrete examples, there are several texts to consult. Perhaps the most obvious is *Der Antichrist*, which constituted the first book of the *Umwerthung aller Werthe* when he wrote it in September 1888, especially the first fourteen sections.[25] Also the chapter, "What I Owe the Ancients" in *Götzen-Dämmerung*, which was written in close association with *Ecce homo*, as well as the rest of that work, contains much interesting information about how Nietzsche viewed his revaluation. Of relevance is also the fifth and last book of *Die fröhliche Wissenschaft*, and especially for aesthetic values, *Der Fall*

Wagner. Of especial interest is also *Also sprach Zarathustra*, which he praises so highly in *Ecce homo*, and especially the chapter "Of Old and New Law-Tables" in the third book of *Also sprach Zarathustra*. Most of this is beyond the scope of this study, which primarily deals with *Ecce homo*, but *Götzen-Dämmerung* is discussed in the last section of this chapter, and here I will briefly discuss the most relevant chapter of *Also sprach Zarathustra*.

For Nietzsche, *Also sprach Zarathustra* is a tragic work.[26] We need to recall that tragedy is for Nietzsche an affirmative art and *Weltanschauung*: "the *affirmative* pathos *par excellence*, I call the tragic pathos."[27] When Nietzsche introduces Zarathustra for the first time, in *Die fröhliche Wissenschaft*, 342, this section is called "*Incipit tragoedia*," that is, "the tragedy begins," and the section also ends with these words. He uses the same words when he refers to *Also sprach Zarathustra* after it was written, in *Die fröhliche Wissenschaft*, V, 382. This section he also quotes in *Ecce homo* at length (EH, Books, Zarathustra, 2). In his review of *Also sprach Zarathustra* in *Ecce homo* he refers to it, or aspects of it, five or six times as the concept of Dionysos and as being Dionysian, and he refers to the language of Zarathustra as dithyrambic. The tragic *Weltanschauung* is, according to Nietzsche, akin to ancient tragedy.

We cannot examine all the values expounded in *Also sprach Zarathustra* here, but those of "that decisive chapter" ("Of Old and New Law-Tables"), so suitable for a study of the revaluation of all values, can be commented upon. The theme of this chapter in *Also sprach Zarathustra* is clearly one of revaluation even if the expression is not used. About half of the thirty sections of this, the longest chapter in *Also sprach Zarathustra*, are critical and give different versions of "shatter the old law-tables"! This critique culminates in the command: "Shatter, shatter the good and the just!" The new law-tables are only half-written, lying among the old shattered ones. We are given a rather long list—in the form of metaphors and similes—of virtues, descriptions, and imperatives, summarizing much of what has been said earlier in *Also sprach Zarathustra*. (Nietzsche did not publish part four of *Also sprach Zarathustra* and therefore this section which is placed near the end of part three, can well be seen as a summary.) The affirmative part of this chapter claims that what is good and bad depends on the goal, and the goal is the *Übermensch*. To this theme a number of concepts are associated: the future, a new nobility, wanting to rule, and life and society as an experiment. We are further given a description of "the highest soul," while numerous "virtues" are described and recommended: the bestowing virtue, honesty (realism), creativity, courage, dance and laughter, pride and self-love, self-overcoming and becoming better than the best (compare Nietzsche's interest in and praise of the

Greek concepts *agon* and *aristeuein*), and willingness to sacrifice oneself and one's neighbors. It culminates in "This new law-table do I put over you, O my brothers: *Become hard*!"—for the noble and the creative are hard.[28]

This interpretation of *Also sprach Zarathustra* as the culmination of Nietzsche's affirmative values is confirmed a little later in *Ecce homo*, where Nietzsche claims that the domination of Christian values was due to the fact that "above all, a *counter-ideal* was lacking—until *Zarathustra*."[29] Thereafter Nietzsche refers to the tremendous task of the revaluation and speaks of it as a shattering thunderbolt, explaining thereby the title of the last chapter: "Why I am a Destiny." In section eight of this chapter Nietzsche reconnects to *Also sprach Zarathustra* and gives several examples of truths and concepts created by Christian morality but absent among healthy values:

> Have I been understood? I have not just now said a word that I could not have said five years ago through the mouth of Zarathustra—The *unmasking* of Christian morality is an event without equal, a real catastrophe. He who exposes it is a *force majeure*, a destiny [. . .] The concept "God" invented as the antithetical concept to life [. . .] The concept "soul," "spirit," finally even "immortal soul," invented so as to despise the body, so as to make it sick [. . .] The concept "sin" invented together with the instrument of torture which goes with it, the concept of "free will" [. . .] Finally—it is the most fearful—in the concept of the *good* man common cause made with everything weak, sick, ill-constituted, suffering from itself [. . .] an ideal made of opposition to the proud and well-constituted, to the affirmative man, to the man certain of the future and guaranteeing the future—the latter is henceforth called the *evil man*. . . . And all this was believed in *as morality*!—*Ecrasez l'infâme*! (*Ecce homo*, "Destiny," 8)

We are here given examples of several values and character traits that Nietzsche approves of and regards as healthier revalued values or concepts (God—life; soul and immortal soul—body; sin—innocence; the weak and sick as ideals—the proud and well-constituted). It is thus time for us to move on to the next section and discuss these and other concrete such values and traits.

6.6 Concrete Revalued or Healthy Values

Can we identify specific values and value-systems that Nietzsche revalues in *Ecce homo* (B)? Yes, as we have just seen it is possible to identify a number of "revaluations" in *Ecce homo*. Some are associated with a number of generally accepted virtues (such as honesty and compassion), with general views (such as pessimism and Christianity) or with other characteristics (such as dialectics and feelings of guilt). Many of them will, on closer inspection, be seen as closely associated with one another, or as partially overlapping. One can distinguish four groups of things being "revalued" in *Ecce homo* (here sometimes listed as a single trait, attitude, or system, but also often as a pair of opposing traits or systems). The first category (1) contains broader systems or views which Nietzsche criticizes or "revalues." The following three categories contain many specific traits, virtues, properties, and attitudes. The first of these (2) contains those which Nietzsche, on the whole, appears to agree with, and thus to accept the "conventional" view and value, the second (3) those whose "traditional" value Nietzsche reverses or changes significantly, while the last one (4) lists new or unusual traits and properties that Nietzsche emphasizes as valuable.

Some readers may feel that only those in the third (and possibly those in the fourth) group are true candidates for being revalued, and it is correct that these are the most obvious candidates. However, all four groups are necessary for an understanding of Nietzsche and his revaluation project. Although a revaluation of a trait most frequently means that its value becomes different or even opposite to its traditional value, this is not always or necessarily so. One of Nietzsche's descriptions, indirectly referred to in *Ecce homo*, of what a revaluation implies states "*In what do you believe?*—In this, that the weights of all things must be determined anew" (*Die fröhliche Wissenschaft*, 269). Some things may, after examination, turn out to have retained their old value. For example, the relatively traditional virtues of courage, wisdom, and honesty (as well as others such as gratefulness and magnanimity), Nietzsche seems to have examined and on the whole found and agreed to be of high value.[30]

Let us examine and list many of the "ideologies," systems, traits, and values which Nietzsche discusses or mentions in *Ecce homo* from this perspective. I have often, but not always, divided them into pairs, and have then placed the alternative which Nietzsche affirms on the right and that which he rejects on the left.

However, one should be aware that these tables as they stand can be very misleading. I have here attempted to stay close to what Nietzsche actually says in *Ecce homo*—and without context it often becomes misleading. Nietzsche is often carried away by rhetoric, and furthermore he (and we) are forced to use conventional language which has been infused with "decadent" values for 2,000 years, and at most he can only hint at or indicate the "new" values and concepts. A full understanding would require a full awareness of Dionysian values and the

Table 6.2 Nietzsche's Explicit Revaluations in *Ecce Homo* Divided into Four Groups and Categories:

(i) Complex ideologies, systems, or views Nietzsche criticizes or "revalues":

Conventional Systems Nietzsche "Revalues"	Nietzsche's Alternative
1. Life- and world-denying	1. Affirmative, Yes-saying
2. Decadent traits, instincts, and views. Illness	2. Healthy traits, instincts, and views. Health. Great health
3. Idealism / metaphysics = "true world"	3. "Reality," realism
4. Moralistic and/or idealistic psychology[31]	4. Psychological realism[32]
5. Moralism and idealism	5. The hidden and forbidden, immoralism
6. Moralistic and/or idealistic truth	6. Hidden and forbidden truth
7. Pessimism and optimism	7. Tragedy
8. Christian values	8. Noble values, Dionysian values, immoralism
9. Christianity[33]	9. Tragedy, atheism, early Greek culture
10. Lies, hypocrisy, the old truth	10. Truth, truthfulness
11. "Improving" humanity = drain life	11. The breeding of a higher humanity
12. The good, the benevolent	12. The "evil" man
13. Saint	13. Satyr
14. Free thinkers and *libres penseurs*	14. Nietzsche also refers to and affirms "free thinkers," but in a different sense
15. Modern ideas (including modern science, art, politics; "objectivity," sympathy with sufferers, the historical sense, scientificality)	15. Noble ideas and values
16. Nationalism	16. "Good European" and cosmopolitan
17. Petty politics	17. Grand politics
18. German *Bildung*	18. Being creative

(ii) Commonly agreed upon valuable traits, aspects, and virtues (which Nietzsche "agrees" with):

1. Courage
2. Honesty, extreme honesty, truthfulness (which he also often refers to as cleanliness)
3. Wisdom
4. Toughness toward oneself, *sophrosyne*, self-discipline, "become hard"
5. Being authentic and not alienated
6. Creativity
7. Decency, politeness

(*Continued*)

Table 6.2 Continued

(iii) Those traits about which Nietzsche challenges traditional or common evaluations:

Nietzsche de-values or decreases the value of:	Nietzsche values or increases the value of:
1. *Mitleid* (pity or compassion)	1. The *importance* of illness, misfortune, and suffering, emergencies, *Mitfreude* (shared joy)
2. Dialectics (reason and the conscious)	2. Profundity, instincts, the subconscious
3. Feelings of reaction, revenge, resentment and "free will"	3. Active feelings (such as curiosity, aggression, being "warlike," etc.)
4. Guilt and bad conscience	4. Animal vigor, *virtù* = how to flourish
5. Punishment	5. [Acceptance?]
6. Altruism and selflessness	6. Egoism (but depends on who is egoistic)
7. Selflessness	7. Pride, proud man, being authentic
8. Humility	8. Loving oneself, "the soul that loves itself the most," self-respect
9. Seeking comfort and happiness	9. Self-discipline, "Become hard!"
10. The "good" humans	10. Conventionally bad/evil/destructive humans
11. The soul, the spirit	11. The body, physiology (but including sublimation)
12. (Forced sexual abstinence)	12. Sexual love (but including sublimation)
13. Seriousness	13. Cheerfulness, playfulness
14. The saint	14. Satyr
15. The "good man"	15. *Gentilhomme*
16. Herd animal, the most revered types of man.[34]	16. Exceptional man, *Übermensch*, those turned out well, yes-saying, future-assured, future-confirming

(iv) "New" or unusual traits which Nietzsche emphasizes as valuable with some obvious "opposites" placed in brackets:

1. Psychological cleanliness [contra mental laziness and cosiness]
2. Self-overcoming [contra *stasis*, not developing]
3. Physical activity [contra physical inactivity, being merely reactive]
4. Mental activity (out of oneself) [contra mental inactivity and laziness, being merely reactive]
5. Feeling a sense of distance / order of rank [contra equality, feeling community with others]
6. Solitude (valuable for psychological cleanliness and authenticity) [feeling community with others]
7. Exceptional man, *Übermensch*, those turned out well, yes-saying, future-assured, future-confirming [contra the herd animal, the most revered types of man]

associated worldview which is not yet possible. In many cases Nietzsche actually affirms both alternatives, such as seriousness and cheerfulness. In fact, Nietzsche often denies the dichotomy. One can thus not read these tables straight off.

One way to better understand what Nietzsche says in regard to the two value-systems (Christian versus Dionysian) is to realize that what he is talking about is similar to what later has been called two paradigms (as two systems of thought, most famously those of geo- and heliocentric worldviews). When one belongs to one paradigm, or set of values, one almost cannot understand those of the other for they are on a fundamental level so different, although often using the same or similar words and language. We are often blind to the values of our own time, and often find it difficult to realize fundamental alternatives. The degree to which nineteenth- and twentieth-century values were influenced by Christianity, and to a rejection of life and reality, is much more visible when one examines how they are related to seventeenth- and eighteenth-century, and earlier, values (especially since many today do not feel particularly Christian).

Already in 1883 Nietzsche felt that there existed two movements, one leading to "the last man" and the other to the *Übermensch* (both of which he describes in the prologue to *Also sprach Zarathustra*).[35] He thereafter often speaks of opposing values, and in his plan for the fourth book of his *Hauptwerk* in late August 1888 (i.e., shortly before he wrote *Ecce homo*), see Table 3.1, p. 52, it consisted of only three chapters: the first one on order of rank (of values), the second called "The two ways" or "The two roads," which probably refers to the two paradigms of values, and the third about eternal recurrence (probably as a test of values).[36]

Many of the traits and attitudes listed in Table 6.2 can be summarized here as pairs of traits (with those Nietzsche affirms now listed first). Some of these may seem to be far too rhetorical, and only a closer inspection and analysis can determine to what degree they can constitute a fair and useful dichotomy. Some of the most important such dichotomies are the following:

Egoism ↔ altruism
Pride (self-affirmation) ↔ humility
Sharing in the feeling of joy [*Mitfreude*] ↔ pity or compassion [*Mitleid*]
Realist (affirming reality as it is) ↔ idealist (denying reality)
Brave ↔ coward
Truthful ↔ "hypocritical" (idealist)
Possessing self-discipline ↔ depersonalization
Adventurer ↔ traditionalist
Experimenter ↔ dogmatist

Life-affirming ↔ life-denying
Amor fati ↔ reality-denying
Future-confirming ↔ future-sacrificing

Some of these, especially the last ones, are such that one would perhaps expect most readers to prefer the alternatives listed to the left—which to me implies that they are too rhetorical or that we view them still, almost unavoidably, from within our basically Christian and modern value-system.

Although perhaps most or many readers would choose the first alternative when listed as here, in actual fact and in their lives, Nietzsche would argue, they and many of their values are based on and are aimed at the second alternative.

Let us briefly examine and comment on one of these pairs, the third one on *Mitfreude* versus pity/compassion, as an example of how they can be analyzed.

The value which perhaps most clearly characterizes modern ethics and ideals (though it was perhaps even more central during the early process of modern secularization in the nineteenth century, and for Nietzsche's philosophical teacher, Schopenhauer, it constituted the core of ethics) is *Mitleid*, pity or compassion. Nietzsche recommends an understanding of his own relation to pity as a "secret door" to comprehending his whole philosophy,[37] and writes in section 6 of the preface to *Zur Genealogie der Moral*:

> This problem of the *value* of pity and of the morality of pity (I am an opponent of the disgraceful modern immaturity of feelings) appeared at first to be only something isolated, a detached question mark. But anyone who remains there for a while and *learns* to ask questions, will experience what happened to me—a huge new vista opens up before him, a possibility grips him like an attack of dizziness, all sorts of mistrust, suspicion, and fear spring up—his belief in morality, in all morality, starts to totter, and finally he hears a new demand. Let us proclaim this *new demand*: we need a critique of moral values, and *we must first question the very value of these values*.

The fact that pity was held in such high regard during the nineteenth century and by Nietzsche's early inspirer Schopenhauer is one of the reasons why Nietzsche criticizes it with such vehemence in his later writings, as a variant of nihilism. For Nietzsche, who distinguishes between that which is life-affirming and life-denying, pity (especially the *ideal* of pity) is something which makes life less worth living, compatible with decadence and nihilism. He objects to its sense of generality, and claims that it pacifies ("it has a depressive effect. One loses force when one pities").[38] Nietzsche frequently criticizes pity for being a "*von oben*" attitude, which is patronizing to the one who suffers. For Nietzsche, pity is the mental or psychological equivalent to letting oneself be infected or to mutilate oneself for the purpose of sharing another being's illness or injury ("suffering itself becomes contagious through pity"). Nietzsche does not argue against helping those in need, it is the *ideal* of compassion he rejects.

Apart from these more psychological approaches, Nietzsche presents three philosophical arguments against pity. The first, and less important one, is an argument of consequence, that pity does not reduce the amount of suffering in the world, but, instead, increases it. His second argument is that pity is decadent and nihilistic, that is, that it reflects the weak and life-denying (or that which is weak and life-denying within us), whose first response when it encounters pain and suffering is to lower oneself to this lower degree of life-intensity. Pity as ideal is nihilistic, since it lacks any positive goal, it does not "lift," it only says what one should reduce, what should *not* be, what one should not do. It has only a negative goal. *It thus lacks a positive content*: "pity is *practical* nihilism."[39] He also points out that "in every *noble* morality it counts as weakness," and approvingly refers to Aristotle's critical view of pity.[40] Instead, Nietzsche sometimes contrasts pity (*Mitleid*) with "*Mitfreude*," the feeling of joy with someone else, which does have a "lifting," a positive, content. "I want to teach them what is understood by so few today, least of all by these preachers of pity: *to share not suffering but joy*."[41] Third, Nietzsche accepts suffering, much more than seems to be accepted by modern and Christian values, suffering as a part of life and perhaps as a necessary means to and motive for human striving and development. The pair *Mitfreude—Mitleid* seems to reflect important aspects of the two major value-systems.

Nietzsche's severe critique of pity as a supreme value has often been misunderstood and interpreted psychologically (against him, as being callous). It is thus worth noting that Nietzsche approved of pity during his youth and early period, but changed his view at the time of his break with Schopenhauer around 1876.[42] Furthermore, he, as seems true, claimed that he was personally very sensitive and susceptible to the feeling of pity. For example, the whole fourth part of *Also sprach Zarathustra* deals with the danger of pity, and in several letters from after 1876 he emphasizes that he easily feels pity, and that he therefore recognizes and suffers from its consequences.[43]

These values and traits have all been mentioned in *Ecce homo*. Let us briefly look beyond that into what he says about affirmative values in his notes from 1887 and 1888. Nietzsche occasionally not only mentions but even lists different values, character traits, emotions, and properties which he affirms and seems to regard as belonging to the life-affirmative side of the dichotomy. For example, in one note from April 1888, he writes:

> The *yes-saying* affects
> Pride
> joy
> health
> the love of the sexes
> enmity and war
> reverence
> beautiful gestures, manners, objects
> strong will
> the discipline of high intellectuality
> will to power
> gratitude towards earth and life
> : everything that's rich and wants to give away, and bestows gifts on life and gilds and immortalises and deifies it—the whole power of *transfiguring* virtues . . . everything that calls good, says Yes, does Yes—[44]

We can note that many of these are similar to, or overlap with, the ones from *Ecce homo* that we have discussed earlier.

To mention just one earlier such expression of revaluations: In the summer-autumn of 1884 Nietzsche discusses eternal recurrence and what is necessary to live with that thought, and twice answers "the revaluation of all values." Nietzsche's meaning is that with present values we will not be able to affirm reality and life sufficiently to affirm eternal recurrence, that is the thought of reliving our life again and again in exactly the same way—for that we need new values, that is, revalue values. He thereafter gives some examples of such revaluations (joy at uncertainty rather than certainty, belief in creativity rather than in "cause and effect," no longer will to survival but to power, and not to possess defensive but proud subjectivism).[45]

More can be found in Nietzsche's extensive notes, but that is part of a different project than this one which is primarily concerned with *Ecce homo* and its relation to the *Umwerthung aller Werthe.*

6.7 The Revalued Values as Related to Ancient Values

Let us turn to the third question: the nature of these revalued values (C). When we wish to clarify the general nature of the set of revalued values, those Nietzsche refers to as life-affirming and noble, rather than just clarifying a number of specific values that are characteristic of the two value-systems, we can note that we were given only a few clues as to their general nature in the last chapter of *Ecce homo*. Let us first summarize those few clues, and thereafter go beyond *Ecce homo* to other late books and his late notes.

Nietzsche's allusions to the general nature of these values in the last chapter of *Ecce homo* seem so vague, rhetorical, and value-laden that one can lose hope of ever acquiring a better and more concrete understanding of it. He refers to the revalued values, apart from being opposed to Christian values, as life-affirming, reality-affirming, and associated with ascending life. This seems primarily to be the rhetorical mirror-image of the values he is criticizing.

However, a more careful reading gives us reason to suspect that Greek antiquity constitutes an important source of inspiration and reference point for him, especially the last sentence of the whole book: "Have I been understood?—*Dionysos against the crucified one* . . . ."[46]

We can learn much more by going on to Nietzsche's other late books and late notes. These confirm how important antiquity was for Nietzsche,[47] not just in general, but also as a source of alternative values and human ideals.[48] Furthermore, the importance of history and a historical approach, for the revaluation, and more concretely, *what* in history is expressed in a note from the first half of 1888, quoted earlier: "I sought in history the beginning of the construction of reverse ideals (the concepts 'pagan,' 'classical,' 'noble' newly discovered and expounded—)."[49]

There are several concepts and historical epochs which can help to illuminate the set of revalued values: antiquity, classical, tragedy, the Renaissance, the dichotomy of master- and slave-morality, noble, and pagan. By examining what the late Nietzsche says regarding these concepts and epochs we can get a better grasp of his ideas of healthy values. Most of these are important concepts in Nietzsche's writings, and we will be able to only briefly touch on some of the most obviously relevant aspects of them here for the question of better understanding the general nature of the revalued set of values.

Nietzsche frequently refers to a dichotomy of values (and to related phenomena) in *Ecce homo*, and examining these can help us get a better view of the revalued values. For example, in his review of *Die Geburt der Tragödie* in *Ecce homo*, section 2, he sets up the dichotomy and writes: "I was the first to see the real opposition—*degenerating* instinct turning against life with subterranean vengefulness [. . .] and a formula born of abundance, superabundance, for the *highest affirmation*, a yes-saying without reservation, even to suffering."[50] In *Götzen-Dämmerung*, he frequently refers to two forms of life and the corresponding sort of persons: ascending and descending types. Later in this review, in section 4, Nietzsche makes clear that the healthy side of the dichotomy is related to a revival of Greek values: "Everything in this essay is prophetic: the proximity of the return of the Greek spirit, the necessity for *counter-Alexanders* to *retie* the Gordian knot of Greek culture after it had been untied." This strong belief in Greek culture and values is, in fact, a constant in Nietzsche's thought.[51] We can, for example, take his view of a dichotomy of values in the 1870s, and realize that a revaluation of our present values are a natural development of that attitude: "My aim is: to create complete hostility between our modern 'culture' and the ancient world. Whosoever wants to serve the former must *hate* the latter."[52] Many other expressions of Nietzsche's high appreciation of Greek antiquity abound in his writings. To mention just a few from his later writings: "The highest types hitherto, the Greeks"[53] and "the highest type [of ideal]: the *classical* ideal."[54]

Occasionally, Nietzsche also attempts a valuation of present phenomena, values and thought in terms of antiquity or by asking, for example, what Aristotle would have thought of it: "The *ancient world* has in fact always been understood only *in terms of the present*—and will *the present* now be understood *in terms of the ancient world*?"[55] And in *Jenseits von Gut und Böse*, 267, he states: "I do not doubt that the first thing an ancient Greek would remark in us Europeans of today would also be self-diminution—through that alone we should be 'contrary to his taste.'"

The importance of antiquity is not particularly prominent in the last chapter of *Ecce homo*, but it is elsewhere in the book. The importance of antiquity is also visible in the two Wagner-oriented books from 1888, *Der Fall Wagner* and *Nietzsche contra Wagner*. In both of them Nietzsche strongly separates "*an aesthetics of décadence* and a classical aesthetics." The shorter latter work also ends with high praise of the Greeks. The last paragraph states:

> Oh, those Greeks! They knew how to live. What is required for that is to stop courageously at the surface, the fold, the skin, to adore appearance, to believe in forms, tones, words, in the whole Olympus of appearance. Those Greeks were superficial—*out of profundity*. And is not this precisely what we are again coming back to, we daredevils of the spirit who have climbed the highest and most dangerous peak of present thought and looked around from up there—we who have looked *down* from there? Are we not, precisely in this respect, Greeks? Adorers of forms, of tones, of words? And therefore—*artists?*[56]

The importance of antiquity is even more pronounced in the last chapter of *Götzen-Dämmerung*, "What I Owe the Ancients," which began as part of *Ecce homo* and was moved to *Götzen-Dämmerung* only at the time of proofreading that work. This chapter can reasonably be read as part of *Ecce homo* (containing much biographical material, especially about his reading), but also on the importance of Dionysos, the Greeks, and the idea of eternal recurrence for him. In its very last section Nietzsche again gives a specific meaning to the revaluation of all values:

> Tragedy [. . .] affirmation of life [. . .] is what I called Dionysian [. . .] the eternal joy of becoming [. . .] And with that I again return to the place from which I set out—the *Birth of Tragedy* was my first revaluation of all values: with that I again plant myself in the soil out of which I draw all that I will and *can*—I, the last disciple of the philosopher Dionysos.—I, the teacher of the eternal recurrence . . .

An attempt at understanding and affecting a revival of tragedy was Nietzsche's first revaluation! The theme of *Die Geburt der Tragödie* is the death of tragedy due to the new anti-tragic *Weltanschauung* introduced by Socrates, Euripides, and Plato. While describing this Nietzsche attempts an intellectual and scholarly reappraisal of tragedy. Equally important as the classification of this as a revaluation is his more general statement that tragedy and the Greeks constitute "the soil out of which I draw all that I will and *can*." It is difficult for him to be more explicit as to where the foundation of his own affirmative values lies. He makes a similar claim in a notebook from 1884: "Knowledge of the great Greeks has formed me."[57]

In the penultimate section of the *Der Antichrist*, we are presented with perhaps the clearest expression of what the revaluation of all values means and what sort of values it implies. Nietzsche claims here that a second revaluation already has been attempted and for a time succeeded, but in the end it failed:

> [. . .] *what* the Renaissance was? The *revaluation of Christian values*, the attempt, undertaken with every expedient, with every instinct, with genius of every kind, to bring about the victory of the opposing values, the *noble* values. . . . Up till now *this* has been the only great war, there has been no more decisive questioning than that conducted by the Renaissance—*my* question is its question—: [. . .] to set the *noble* values on the throne, which is to say to set them *into* the instincts, the deepest needs and desires of him who sits thereon [. . .] Christianity would thereby have been *abolished*!—What happened? [. . .] Luther *restored the Church*: he attacked it. . . . The Renaissance—an event without meaning, a great *in vain*!—[58]

As we have seen earlier, Nietzsche constantly praises the Renaissance and antiquity highly.

Nietzsche prefers values and a morality that uses honor as the criterion rather than goodness or utility.[59] This is very noticeable in the last chapter "What Is

Noble?" in *Jenseits von Gut und Böse*. A condensed expression of this can be found in a note: "the *value of a human being* is *not* to be measured by her effect. 'Noble,'" and Nietzsche makes clear in this note that this was a theme he intended to discuss in volume 4 of his *Hauptwerk*.[60] Nietzsche summarizes many of the more personal traits which characterize nobility in a letter to Gast:

> Yesterday I noted [. . .] a quantity of traits by which I detect "distinction" or "nobility" in people—and, vice versa, what pertains to the "rabble" in us. [. . .] It is distinguished to give a steadfast impression of frivolity, which masks a stoic hardness and self-control. It is distinguished to go slowly, in every respect, also to have the slow-paced eye. It is difficult for us to wonder at things. There are not many valuable things; and these come to us of their own accord, and *want* to come to us. It is distinguished to avoid small honours and to distrust anyone who is quick to praise. It is distinguished to doubt the communicability of the heart; solitude is distinguished—not chosen but given. To be convinced that one has duties only to one's equals, and to act toward others as one thinks fit; to feel always that one is a person who has honours to give, and seldom concedes that another has honours to give that are meant for us; to live almost always in disguise, to travel *incognito*, as it were—so as to spare oneself much shame; to be capable of *otium* [idleness], and not only be busy as a chicken—clucking, laying an egg, clucking again, and so on. And so on.[61]

The importance of self-love, self-respect, and self-esteem, so closely related to the noble, is frequently emphasized by Nietzsche, for example, in *Jenseits von Gut und Böse*, 287:

> What is noble? [. . .] What [. . .] betrays and makes evident the noble human being? It is not his actions which reveal him—actions are always ambiguous, always unfathomable—; neither is it his "work." [. . .] It is not the works, it is the *faith* which is decisive here, which determines the order of rank here [. . .] some fundamental certainty which a noble soul possesses in regard to itself, something which may not be sought or found and perhaps may not be lost either.—*The noble soul has reverence for itself.*—

6.8 Concluding Remarks

Is there more to Nietzsche's philosophy than what can be found in his published books? The answer is yes, there is. Nietzsche collapsed unexpectedly in early January 1889, forty-four years old, after feeling that he had moved into a new phase of his development in 1887/88, and with extensive notes for future works, especially the three further volumes of *Umwerthung aller Werthe*. It ought to be our task to mine and quarry this source much more thoroughly than what has been the case until now.

Many readers of Nietzsche find it surprising and frustrating that he himself claims that the idea of eternal recurrence is so profound and fundamental, but that he hardly elaborates on it at all. In fact, his most comprehensive "discussion" of it is in its very first presentation in *Die fröhliche Wissenschaft* (in the penultimate section, 341, of the first edition) and more poetically in *Also sprach Zarathustra*. Thereafter he sometimes alludes to it but does not carry out any discussion of it or its consequences. *There was, however, a reason for this, and that was that he saved it to constitute the pinnacle of his "Hauptwerk,"* as is shown in almost all of his drafts for that work. The same frustrated expectation can be held about several other aspects and topics of Nietzsche's late thought, especially regarding the revaluation of all values and nihilism. In fact, for the latter case, Nietzsche has even at the end of *Zur Genealogie der Moral* promised (as we have seen earlier) that he would elaborate more extensively on "the history of European nihilism" in the future (and there are ample notes on this theme among his late notebooks) while there is relatively little on nihilism in his published books. To deny that Nietzsche had such intentions, and to ignore the late Nietzsche's many interesting notes, has been a failure and a sign of poverty in Nietzsche research in the last decades.

To achieve a better grasp and understanding of the planned contents of the *Umwerthung aller Werthe*, one needs to examine Nietzsche's other late books in a similar manner as we have done with *Ecce homo* here. This is especially pertinent for *Götzen-Dämmerung*, which, like *Ecce homo*, was written to attract attention to the *Umwerthung aller Werthe*, and which contains significantly more philosophy than *Ecce homo*. Valuable would also be studies of *Der Antichrist*, not primarily as a critique of Christianity, but as being the first of four volumes of the *Umwerthung aller Werthe*, and thus what this work can say about the planned contents of the last three unwritten volumes. Even more important and rewarding would, of course, be to perform a detailed examination of his late notes in regard to both the philosophical and the literary project of a revaluation of all values. Another task would be to go beyond Nietzsche and examine our values and perhaps other systems of values from this or a related perspective.

Appendix

Outline, Summary, and Chronology of *Ecce Homo*

By far the greater part of the manuscript was written from mid-October to early November 1888. I primarily comment on the timing of the texts which were added or significantly revised later than this.

The Table of Contents of *Ecce Homo*

Foreword

1. Why I Am So Wise
2. Why I Am So Clever
3. Why I Write Such Good Books
   - The Birth of Tragedy
   - The Untimelies
   - Human, All Too Human
   - Daybreak
   - The Gay Science
   - Thus Spoke Zarathustra
   - Beyond Good and Evil
   - Genealogy of Morals
   - Twilight of the Idols
   - The Wagner Case
4. Why I Am a Destiny

Outline, Summary, and Chronology of *Ecce Homo*

Foreword, 1 to 4 [All four sections written in early November.]

1. Nietzsche will shortly confront mankind with the heaviest demand (a revaluation of all values)—which was also the planned title of his

coming *magnus opus*. Compare Nietzsche's letter to Gast, dated October 30, 1888: "I wanted to introduce myself before the completely uncanny solitary act of the *Revaluation*." Nietzsche says who he is for this purpose (compare planned subtitle "Why I know a thing or two more").

2. Nietzsche as a disciple of Dionysos. More satyr than saint. No moralist. Humanity has come to praise the opposite values from the life-affirming ones.
3. Dichotomy: moralism and idealism contra secret motives. Idealism contra truth.
4. Praise of *Thus spoke Zarathustra*. Quotes: *Thus spoke Zarathustra* I.

Summary: The purpose of *Ecce Homo* is to present himself and his task before publishing his planned four-volume *Revaluation of All Values*, so that he and his coming work will not be misunderstood or ignored.

Table of contents

Prologue. "On this beautiful day . . ." [Written and originally dated October 15, 1888.]

Why I Am So Wise, 1–8 [3 exchanged at a very late stage, mad? And 8 added late in November.]

1. Nietzsche was both decadent and anti-decadent—both ill and healthy. This made him good at inverting perspectives and revaluing values.
2. The above continued. Nietzsche's illness helped him turn to life, to turn out well.

3 [Original version]. This double nature, also in family and nationality.

3 [Very late December 88/early January 89]. Father idealized, severe critique of mother and sister; Nietzsche as Polish, aristocratic, and his relation to Wagner.

4. Nietzsche has had no negative experiences. Critique of pity.
5. Critique of reactive feelings, resentment, revenge, and guilt.
6. Nietzsche's illness freed him from resentment. Rejects revenge (*Amor fati*).
7. One needs active feelings, for example, aggressive pathos—against equal opponents. Opponent to Christianity.
8. Nietzsche's sense of cleanliness and solitude. Praise of and quotation from *Thus spoke Zarathustra* II.

Summary: In this chapter Nietzsche describes himself and his psychology, and why he is able to revalue values. He shows that he is different and has experienced much, both out of strength and out of weakness, and this multifarious capacity has made him able to revalue values. He is both sickly and healthy—decadent and anti-decadent. He claims to feel no resentment, but to possess aggressive pathos and intellectual cleanliness.

Why I Am so Clever, 1 to 10 [4 added on December 29; 6 and 7 added somewhat earlier; 3 revised; and 10 added in early December.]

1. "Why do I know a thing or two *more*" [so that I can revalue values]. The central sentence of this section and the whole chapter is "how *you* personally have to nourish yourself in order to attain your maximum." Nietzsche has not wasted himself on non-questions (idealism, Christianity). Instead, questions of nutrition. Physical activity.
2. Question of place and climate (the importance of dry air and clear skies).
3. Question of relaxation. Reading (Nietzsche claims to read primarily French authors).
4. Continued: Poetry
5. Continued: Wagner
6. Continued: Wagner is poison, but also "the greatest benefactor of my life."
7. Continued: Music (should be cheerful and profound).
8. Conclusion of 1 to 7: It is self-preservation to react as little and as rarely as possible. This is taste.
9. Summary: how does one become what one is? In Nietzsche's case this means to be able to revalue values—it was necessary that he accepted his egoism and that he lacked knowledge about his task and himself. Nietzsche contrasts this to the Socratic "Know Thyself." Fatalism. Nietzsche's *amor fati.*
10. Summary: These "small things," nourishment, climate, etc., are more important than the lies (God, soul, morality) generally emphasized. We have also had the wrong human exemplars (those who deny life). Nietzsche wants to rectify this—suggests himself as *exemplum* (cf. title of the book). *Amor fati* as sign of greatness.

Summary: In this chapter Nietzsche discusses how to "attain your maximum"; ignore false questions (religion, idealism, morality), but maximize the true conditions of life: nourishment, place, climate, relaxation, accepting one's egoism, lack of knowledge of one's *telos* (fatalism). *Amor fati*—accept reality and one's fate.

Why I Write Such Good Books, 1 to 6 [2 exchanged after December 6; 3 rewritten; and 6 added around December 6.]

1. How and why have Nietzsche's books been misunderstood? One reads in them one's own experiences. "Ultimately no one can hear in things—

books included—more than he already knows." Nietzsche's views and experiences are too original.

2. Germans misunderstand Nietzsche, but others understand better. Nietzsche claims to have important readers (Brandes, Strindberg, Taine, . . .). "I am the *anti-ass* par excellence and hence a world-historic monster—I am, in Greek, and not only in Greek, the *Antichrist* . . ."
3. Why Nietzsche is misunderstood: One needs "loftiness" of will to understand his books. What sort of readers he wants and needs: brave, adventurous.
4. Nietzsche's style: "Every style is *good* that really communicates an inner state."
5. Nietzsche's books contain much psychology, also of women. "The Circe of humanity, morality, has falsified beyond recognition—*infected*—all *psychologica*."
6. Nietzsche exemplifies his psychology—by quoting *Beyond Good and Evil*, 295, and his description of Dionysos there.

Summary: Why Nietzsche is misunderstood his experiences are too unique. Nietzsche's style and psychology. -

Reviews of all his books, at least in large part, to indicate their relevance for the revaluation project [the majority of these texts were written in mid-November, excepting *Also sprach Zarathustra*, which was revised or added on December 6, and later. The texts for part of the later books, from *Beyond Good and Evil* onward, were written before mid-November.]

The Birth of Tragedy, 1 to 4 [Section 4 added on December 6.]

1. The Wagnerian content of *The Birth of Tragedy* was according to Nietzsche a mistake. Nietzsche's summary: the Dionysian-Apollonian opposition—translated into metaphysics—becomes a unity in tragedy. Innovations according to Nietzsche: (1) the Dionysian. (2) Socrates as decadent. Critique of Christianity.
2. *The Birth of Tragedy* remarkable as beginning: Nietzsche discovered the Dionysian. "Morality itself as a symptom of *decadence* is an innovation." Affirmation versus degeneration. Affirming reality or fleeing it (idealism).
3. Nietzsche "the first tragic philosopher" (the opposite of pessimism). Nietzsche praises Heraclitus. Eternal recurrence.

4. Nietzsche "promise[s] a *tragic* age." What Nietzsche described in *The Birth of Tragedy* was not Wagnerian music, but the Dionysian music Nietzsche heard. Nietzsche shows this by arguing that "all the psychologically decisive passages" in *Wagner in Bayreuth* "speaks of me alone" —not Wagner. Several examples.

The Untimelies, 1 to 3 [All three sections written and revised at the latest in mid-November.]

1. The *Untimelies* are presented, the first a critique of German education, the second of modern science and the "historical sense." The last two give a new sense of culture and are about Nietzsche (rather than Schopenhauer and Wagner).
2. Nietzsche reviews the reception of the first *Untimely Meditation* on Strauss. Nietzsche represents a new kind of free-thinking (as opposed to Strauss and other moderns).
3. The third and fourth *Untimely Meditations* present a new concept of education and self-discipline. The essays are much more about Nietzsche than about Schopenhauer and Wagner.

Human, All Too Human, 1 to 6 [1 to 5 in mid-November, 6 added in late December.]

1. Nietzsche tells the history of *Human, All Too Human*: With this work "I liberated myself from what in my nature did not belong to me," for example, idealism.
2. *Human, All Too Human* began as "The Ploughshare" at the time of the first Bayreuth Festival in 1876. What Nietzsche saw there was not the old Wagner, but a new Germanic and nationalistic Wagner.
3. Nietzsche noticed that he had forgotten himself, both Wagner and philology were aberrations. He now began to be concerned with *realities* instead, physiology, science, etc.
4. Nietzsche needed to break with his past, and his illness made it a slow process. The illness prevented reading, instead, he thought. Slowly he returned to himself. *The Wanderer and His Shadow* and *Dawn* show this higher kind of recuperation.
5. *Human, All Too Human*, a monument to self-discipline. Nietzsche tells of its construction. He sent it to Wagner, and received *Parsifal*. Wagner had become pious.

6. [This section was added long after the rest.] Nietzsche here interprets *Human, All Too Human*, 37, as foreshadowing his present views (a bit odd since he is actually quoting Paul Rée's words: "there is no intelligible world" and saying that we can read it as Nietzsche's). This anti-metaphysical and anti-idealistic principle —through the *Revaluation of All Values*—will perhaps in 1890 (with the publication of the *Revaluation of All Values*) serve as the axe to humanity's "metaphysical need."

Daybreak, 1 and 2 [Both sections written in mid-November.]

1. The first and last sentences of the review state that his campaign against morality—the morality of un-selfing oneself—began with this book. But the book is affirmative and mild (unlike the present and coming critique of morality). The motto "many dawns that have not yet broken" is here related to a revaluation of all values.
2. This section is not about *Dawn* (except the last sentence), but about the *Revaluation of All Values.*

The Gay Science [One section, written in mid-November.]

The book described as affirmative and generous. Nietzsche connects it to *Thus spoke Zarathustra* and (in a rather hidden manner) to the revaluation of all values.

Thus Spoke Zarathustra, 1 to 8 [Mostly written around December 6, except for the last two, from mid-November. The last third of section 5 was completely revised during the end of December.]

1. Nietzsche tells of the history of his first book of *Thus spoke Zarathustra* (February 1883). He was "pregnant" with it for one and a half years before writing it (since August 1881, that is, when he discovered the idea of eternal recurrence), including when writing *The Gay Science.* He strongly emphasizes eternal recurrence: "The basic conception of the work—the *thought of eternal recurrence*, this highest attainable formula of affirmation [. . .] Zarathustra's fundamental thought."
2. Nietzsche quotes *The Gay Science*, V, 382, the whole of the last section before the epilogue, about great health and the search for new values and ideals.
3. Nietzsche describes the inspiration he felt while writing *Thus spoke Zarathustra.*

4. Description of the period of exhaustion which occurred after the first book of *Thus spoke Zarathustra*, and then the writing of books two and three. (Book four is not mentioned.)
5. During and after writing the three books of *Thus spoke Zarathustra* (only ten days each) were times of crises. The regret of the great solitude. Absurd sensitivity.
6. High praise of *Thus spoke Zarathustra*. The symbols Zarathustra and Dionysos merge. Zarathustra says and does—no!—to previous ideals, but is nevertheless the opposite of a no-saying spirit. Zarathustra knows eternal recurrence and yet affirms existence.
7. Zarathustra, Dionysos, and those who totally affirm reality use the language of the dithyramb, of which Nietzsche is the [modern] inventor. Long quotation from *Thus spoke Zarathustra*.
8. Zarathustra's task is also Nietzsche's, total affirmation, even of the past. Quotation from *Thus spoke Zarathustra*. Also to create a new ideal of the human, the overhuman. Quotation from *Thus spoke Zarathustra*. For this one needs to "become hard!" the true badge of a Dionysian nature.

Beyond Good and Evil, 1 and 2 [Written before mid-November, but at first having only section 2.]

1. The yes-saying task done in *Dawn*, *The Gay Science*, and *Thus spoke Zarathustra*. Now, in 1886–8, it is time for the no-saying task, "the revaluation of previous values." All books from this period were fishhooks, but there were no fish.
2. [Originally, this section stood alone, later section 1, *not* about *Beyond Good and Evil*, but about the whole post-Zarathustra period, was added.]*Beyond Good and Evil* is a "critique of modernity," including modern science, art, and politics, but also contains pointers toward an opposite, noble type. Both the style and much of the content of *Beyond Good and Evil* are regarded by Nietzsche as necessary recuperation after *Thus spoke Zarathustra*. (A last sentence about what "my great teacher Dionysos" says at the end of *Beyond Good and Evil* deleted by Nietzsche.)

On the Genealogy of Morals, one section [Written before mid-November.]

"The truth of the *first* essay is the psychology of Christianity [. . .] The *second* essay gives the psychology of *conscience*" and the third explains the power of the ascetic ideal "because it was the only ideal till now."

"Above all there was no *counter-ideal—till Zarathustra.*" Three decisive preliminary works of a psychologist toward a revaluation of all values."

Twilight of the Idols, 1 to 3 [1 and 2 written in mid-November, section 3 added in late November (with minor revisions during the end of December).]

1. *Twilight of the Idols* is a short cheerful work which shows "how topsy-turvy everything was before" Nietzsche came along, and with a title which means that "the old truth is coming to an end."
2. The first half of this section is about *Twilight of the Idols*: it contains so many truths. The second half is about the *Revaluation of All Values* project. Nietzsche is the first one to have a yardstick for [the new] "truths," he knows the way to culture, the way upwards. Therefore "I am also a destiny."
3. Immediately after *Twilight of the Idols*, Nietzsche began work on *The Antichrist* and finished it on September 30.

The Wagner Case, 1 to 4 [Written or revised in mid-November. Section 4 completely revised at the end of November, and then again lightly in early December.]

1. Nietzsche objects "that music has been robbed of its world-transfiguring, yes-saying character—that it is *décadence* music and no longer the flute of Dionysos." But his critique goes beyond Wagner, to a critique of what Germany stands for.
2. Critique of the Germans. They are cowards in the face of reality—they are idealists. Critique of their view of history, nationalism, Christianity, and Luther. They have committed "all the great cultural crimes of four centuries." Who except me know "a way out of this blind alley?"
3. The Germans and their philosophers are all unconscious counterfeiters—from Leibniz and Fichte to Kant. They lack cleanliness and are superficial.
4. Nietzsche contra the Germans. They have shown complete silence in regard to Nietzsche's books. Nietzsche published *The Wagner Case* roughly two years before the *Revaluation of All Values*. "For I am carrying the destiny of humanity on my shoulders."

Summary: Nietzsche discusses and summarizes all of his books, with reference to his own development and how they relate to his task of revaluating values and his coming work, the *Revaluation of All Values*.

Why I Am a Destiny, 1 to 9 [Originally seven sections, 3 to 9; 1 and 2 added around December 6]

1. The revaluation of all values. Nietzsche wants to publish *Ecce Homo* before the *Revaluation of All Values*. The section introduces the revaluation of all values and its effects in general.
2. Nietzsche is both a creator and a destroyer.
3. What does the name Zarathustra mean? Zarathustra, the original inventor of moralism —metaphysical morality—becomes an immoralist.
4. Immoralism incorporates two denials: (1) The good persons. (2) Decadence and Christian morality. The psychology of the good—they deny reality. Quotations from *Also sprach Zarathustra*. Reference to future work: "I shall have a great opportunity to demonstrate . . . the uncanny consequence of *optimism*" in the *Revaluation of All Values*.
5. Revaluation. Zarathustra is a friend of the evil (those opposite of the good). Quotations from *Thus spoke Zarathustra*.
6. Psychology: To be an immoralist also means to feel Christian morality to be beneath oneself. This can lead to disgust at man.
7. Nietzsche is the first to have unmasked Christian morality, the morality of un-selfing oneself—which is based on a denial of reality. Revaluation of all values—with several examples (soul, purity, egoism, etc.). Mankind has always been taught decadence values.
8. Continues the themes from previous section. The unmasking of Christian morality. Revaluation of all values—with many examples. Destroy morality.
9. "*Dionysos against the crucified one.*"

Summary: Nietzsche is a destiny because he revalues values and destroys Christian and decadence morality. He sets up a dichotomy between Christian and Dionysian (tragic) values.

Notes

Chapter 1 (pages 1–23)

1 All italics in quotations (here and in subsequent instances) are original. This also applies for the few bold cases.

2 To quote one of them here, as an example: "And so, roughly two years before the shattering lightning bolt of the *Revaluation*, which will have the earth in convulsions, I sent *Der Fall Wagner* out into the world" (EH, Books, *The Case of Wagner*, 4). I am mostly writing the title *Ecce homo* in German. In English it is usually written as *Ecce Homo*.

3 *Ecce homo: Oder: warum ich Einiges mehr weiss*, see KSA 13, 24[1], p. 615 and KSA 14, p. 465. Nietzsche also uses this early subtitle in *Ecce homo*, in the first sentence of the second chapter, "Why I Am so Clever," and Duncan Large translates it probably better as "Why I Know a Thing or Two More."

4 "bruckstücksweise, so weit es dazu erfordert war."

5 That *Ecce homo* is meant to be preparatory to the *Umwerthung aller Werthe* is also clear in his letter to Gast, dated November 13, 1888.

6 The origin of the philosophical project of a revaluation of values is older. I have in the article "The Origin and Early Context of the Revaluation Theme in Nietzsche's Thinking," *Journal of Nietzsche Studies* 39 (2010) 12–29 argued that the theme can be found in Nietzsche's notes (but without the expression "revaluation," which he coins in 1884) from 1880.

7 The arguments put forward in this text are the result of work done over many years. I especially wish to thank Duncan Large for inviting me to partake as the main speaker at the stimulating *Ecce Homo Centenary Conference* in London in November 2008 and to Helmut Heit for inviting me to hold a seminar on *Ecce Homo* in Berlin in April 2009, in the early phase of my work. I also wish to thank the many students who have actively partaken in the three courses on *Ecce Homo*, and other courses related to Nietzsche's philosophy, which I have taught at Uppsala University.

8 I have in my article "Nietzsche's *magnum opus*," *History of European Ideas* 32 (September 2006), 278–94, criticized biographers for having expressed a remarkably

limited interest in Nietzsche's extensive work on writing a *magnum opus* or "*Hauptwerk*" during the last five years of his active life. He spent more time on that task alone than on writing not only each of his late books but even on all of them together, and yet biographers have hardly discussed it at all.

9 H. G. Hödl makes the same observation: "haben verschiedene Interpreten das Werk [. . .] eher als Symptom denn als philosophische Schrift gewertet; positive inhaltlische Würdigungen scheinen eher die Ausnahme" (465f).

10 "Zunächst versucht Nietzsche, sich über sich selber Rechenschaft zu geben [. . .] denn gerade in letzter Zeit stiess er auf viel Unverständnis und Missverständnisse" (part II, p. 657).

11 "Der so denkt, redet, schreibt, ist gewiss [. . .] nicht mehr bei Sinnen," Ross, p. 766.

12 "Die Schrift 'Ecce homo' enthält keinen neuen Gedanken mehr. Es ist die logische Darstellung seines Wahnes"; Ross, p. 764.

13 "was er am 15. Oktober, seinem Geburtstag, beginnt, ist das, was ihm nun noch allein am Herzen liegt: Selbstdarstellung, Selbstverteidigung, Selbsterklärung, Krieg und Sieg" (p. 762).

14 "Die letzten Werke, die in schneller Folge entstehen, 'Der Fall Wagner,' 'Götzendämmerung,' 'Der Antichrist,' und 'Ecce homo,' entwickeln keine neuen Gedanken mehr, sondern es wird das Bekannte vergröbert oder zugespitzt" (p. 318).

15 "'Ecce homo' kreist fast nur noch um die Frage: wer bin ich denn, dass es mir vergönnt und erlaubt ist, so zu denken wie ich denke?" (p. 318).

16 Nietzsche had spent the majority of his last five active years on working on his *Hauptwerk*, much more time than on any of his actual books, and yet biographers hardly mention it at all. Prideaux is no exception. Her only mention of *The Will to Power* is on page 305, and there she writes: "but on 4 September [. . .] he changed his mind and jotted down what he called the final plan for the revaluation of all values. Intended to shake the very foundations of thought, it would now consist of four books" (305). Thereafter she actually mentions it four times, without discussion or comment, but it is not altogether easy for the reader to notice, since she gives it no title and does not relate it to anything. She paraphrases: "His revaluation would put the world back on course for the first time in centuries" (313), and, in regard to *Ecce Homo*, which Nietzsche began on his birthday, she writes: "this birthday deserved an autobiography. Again he was postponing the great revaluation" (314). Thereafter, writing about December 1888: "There were so many things to occupy him. None of them was the next book in the great revaluation" (319), which seems to refer to the planned second volume of the *Umwerthung aller Werthe*. Thereafter, seemingly talking about November–December, she actually paraphrases a letter from October 18: "The four books of the great revaluation would soon appear, he told Overbeck" (323). The rest is silence.

17 To mention just one example, the Swedish Carl-Göran Ekerwald's *Nietzsche: Liv och tankesätt* (1993) regards it as a sort of autobiography, but dismisses it on a single page as hopelessly self-praising. He makes no mention of its relation to *Umwerthung aller Werthe*.

18 It is probably an inheritance from the pre-1969 era, when the revaluation of all values project and book was generally taken more seriously, until Montinari's severe critique of it.

19 Later, Tanner again vaguely hints at this plan: "he truly thought that he was close to achieving something earth-shattering" (p. x).

20 Andreas Urs Sommer, in his commentary on *Ecce Homo* argues similarly, as does H. G. Hödl, p. 465.

21 "Damit wird gezeigt, dass *Ecce Homo* nicht einfach eine Autobiographie darstellt, sondern eine *Selbst*erzählung, die eine systematische Funktion im Werk Nietzsches in Hinblick auf die 'Umwertung' hat" (465). Compare also similar statements on pages 485, 486, 487, 497, and 503. I wish to thank one of Bloomsbury's anonymous readers for bringing this work to my attention. Hödl's study is full of knowledge and insight, and ought to receive much more attention than it has. I find it to be among the very best Nietzsche studies I have read. Variants of many of the arguments I put forward in this study can be found in Hödl's book. One of the differences is that Hödl accepts the now conventional view that Nietzsche gave up on a four-volume *Umwerthung aller Werthe* in late November 1888 and thereafter regarded it as synonymous with *Der Antichrist*. However, he does not refer to the late proofs from the middle of December where Nietzsche still speaks of the *Umwerthung aller Werthe* as a four-volume work (discussed later). Furthermore, Hödl explicitly states that he is not performing an interpretation [*Gesamtinterpretation*] of *Ecce Homo* (p. 486).

Another seemingly highly interesting German study which may have significant overlap with my study, but which unfortunately came to my attention too late, is Heinrich Meier's *Nietzsches Vermächtnis* (München, 2019).

22 This is reflected in the following three statements from pages 171f: "Ähnlich fühlte auch Nietzsche 1888 spontan den Wunsch, sich selbst sein Leben zu erzählen," "Nietzsche schreibt seine Autobiographie fast im Sinne eines Nachrufes," and "Bei seinem biographischen Rückblick versucht er den Sinn seiner Werke zu erläutern."

23 Although, in truth, this really affected only a small proportion of the text.

24 This essay has also been published, in slightly different forms, in several other publications, including in the commentary volume on Nietzsche's works, KSA 14. Its first publication was in 1975.

25 Montinari, p. 102: "Zum anderen wird von Podach ein Kampf mit einem Hauptwerk postuliert, der nie stattgefunden hat: Nietzsches Nachlass stellt im Ganzen einen Versuch dar; dieser Versuch wurde durch die Krankheit abgebrochen. Zu behaupten, dass dadurch Nietzsches Lebenswerk unvollendet

geblieben ist, ist, wie wir bald sehen werden, beinahe eine Naivität, verursacht durch den mehr als dubiosen Begriff 'Hauptwerk.'"

At the end of the essay, on p. 118, Montinari continues: "*Inhaltlich* gesehen war die *Umwerthung aller Werthe* in einem gewissen Sinne dasselbe wie der 'Wille zur Macht,' aber eben deshalb war sie dessen *literarische* Negation. Oder auch: Aus den Aufzeichnungen zum 'Willen zur Macht' sind die *Götzen-Dämmerung* und *Der Antichrist* entstanden; der Rest ist—Nachlass. [. . .] *Die Turiner Katastophe kam, als Nietzsche wortwörtlich mit allem fertig war.*"

26 Curt Paul Janz, *Friedrich Nietzsche*, 3 volumes (1978, second revised edition 1993), III, pp. 20f.: "Mit dem vermeintlichen Totschlag des paulinischen Christentums als versetztem Platonismus und jüdischer Priestermachtskonstruktion glaubt Nietzsche die philosophische Hauptarbeit getan zu haben. Alles übrige, alle 'Umwertung aller Werte' folgt nun naturnotwendig daraus, und er hat jetzt keine weitere Aufgabe mehr, als über der Ausbreitung dieser letzten 'Erkenntnis' zu wachen. Mit ihm und mit dem 30. September 1888 ist die Philosophie überhaupt am Ende! 'Alles ist fertig,' schreibt er schon am 18. Dezember an Carl Fuchs." This letter is now dated as written on December 11, see KSB 8.

27 I have discussed the relevant information and the arguments for whether Nietzsche gave up the intention to write a four-volume *Hauptwerk* at the end of 1888 in "Nietzsche's *magnum opus,*" *History of European Ideas* 32 (September 2006), 278–94, "The Origin and Early Context of Nietzsche's Revaluation of All Values," *Journal of Nietzsche Studies* 29 (2010), 12-29, and in "The Place and Role of *Der Antichrist* in Nietzsche's Four-Volume Project *Umwerthung aller Werthe,*" *Nietzsche-Studien* 40 (2011), 244–55.

28 I also intend to examine how the plans for a four-volume *Hauptwerk* affected Nietzsche's *Götzen-Dämmerung*, as well as examining *Der Antichrist* from this perspective in two further studies.

29 *Jenseits von Gut und Böse*, 6. Compare also section 5: "They pose as having discovered and attained their real opinions through the self-evolution of a cold, pure, divinely unperturbed dialectic [. . .] while what happens at bottom is that a prejudice, a notion, an 'inspiration,' generally a desire of the heart sifted and made abstract, is defended by them with reasons sought after the event—they are one and all advocates who do not want to be regarded as such, and for the most part no better than cunning pleaders for their prejudices, which they baptize 'truths,'" and JGB, 8: "In every philosophy there is a point at which the philosopher's 'conviction' appears on the scene."

30 *Menschliches, Allzumenschliches* , I, 513. Compare section 198. See also M, 553: "nothing other than the intellectual circuitous paths of similar personal drives?" and *Die fröhliche Wissenschaft*, 241: "ultimately, his work is merely a magnifying glass that he offers everybody that looks his way."

31 *Die fröhliche Wissenschaft*, preface, 2 (1886). See also section 3 of the preface.

32 KSA 9, 4[285]. A few further examples can be given: "These things you know as thoughts, but your thoughts are not your experiences, but the echo of the experience of others: as when your room shakes from a wagon passing by. But I sit in the wagon, and often I am the wagon itself." KSA 9, 6[448], Autumn 1880. In his review of *Morgenröthe* in *Ecce homo*, he writes: "Ultimately I was myself this sea creature." In a letter to Burckhardt, Aug. 1882, Nietzsche writes: "I have reached a point at which I *live* as I *think*, and perhaps I have meanwhile learned really to express what I think." In *Also sprach Zarathustra*, I, "Of Reading and Writing," Nietzsche writes: "Of all writings I love only that which is written with blood." Finally, in an unpublished note from 1879 he writes: "My way of reporting historical facts is really to tell the story of my own experiences *à propos* of past ages and men" and he goes on to defend this method. [I am quoting this after J. P. Stern, p. 116, who refers to KGW, IV.3, p. 390, but this reference is not correct.]

33 *Zur Genealogie der Moral*, Preface, 2.

34 I have discussed this extensively in my book *Nietzsche's Ethics of Character: A Study of Nietzsche's Ethics and its Place in the History of Moral Thinking* (Uppsala, 1995).

35 *Nietzsche: Werke: Kritische Gesamtausgabe* (KGW) I.1, 4[77]. (The autobiography is also published in BAW 1, 1–32.)

36 Of some special interest may be this short presentation of himself in and for the journal *Philosophische Monatshefte*, discovered by me: "An Undiscovered Short Published Autobiographical Presentation by Nietzsche from 1872," *Nietzsche-Studien* 27 (1998), 446 ff. Also discovered by me was a short Latin autobiographical text written for his doctorate graduation at Leipzig 1869: "An Undiscovered Short Published Autobiographical Presentation by Nietzsche from 1869," *Journal of Nietzsche Studies* 17 (Spring 1999), 68–9.

37 Daniel Blue has in his excellent biography of the young Nietzsche, *The Making of Friedrich Nietzsche: The Quest for Identity, 1844-1869* (Cambridge, 2016), emphasized and constructively discussed many of these early autobiographical texts. Hödl also takes up many instances of Nietzsche's "Selbstthematisierung."

38 I suspect that this is one of the main reasons why biographers of Nietzsche have spent such limited time and space on *Ecce homo*, as discussed in Chapter 2 earlier. Many of them have used Nietzsche's letters (and other material), and since that material is more reliable than *Ecce Homo*, the book does not seem to add much and thus does not require much attention.

39 That this relates to Nietzsches own development is still more clear in an early draft, KSA 14, 140f. In this earlier draft, Nietzsche writes in the form of "we" instead of "they," i.e., the note then began: "We at present begin . . . our . . . [etc.]."

40 See, for example, letter to Rohde, July 15, 1882: "It [*Die fröhliche Wissenschaft*] contains a portrait of myself." He also expresses this in a number of other letters.

41 For many examples, see my contribution "*Thus Spoke Zarathustra* as Nietzsche's Autobiography," in *Before Sunrise: Nietzsche's* Thus Spoke Zarathustra, edited by James Luchte, Continuum Publishers (London and New York, 2008), 29–46.

42 For a more extensive discussion of this and other related questions (and a possible identification of the biography of Carlyle), see my *Nietzsche's Philosophical Context: An Intellectual Biography* (Illinois University Press, Urbana and Chicago, 2008).

43 However, note that these claims do not necessarily exclude one another. Nietzsche wanted to present himself (or better, an idealized version of himself) but the reason he wanted to do that was to prepare readers for his coming *magnum opus*. It is this second aspect which has been ignored by almost all commentators.

44 Letter to Naumann, November 6, 1888.

45 This is also true, but perhaps in the weaker sense that a second and third volume is connected to an earlier one, for the three volumes of *Menschliches, Allzumenschliches*, which all follow one upon the other, and likewise with *Morgenröthe* and *Die fröhliche Wissenschaft*. Something similar can be said for the four books of *Also sprach Zarathustra*.

46 Friedrich Nietzsches *Ecce homo*: Faksimileausgabe der Handschrift. Transkription von Anneliese Clauss. Dr. Ludwig Reichert Verlag, Wiesbaden 1985 in the series Manu *script*, Band 2. Faksimileausgaben literarisches Handschriften. Herausgegeben von Karl-Heinz Hahn.

47 These proofs seem to me very valuable for establishing a "final" (or very close to final) version of the first quarter of the text. Montinari does not seem to give detailed information about whether and how his final text differs from these proofs, but only states that they have been taken into consideration ("Diese Korrekturbogen warden in unserem Text berücksichtigt"), KSA 14, p. 459. These proofs are now available on the internet at *Nietzsche Source*, Digitale Faksimile Gesamtausgabe.

48 Most of my account here is based on the work of Montinari, especially his text in KSA 14 and the commentary on the facsimile publication of *Ecce homo*, but I have occasionally interpreted the situation a little differently.

49 KSA 13, 24[1].

50 These are early versions of "Clever," 1; "Wise," 6, 4, 5, 1, and 2. The text already then had the title *Ecce homo*, with the subtitle *Oder: warum ich Eininges mehr Weiss* [*Or: Why I Know a Bit More*].

51 See letter to Gast, October 30, 1888; letter to his publisher, Naumann, November 4; and thereafter in many letters. In these letters Nietzsche never uses the term "autobiography."

52 Montinari argues that Nietzsche, on December 29, wrote to the publisher that both of them should be withdrawn from the manuscript, KSA 14, 469, see also pages

453f. This note to the publisher seems not to be included among Nietzsche's letters (as the other revisions are).

Chapter 2 (pages 25–45)

1 This is true already for the young Nietzsche, before he became professor in Basel in 1869. This is a main theme in Daniel Blue's excellent biography of him, *The Making of Friedrich Nietzsche* (Cambridge, 2016).

2 I have used the translation of this letter in Christopher Middleton, *Selected Letters of Friedrich Nietzsche* (Cambridge, 1969, 1996).

3 During 1875 and 1876, Nietzsche went through an intellectual and emotional crisis and changed fundamental aspects of his *Weltanschauung*, including "breaking" with Schopenhauer, Kant, and Wagner. In the preface to *Human, All Too Human* (added in 1886), Nietzsche called the change a "great liberation," and in *Ecce Homo* he wrote: "*Human, All Too Human* is a memorial of a crisis. [. . .] with this book I liberated myself from that in my nature which *did not belong to me*. Idealism does not belong to me [. . .] *realities* were altogether lacking in my knowledge, and the 'idealities' were worth damn all! A downright burning thirst seized hold of me: thenceforward I pursued in fact nothing other than physiology, medicine, and natural science" (*Ecce Homo*, "Human, All Too Human," 1 and 3). The change seems not to have been a simple gradual one, nor a revolutionary one, but one in which Nietzsche several times during 1875 and 1876 appears to have switched back and forth between the old and the new way of thinking. He then exchanged his earlier enthusiasm for metaphysics, idealism, pessimism, art, and aesthetics for a position that was skeptical, free-spirited, and placed science above art and praised the Enlightenment. He even went so far as to write a note in 1877, intended to be included in his next book, where he rejected his earlier writings. "I want expressly to inform the readers of my earlier writings [i.e., *The Birth of Tragedy* and the *Untimely Meditations*] that I have abandoned the metaphysical-artistic views which fundamentally govern them: they are pleasant but untenable. He who speaks publicly early is usually quickly forced to publicly retract his statements," KSA 8, 23[159]. Several similar notes can be found from this period. Compare *Menschliches, Allzumenschliches*, 599, in which an echo of this note reverberates. In it he claims that a "first maturity, with a strong residue of acidulousness" occurs between the age of twenty-six and thirty (i.e., in Nietzsche's case, c. 1870–4) in which everything one writes is reactive and a form of revenge for not receiving recognition. Many of his later discussions of his own thought and development, in new prefaces etc., refer to this break and how the character of his writing and thinking changes. For example, in a note from 1883 he critically characterizes

his early thought: "Behind my *first period* grins the face of *jesuitism*: I mean the deliberate holding on to illusion and the forcible annexation of illusion as the *foundation of culture*. Or put differently: **Buddhism** and a longing into nothingness (the Schopenhauerian opposition between theory and praxis is untenable). The first danger was given to W[agner]" (KSA 10, 16[23]).

Also in numerous letters from 1882–4, Nietzsche refers to having passed through a period of his life, often referring to it as six years long, for example, in letters to Elisabeth, on July 2, 1882; to Lou Salomé, July 3, 1882 ("der allerletzte Theil des Manuscriptes [of *Die fröhliche Wissenschaft*] fertig geworden und damit das Werk von 6 Jahren (1876–82), meine ganze 'Freigeisterei'! Oh welche Jahre! Welche Qualen aller Art, welche Vereinsamungen)," and letters to Bülow, in early December 1882 and to Gersdorff, end of June 1883. See also his notes KSA 8, 1[5] and KSA 10, 9[9].

4 The break between the middle, more positivistic, period and the late period occurred in 1881–2, with the discovery of the idea of eternal recurrence (in August 1881), and came to be publicly expressed in the last sections of the fourth book of *Die fröhliche Wissenschaft* (1882) and then much more intensively in *Thus Spoke Zarathustra* (1883–5).

By the time he published *Die fröhliche Wissenschaft* in the summer of 1882 Nietzsche had moved into a new phase, and was certain enough about it to write on the back of the book: "This book marks the conclusion of a series of writings by FRIEDRICH NIETZSCHE whose common goal it is to erect *a new image and ideal of the free spirit*. To this series belong [here he lists the title of the three volumes of *Human, All Too Human*; *Dawn*; and *The Joyful Science*]." In several letters to Lou Salomé, Nietzsche had stated that he was leaving the free-spirit phase, see letters to Salomé, June 27–28, July 3, and November 24, 1882 ("Do not let yourself be led astray about me—you do not believe, do you, that 'the free spirit' is my ideal?! I am—Forgive me! Dear Lou, be what you must be" ["Lassen Sie sich nicht über mich täuschen—Sie glauben doch nicht, daß 'der Freigeist' mein Ideal ist?! Ich bin—Verzeihung! Liebste Lou, seien Sie, was Sie sein *müssen*])."

Later in the prefaces to *Human, All Too Human* and *Assorted Opinions and Maxims*, written in 1886, Nietzsche spoke extensively about his free-spirit period as an illness, of his being "beside himself" and of his coming back to health in 1882–3: "And, to speak seriously: to become sick in the manner of these free spirits, to remain sick for a long time and then, slowly, slowly, to become healthy, by which I mean 'healthier,' is a fundamental *cure* for all pessimism."

5 Somewhat surprisingly, Nietzsche here speaks of a "ten years" and "over ten years" period of illness which would include the whole middle and late periods, including all of the *Zarathustra* period.

6 "Ich fühle, daß es jetzt einen Abschnitt in meinem Leben giebt—und daß ich nun die ganze große Aufgabe vor mir habe! Vor mir und, noch mehr, *auf* mir!"

Compare his letter to his sister, dated March 31, 1888: "Trotzdem glaube ich, daß es in der Hauptsache *vorwärts* gegangen ist und daß ich einen Schritt mehr aus der vieljährigen Misère und Décadence herausgetreten bin" and his letter to Overbeck, dated March 24, 1887: "Die Nöthigung andererseits liegt auf mir mit dem Gewicht von hundert Centnern, einen zusammenhängenden Bau von Gedanken in den nächsten Jahren aufzubauen—und dazu brauche ich fünf sechs Bedingungen, die mir alle noch fehlen und selbst unerreichbar scheinen!"

7 In several letters Nietzsche defines his "task" as the work on his *magnum opus*, for example, letter to Brandes, May 23, 1888; letter to Deussen, September 14, 1888; and letters to Meysenbug, October 4 and 20, 1888.

8 I discuss Nietzsche's discoveries of these in *Nietzsche's Philosophical Context: An Intellectual Biography* (Urbana and Chicago, 2008), pp. 82–9, with extensive notes, pp. 162–69.

9 There are two separate letters, both from September 2, 1884, one to Gast and one to Resa von Schirnhofer. In the first letter Nietzsche writes: "Ich bin überdies mit der Haupt-Aufgabe dieses Sommers, wie ich sie mir gestellt hatte, im Ganzen *fertig* geworden—die nächsten 6 Jahre gehören der Ausarbeitung eines Schema's an, mit welchem ich meine 'Philosophie' umrissen habe. Es steht gut und hoffnungsvoll damit. Zarathustra hat einstweilen nur den ganz persönlichen Sinn, daß es mein 'Erbauungs—und Ermuthigungs-Buch' ist—im übrigen dunkel und verborgen und lächerlich für Jedermann," and in the second: "In summa: ich bin mit dem Sommer zufrieden, insofern ich für 6 Jahre den Entwurf gemacht habe, den Entwurf meiner 'Philosophie' oder 'Religion' oder was weiß ich? Genug, es **muß** noch gelebt werden."

10 See Nietzsche's words from 1886 quoted in KSA 14, p. 345: "Was ihm [*Jenseits von Gut und Böse*] zu Grunde liegt, Gedanken, erste Niederschriften und Hinwürfe aller Art, das gehört meiner Vergangenheit an: nämlich jener räthselreichen Zeit, in der '*Also sprach Zarathustra*' entstand: es dürfte schon um dieser Gleichzeitigkeit willen nützliche Fingerzeige zum Verständniss des eben genannten *schwerverständlichen* Werkes abgeben."

11 KSA 11, 26[259].

12 It is not visible in *Nietzsche contra Wagner*, but then, this work is just a short anthology of some of Nietzsche's discussions of Wagner between 1877 and 1888.

13 The main Nietzsche editor, M. Montinari, agrees with this. See Montinari, 103, and also KSA 14, pp. 345f.: "Dass *Jenseits von Gut und Böse* sich *nicht* aus dem Material des sogenannten *Willens zur Macht* abgelöst hat, erhellt aus dieser Entstehungsgeschichte. Es war tatsächlich eine Vorbereitung, ein 'Vorspiel' für etwas, das noch kommen sollte und—zumindest als *Wille zur Macht*—nicht kam."

14 This was printed on the back cover of *Jenseits von Gut und Böse*, unfortunately not reproduced in any of the English translations. See KGW VI.2, p. 257.

15 The end of the preface to *Jenseits von Gut und Böse*, Hollingdale's translation.

16 ". . . ich, der letzte Jünger und Eingeweihte des Gottes Dionysos: und ich dürfte wohl endlich einmal damit anfangen, euch, meinen Freunden, ein Wenig, so weit es mir erlaubt ist, von dieser Philosophie zu kosten zu geben?" *Jenseits von Gut und Böse*, 295. It seems as if all earlier English translations have skipped or ignored the word "einmal," —which here surely has the meaning of "one day," "some day," or "later on," and thus have made it look like Nietzsche is expounding on Dionysos' philosophy here, in 295, rather than it being a promise of doing so in the future, that is, in the *Umwerthung aller Werthe*. That this is a promise, and a promise about disclosing more about Dionysos' philosophy in the future (i.e., in his planned four-volume *magnum opus*) is still more visible in the early draft of this section, where he writes: "vielleicht kommt mir auch ein Tag von so viel Stille und halkyonischem Glück [. . .] daß ich Euch, meine Freunde, die Philosophie des Dionysos erzähle" (KSA 14, p. 374).

17 Burnham and Lampert who in their often profound and insightful commentaries and interpretations of *Jenseits von Gut und Böse* respectively, fail to see and comment on that this book, and especially the final sections, point forward to the *Umwerthung aller Werthe*. The same is true for the study by Acampora and Ansell Pearson, *Nietzsche's Beyond Good and Evil* (London, New York, 2011). They strongly emphasize that *Jenseits von Gut und Böse* builds up an "anticipation for great things to come throughout *Beyond Good and Evil*" (p. 192), and they emphasize the penultimate section of *Jenseits von Gut und Böse*, 295, and Dionysos in it—but they remain throughout the study *within* the book—and thus never mention Nietzsche's plans to write a *Hauptwerk* (which is stated both in the subtitle of *Jenseits von Gut und Böse*—"Prelude to a Philosophy of the Future"—and on the cover, where he had listed *Der Wille zur Macht* in four volumes as a work in progress. The expectation Nietzsche is building up in *Jenseits von Gut und Böse* is obviously for his planned *Hauptwerk*.

18 For example, Nietzsche's work and plans for a *Hauptwerk* are not even mentioned in the two recent English-language commentaries on *Jenseits von Gut und Böse* by Burnham and Lampert.

19 On the inside of the title page was printed: "Published to supplement and clarify the last work made public, 'Beyond Good and Evil.'"

20 This text, which I have here paraphrased, is given in KSA 14, p. 378.

21 KSA 13, 11[416]. He considered the title "der Misosoph" for the second volume. Compare also KSA 13, 22[24].

22 "*Die Kunst*, vorweg gesagt, denn ich komme irgendwann des Längeren darauf zurück."

23 *Zur Genealogie der Moral*, III, 27. The sentence before the quoted one is as follows: "*our* problem, the problem of the *meaning* of the ascetic ideal, can dispense with

them; what has this problem to do with yesterday or today!" As a typical example of how Nietzsche's intention and work on this *Hauptwerk* is assumed to be irrelevant (since no such work was finished) and is associated with the problematic selection of Elisabeth and Gast, and thus, it is implied, is best ignored, see Maudemarie Clark and Alan Swensen's translation of and comments on this work, p. 167 (1998).

24 KSA 14, 382. " . . . mein in Vorbereitung befindliches Hauptwerk."

25 See letters to Overbeck, August 30 and September 17, 1887: "Trotzdem schien es mir nothwendig, diesem 'Jenseits' von mir aus etwas zu Hülfe zu kommen: und so habe ich ein paar gute Wochen benutzt, um in Gestalt von 3 Abhandlungen [*Zur Genealogie der Moral*] das Problem des genannten Buchs noch einmal zu präcisiren. Damit glaube ich *am Ende* mit den Bemühungen zu sein, meine bisherige Litteratur 'verständlich' zu machen: und nunmehr wird für eine Reihe von Jahren nichts mehr gedruckt—ich muß mich absolut auf mich zurückziehn und abwarten, bis ich die letzte Frucht von meinem Baume schütteln darf. *Keine* Erlebnisse; *nichts* von *außen* her; nichts *Neues*—das sind für lange jetzt meine einzigen Wünsche" (Letter to Overbeck, August 30, 1887). Compare also: "Mit dieser Schrift (drei Abhandlungen enthaltend) ist übrigens meine vorbereitende Thätigkeit zum Abschluß gelangt: im Grunde gerade so, wie es im Programm meines Lebens lag, *zur rechten Zeit noch*, trotz der entsetzlichsten Hemmnisse und Gegen-Winde: aber dem Tapferen wird Alles zum Vortheil" (Overbeck, September 17, 1887).

26 "Denn in der Hauptsache steht es *gut*: der *Ton* dieser Abhandlungen wird Ihnen verrathen, daß ich *mehr* zu sagen habe als in denselben steht."

27 See especially note KSA 12, 9[83].

28 See letter to Deussen, September 14, 1888.

29 *Der Fall Wagner*, 7. The sentence before the quoted one is as follows: "The latter, the decay of a character, could perhaps find preliminary expression in this formula: the musician now becomes an actor, his art develops more and more as a talent to *lie*." Compare also KSA 13, 17[9].

30 I am working on a commentary to this book, with the title *Nietzsche's Philosophy in a "Nutshell": A Discussion of and Commentary to Nietzsche's* Twilight of the Idols.

31 See my article "Götzen-Hammer: The Meaning of the Expression 'To Philosophize with a Hammer,'" *Nietzsche-Studien* 28 (1999), 38–41.

32 Nietzsche here plays with the title of his *Hauptwerk*, and immediately after the quoted text he will in a similar manner play with the title of his *Der Fall Wagner*. The German text is: "Eine *Umwerthung aller Werthe*, dies Fragezeichen . . . ," which probably refers both to a *revaluation of all values* and to the (projected) title *Revaluation of All Values*.

33 Nietzsche at a very late stage added the final chapter "What I Owe to the Ancients" (which actually was part of the earliest version of the *Ecce Homo* manuscript) to *Götzen-Dämmerung*.

34 Letter to Gast, September 12, 1888: "so daß die Schrift [*Götzen-Dämmerung*] als *einweihend* und *appetitmachend* für meine *Umwerthung der Werthe* (deren erstes Buch beinahe in der Ausarbeitung fertig ist) dienen kann."
35 Letter to Deussen, September 14, 1888.
36 Letter to Taine, December 8, 1888: ". . . und in Hinsicht auf das, was es *vorbereitet*, beinahe ein Stück Schicksal."
37 "Sie ist kurz und im höchsten Grade vorbereitend."
38 See my article "The Place and Role of *Der Antichrist* in Nietzsche's Four-Volume Project *Umwerthung aller Werthe*," *Nietzsche-Studien* 40 (2011), 244–55.
39 *Der Antichrist*, 6.
40 He uses the word *Hauptwerk* six times in at least four letters (written September 2, 1886; October 15, 1887; September 7, 1888; and November 6, 1888), but also, in many more letters, uses many synonyms for it or directly uses the projected titles "Der Wille zur Macht" and "Umwerthung aller Werthe."
41 "Jedermann, der meinen Engadiner Arbeits-Sommer d. h. die Förderung meiner *Aufgabe*, *meines* 'Eins ist noth' *unterbricht*, als meinen Feind betrachte. [. . .] Ich habe keine Zeit mehr zu verlieren und habe schon viel zu viel verloren; wenn ich nicht mit meinen guten Viertelstunden geize, so habe ich ein schlechtes Gewissen. Du kannst nicht wissen, was ich noch von mir verlange."
42 We can note that the expression "Nun habe ich zum ersten Male meinen Hauptgedanken"—"for the first time" —suggests that he knew that he was going to do it again later, that here he is already referring to his long-term project of a *Hauptwerk*.
43 "Haben Sie davon gehört, daß mein Zarathustra fertig ist? (in 3 Theilen—Sie kennen den ersten davon)."
44 "Eine Vorhalle zu meiner Philosophie—für mich gebaut, mir Muth zu machen. Schweigen wir davon."
45 In this letter he states that it is under the clear sky of Nice that he wants "schon das Werk meines Lebens vorwärts bringen, das härteste und entsagungsreichste Werk, das sich ein Sterblicher auflegen kann.—Ich habe Niemanden, der darum weiß: Niemanden, den ich stark genug wüßte, mir zu helfen." Further on he writes: "Die Hauptsache aber ist die: ich habe Dinge auf meiner Seele, die hundert Mal schwerer zu tragen sind als la betise humaine. *Es ist möglich*, daß ich für alle kommenden Menschen ein Verhängniß, das Verhängniß bin—und es ist folglich *sehr möglich*, daß ich eines Tages stumm werde, aus Menschen-Liebe !!!"
46 "Himmel! wer weiß, was auf mir liegt und was für Stärke ich brauche, um es mit mir selber auszuhalten! Ich weiß nicht, wie *ich* gerade dazu komme—aber es ist möglich, daß mir *zum ersten Male* der Gedanke gekommen ist, der die Geschichte der Menschheit in zwei Hälften spaltet. Dieser Zarathustra ist nichts als eine Vorrede, Vorhalle—ich habe mir selber Muth machen müssen, da mir von überall her nur die Entmuthigung kam: Muth zum *Tragen* jenes Gedankens! Denn ich bin

noch weit davon entfernt, ihn aussprechen und darstellen zu können. Ist er wahr oder vielmehr: wird er als wahr geglaubt—so ändert und dreht sich *Alles*, und alle bisherigen Werthe sind entwerthet" (Letter to Overbeck, March 8, 1884).

47 "In Summa: es gehört zu meinen Aufgaben, auch darüber Herr zu werden und fortzufahren, alle meine Schicksale zu Gunsten meiner Aufgabe '*in Gold zu verwandeln*.' Es gab doch wieder Stunden, wo diese Aufgabe ganz deutlich vor mir steht, wo ein ungeheures Ganzes von Philosophie (und von Mehr als je Philosophie hieß!) sich vor meinen Blicken auseinander legt. Dies Mal, bei dieser gefährlichsten und schwersten 'Schwangerschaft,' muß ich mir begünstigende Umstände zusammenholen und alle Sonnen mir leuchten machen, die ich noch kennen lernte" (Letter to Overbeck, August 18, 1884) and "Im Ganzen sind alle Dinge diesen Sommer bei mir von der Stelle gekommen, und der Hauptzweck ist erreicht worden, freilich sehr auf Unkosten der Gesundheit: namentlich ist eine plötzliche auffallende Verdunkelung der Augen hinzugekommen [. . .] Die Gesammt-Depression, an der ich leider bei unserm Zusammensein in Basel litt, ist aber gehoben [. . .] Welch sonderbares Schicksal, 40 Jahr alt werden und alle seine wesentlichsten Dinge, theoretische wie praktische, als Geheimnisse mit sich noch herumschleppen!" (Overbeck, September 14, 1884).

48 Montinari has also observed this and writes in KSA 14, p. 281 that Nietzsche until the autumn 1884 was occupied by "intensiver theoretischer Beschäftigung."

49 See, for example, KSA 11, 27[58, 80, and 82], but also much of the contents of the notebooks W I 1 and 2 (published as KSA 11, 26[1–469] and perhaps also 25[1–526]), written during the spring of 1884. Compare also Nietzsche's letter to Overbeck, July 23 and August 18, 1884, where he alludes to this project.

50 See KSA 11, 39[1], August/September 1885.

51 See KSA 12, 2[100] and several of Nietzsche's letters: "Scheint es nicht, daß eine Wallfahrt dorthin [Corte auf Corsika] eine geziemende Vorbereitung für den 'Willen zur Macht.' Versuch einer Umwerthung aller Werthe ist?" (Letter to Gast, August 16, 1886). "Es handelt sich jetzt auch bei mir um eine conceptio [in the sense of a teaching, a program, a totality]: Du wirst es aus dem Umschlage meines letzterschienenen Werks errathen, welches ich Dir (wie sich von selbst versteht) zugesandt habe" (Seydlitz, August 17, 1886)."Das ganze Jahr ist damit draufgegangen: gut, salvavi animam, es war eine Gewissenssache, aber nunmehr ist's genug!—Ich brauche jetzt, für lange lange Jahre, tiefe Ruhe: denn es steht die Ausarbeitung meines ganzen Gedankensystems vor mir" (Letter to Fritzsch, end of December 1886).

52 KGW VI.2, page 257.

53 "In der Hauptsache fühle ich mehr als je die große Ruhe und Gewißheit, auf meinem Wege und sogar in der Nähe eines großen Ziels zu sein" (Letter to Overbeck, September 14, 1888).

54 Compare also "Aufrichtig gesagt, einen *Wagner abthun* gehört, inmitten der über alle Maaßen schweren Aufgabe meines Lebens, zu den wirklichen Erholungen. Ich schrieb diese kleine Schrift im Frühling, hier in Turin: inzwischen ist das erste

Buch meiner *Umwerthung aller Werthe* fertig geworden—das größte philosophische Ereigniß aller Zeiten mit dem die Geschichte der Menschheit in zwei Hälften auseinander bricht . . ." (Letter to Meysenbug, October 4, 1888).

55 KSA 13, 23[8 and 13].

56 There are two further sections in KSA 13, sections 24 and 25. However, section 24 consists of the earliest draft of *Ecce Homo* (already from before it had become *Ecce Homo*) and was written shortly before October 15, 1888, and is thus approximately simultaneous to the notes in section 23. The last section, 25[1–21], of ten pages, consists of notes written in December 1888 and early January 1889, which are mostly politically oriented and clearly affected by Nietzsche's mental deterioration.

57 See, for example, the letter to Tenischeff, December 8, 1888: "In diesem Augenblick, wo eine Aufgabe mich gleichsam heraustreibt aus menschlischer Beziehung."

In earlier letters during the last year he frequently speaks of having a task for the future, for example, letters to Gersdorff, December 20, 1887: "In einem bedeutenden Sinn steht mein Leben gerade jetzt wie im vollen Mittag: eine Thür schließt sich, eine andre thut sich auf. Was ich nur in den letzten Jahren gethan habe, war ein Abrechnen, Abschließen, Zusammenaddiren von Vergangnem, ich bin mit Mensch und Ding nachgerade fertig geworden und habe einen Strich drunter gezogen. Wer und was mir übrig bleiben soll, jetzt wo ich zur eigentlichen Hauptsache meines Daseins übergehn muß (überzugehn verurtheilt bin . . .) das ist jetzt eine capitale Frage. Denn, unter uns gesagt, die Spannung, in welcher ich lebe, der Druck einer großen Aufgabe und Leidenschaft, ist zu groß, als daß jetzt noch neue Menschen an mich herankommen könnten," and to Deussen, January 3, 1888: "Jetzt begehre ich für eine Reihe Jahre nur Eins: Stille, Vergessenheit, die Indulgenz der Sonne und des Herbstes für etwas, das *reif* werden will, für die nachträgliche Sanktion und Rechtfertigung meines ganzen Seins (eines sonst aus hundert Gründen ewig problematischen Seins!)."

In other letters he speaks about his need to have good working conditions for several years ahead, for example, letter to Overbeck, September, 1888.

58 Letter to Overbeck, April 7, 1884.

59 "gelehrten Zwecken, denn ich habe in Hinsicht auf das nunmehr zu absolvirende Hauptpensum meines Lebens noch viel zu lernen, zu fragen, zu lesen" (Letter to Gast, September 15, 1887). For a detailed discussion and listing of Nietzsche's known philosophical reading, see my study *Nietzsche's Philosophical Context: An Intellectual Biography* (Urbana and Chicago, 2008).

Chapter 3 (pages 47–80)

1 Some of this is discussed in Nicholas More's *Nietzsche's Last Laugh: Ecce Homo as Satire* (Cambridge, 2016).

2 Ronald Hayman's *Nietzsche: A Critical Life* (1980), p. 332.
3 Nietzsche's last outline for the last three volumes of *Umwerthung aller Werthe* is in KSA 13, 23[13], from October 1888. It consists of the following text: [Volume 2] *The Free Spirit*/ Critique of Philosophy as a Nihilistic Movement. [Volume 3] *The Immoralist*/ Critique of Morality as the Most Dangerous Kind of Lack of Knowledge. [Volume 4] *Dionysos philosophos*.

   From earlier notes it is possible to acquire much more detail about the planned contents of the different books, although one, of course, must assume that some rearrangements occur as the project develops. From early 1888 it is possible to gain much detailed information. Note KSA 13, 12[2] arranges twelve chapters into the four books (as do several other notes). More extensively, note KSA 13, 12[1] summarizes 374 notes, each in a few words, and then lists to which of the four books each belongs.
4 KSA 13, 19[8], 11[416] (this note is placed at the end of an earlier notebook, but was written at the end of the summer according to Montinari), 22[3, 14, 24], 23[8 and 13].
5 Except that books 2 and 3 have exchanged places in two of them.
6 These three more detailed tables of contents are KSA 13, 12[2], 16[51], and 18[17]. It is true that it is unclear where two distinct themes mentioned in them, critique of modernity and aesthetics, belong (or if they fall away), but it is easy to imagine that aesthetics were then meant to be discussed in the third volume (mostly dealing with morality), and that the theme of critique of modernity probably now fell apart and was meant to be discussed in all three of the first volumes (in relation to Christianity, nihilism, and morality).
7 Jing Huang has recently well summarized much of the discussion of the value of Nietzsche's notes in her "Did Nietzsche want his notes burned? Some reflections on the *Nachlass* problem," *British Journal of the History of Philosophy* 27, 1194–214 (2019).
8 I follow the usual English translation, but the German word "Klok" seems to me better translated as "sagacious" than as "clever."
9 The only other time Nietzsche used the expression, in *Götzen-Dämmerung*, "Morality as Antinature," 6, it is also used without reference or allusion to Christ.
10 In his letter to Meta von Salis, November 14, 1888, Nietzsche writes, referring to the title *Ecce homo*: "Dieser *homo* bin ich nähmlich selbst, eingerechnet das *ecce*; der Versuch, über mich ein wenig Licht *und Schrecken* zu verbreiten, scheint mir fast zu gut gelungen."
11 We can note that for the pessimistic philosopher Schopenhauer, the saint represented one of the highest states of man, as it did for the early Nietzsche.
12 Nietzsche may seem, especially in this section, to claim not really to revalue values, but only to question and criticize them: "The last thing *I* would promise would be to 'improve' humanity. I do not set up any new ideals, let the old ones learn what

it means to have legs of clay. *Toppling idols* (my word for 'ideals')—that is more my kind of handiwork." However, these claims are not completely correct. Not only does he suggest a number of "constructive" or "new" ideals (such as the existential "become who you are," and to accept reality, ignore a false metaphysical world, etc.), he clearly works on and proclaims a revaluation of values, and later he, for example, refers to "an unprecedented overturning and rebuilding" (EH, Clever, 10). His claim in this section of the foreword is probably instead that he does not set up new dogmas, which is done by prophets, fanatics, and priests, but, instead, suggests the more existential claims that we should each find our own (different) ideals. (However, on a few occasions he may seem to go against this. When he speaks of "grand politics" and then he says that humanity "for the first time asks the question 'why?' 'what for?' *as a whole.*" However, he does not here tell us what that common purpose would be, and if it is, as seems likely, related to *amor fati* and eternal recurrence, and basically says that you and we should affirm reality—then that is so broad and general that it cannot be regarded as a dogma in the same sense as the ideals Nietzsche criticizes.)

13 This question was so important for him that he had marked it as a serious candidate for the subtitle of the whole book: "warum ich Einiges mehr weiss," KSA 13, 24[1].

14 Another candidate for the subtitle to *Ecce homo* was "Aufzeichnungen eines Vielfachen" ("Notes of a Multifarious Man"), KSA 13, 24[3]. The word "multifarious," *Vielfachen*, echoes the description of Homer's Odysseus, who is called *polytropos* (versatile, multifarious or "man of many moves"). This is relevant, since early Greek antiquity constitutes the most obvious source of inspiration and of alternative values for Nietzsche. Homer, including Odysseus, like Goethe, is one of Nietzsche's foremost "heroes."

15 I take him to mean either in 1887/88 or possibly shortly before he wrote *Also sprach Zarathustra* (1883–5), probably in 1881, when he discovered the idea of eternal recurrence and several other late *topoi*.

16 It has been suggested that the last claim should be interpreted as that Nietzsche had just received a postcard with a picture of Dionysos' head. This would explain Nietzsche's statement, but not quite his expression, that is, his assumption that his reader could understand it. Furthermore, there is no evidence that he did receive such a postcard. I have examined his known and extant post, and found nothing that would suit such a description.

17 Nietzsche's claim here that "for years I read nothing—the *greatest* favour I have ever done myself!" is certainly incorrect and misleading. The period to which he was referring was primarily the year 1877, but also 1876. At that time he had continuous and serious health problems, and was completely released from teaching at both the University of Basel and the associated gymnasium for a full academic year, from October 1876 to October 1877. It is true that he read much less then than in

other years—but still much more than "nothing." In 1876 we have evidence that he read at least twelve books (which he discussed in letters or from which he copied passages), and is likely to have read further ones. We know that he this year also bought twenty-one titles and borrowed twenty-six titles from the university library in Basel. In 1877, it is true, he read very few books himself (he also bought very few books and borrowed none at all from the university library, since he was away on sick leave most of the year). However, he did read a few—Taine, Plato, Rée, Meysenbug, Deussen, Seydlitz, Lipiner, Sterne (and probably several others)—and, more importantly, a very large number of books were read to him, mainly by the other members of the Sorrento group (Rée, Meysenbug, and Brenner), and at other times by Peter Gast, Seydlitz, and possibly by his sister Elisabeth. We know of well over twenty titles that were read to Nietzsche that year, including works by Voltaire, Diderot, Burckhardt, Ranke, Thucydides, Herodotus, Lope de Vega, Calderon, Cervantes, Michelet, Daudet, Ruffini, Turgenev, Charles de Rémusat, Renan, A. Herzen, and Mainländer, as well as the New Testament.

18 He made a similar claim in *Die fröhliche Wissenschaft*, V, 366: "We do not belong to those who have ideas only among books, when stimulated by books. It is our habit to think outdoors [. . .] We read rarely, but not worse on that account."

19 Letter to Elisabeth Förster, November 3, 1886. Nietzsche continued in the letter: "Between us, my dear sister, the way I stand toward life and the task I have to perform, Europe is for me necessary, since it is the seat of science on Earth." In an earlier letter, from November 23, 1885, Nietzsche had written in regard to Paraguay: "The lack of larger libraries is perhaps not sufficiently emphasized [in the advertisement for Elisabeth and Bernhardt Förster's planned new colony in Paraguay]. Please forgive me, my dear Lama [Elisabeth's pet name], when the sickly cultural animal, your brother, allows himself a joke." Nietzsche also quoted Cicero in a short note written between November 1887 and March 1888, KSA 13, 11[18], which consists of just the words: "si hortum cum bibliotheca habes, nihil deerit. Cicero," which means "he who has a garden with a library lacks nothing."

In a letter from Chur, May 20, 1887, Nietzsche wrote: "The library in Chur, ca 20,000 volumes, gives me for education this and that." He then went on and discussed three books he had been reading there.

20 Letter to Franz Overbeck, April 14, 1887: "I need a place with a large library for my next work: I have considered Stuttgart. They have sent me the very liberal rules of the Stuttgart Library."

21 "Obviously, we spoke much about books and authors. Nietzsche had the *le flair du livre* and read much in spite of his eye-problems. [. . .] Like almost all good readers he annotated specific places in the text. Thus, a part of his intellectual life remains in the books he possessed." Meta von Salis-Marschlins, *Philosoph und Edelmensch: Ein Beitrag zur Charakteristik Friedrich Nietzsches* (Leipzig, 1897), p. 51.

22 See my article "Nietzsche's Reading and Private Library, 1885–89," *Journal of the History of Ideas* 58 (1997), 663–93, for further information about these authors and books.
23 He also claims not to read Pascal, although he had read him intensively for many years.
24 *On the Genealogy of Morals*, III, 22.
25 This is a listing of the persons Nietzsche most often praised in his published works. For a fuller discussion, see my *Nietzsche's Ethics of Character* (Uppsala, 1995).
26 KSA 14, p. 476f. This earlier listing was written in October 1888, but replaced by the printed version in early December 1888.
27 For a more general discussion of Nietzsche's reading, with focus on his philosophical reading, see my study *Nietzsche's Philosophical Context: An Intellectual Biography*, University of Illinois Press (Urbana and Chicago, 2008).
28 See, for example, the essay by Ralph-Rainer Wuthenow, *Nietzsche als Leser* (Hamburg, 1994). In other respects, this essay is very readable.
29 KSA 14, p. 477f.
30 We can note that Nietzsche in the previous section had described himself in just this manner: "I have not the slightest wish for anything to be other than it is; I myself do not want to be different."
31 Considering that *Ecce homo* usually has been read as an autobiography, it is tempting to go through and list all instances when Nietzsche is misleading or mistaken about his life. However, I believe that showing that the whole purpose of and intention with the book was very different than that of an autobiography, and the scattered examples I have shown (especially regarding his reading, earlier) ought to be sufficient, in the future, to prevent straightforward autobiographical readings.
32 The translation is taken from Middleton, p. 289.
33 The sentence was added after the rest of the text.
34 It has been thus understood by many commentators.
35 KSA 14, p. 485.
36 Oddly enough, Nietzsche contradicts these fifteen lines below in his claim: "*non legor, non legar*," that is, "I am not read, I will not be read."
37 In fact, his comment later in *Ecce homo* that he is "not a man but dynamite" is taken from the review referred to in this chapter of *Jenseits von Gut und Böse* by Widmann entitled "Nietzsche's Dangerous Book," published on September 16–17, 1886. Spitteler's essay, "Friedrich Nietzsche in His Books," was published on January 1, 1888. Originally, Nietzsche appreciated both reviews, but already by February 10, 1888, Nietzsche in a long letter to Spitteler explains why he was dissatisfied with it. Both these reviews have been published in KGB III.7/3.2.
38 KSA 14, p. 374.

39 In 1872 the highest form of art was regarded as a synthesis of the Apollonian and Dionysian, while now, in *Ecce homo*, he (falsely) writes that in *Die Geburt der Tragödie*, the Dionysian was regarded "as the single root of all Greek art."
40 At the end of *Die Geburt der Tragödie*, 24.
41 Wolfgang Groddeck's "Die Geburt der Tragödie" in 'Ecce homo': Hinweise zu einer strukturalen Lektüre von Nietzsches 'Ecce homo,'" *Nietzsche-Studien* 13 (1984), 325–33, contains many interesting discussions and observations of *Ecce homo*, and a few comments which overlap with mine, but his overall thesis is different.
42 For Nietzsche's view of and relation to Christianity and how it developed, see my two essays "Nietzsche's Changing Relation to Christianity: Nietzsche as Christian, Atheist and Antichrist," in *Nietzsche and the Gods* (SUNY), edited by Weaver Santaniello (New York, 2001), 137–57, and "Nietzsche's Atheism," in *Nietzsche and the Divine*, edited by Jim Urpeth and John Lippitt (Clinamen Press, Manchester, 2000), 1-13.
43 The last fifteen lines of this section, 6, from "The passage reads:" is thus a slightly changed quotation from Nietzsche's *Menschliches, Allzumenschliches*, 37 (including a number of comments which one would normally place in brackets), in which he discusses and quotes Paul Rée. The quotation within the quotation does not quite follow what he wrote in *Menschliches, Allzumenschliches*, 37. There he had added "(metaphysical)" as an explanatory comment immediately after the word "intelligible"—this is not in Rée's original text, on page viii of the book. The comment after this sentence "*—for* there is no intelligible world . . ." is a clarifying addition which Nietzsche makes now in 1888—but is fully in line with, and assumed by, Rée.
44 Nietzsche is a skillful user of hermeneutical reading, that is, of placing himself in the role of the author, so a certain sense of identification would perhaps not be surprising. However, this seems to be a bit more than that (unless the meaning is that it was he who inspired his friend Rée to write it—Rée and Nietzsche wrote their respective books while sharing quarters in 1877), especially when we know the future. This sense of strong identification becomes pathological in early January 1889, as can be seen in his last letter to Jakob Burckhardt on January 6, 1889: "The unpleasant thing and one that nags my modesty, is that at root every name in history is I."
45 In fact, Nietzsche gives most of the titles of his own books in a slightly changed form, but this is the only one which is of greater relevance.
46 However, I have in a different publication, "The Origin and Early Context of Nietzsche's Revaluation of All Values," *Journal of Nietzsche Studies* 29 (2010), 12–29, examined the case for and argued that one can find the origin of his philosopheme 'revaluation of all values' among his notes from this time, 1880/81.
47 See KSA 14, p. 494.

48 The last eight aphorisms of book three were added to it while proofreading the book. All of them are of high quality and of great interest. The one following the one quoted in the text above, 270, is of especial interest in relation to *Ecce homo*, for Nietzsche here too uses Pindar's words and the theme of the first two chapters of *Ecce homo*: "*What does your conscience say?* —'You shall become the person you are.'"

49 In the preface to *Die fröhliche Wissenschaft* from 1886, Nietzsche emphasizes the book as a work of "the intoxication of convalescence." In line with the two 1886 prefaces to *Menschliches, Allzumenschliches*, Nietzsche seems to argue that he was first a romantic, and then turned against this with revulsion during the positivistic phase of *Menschliches, Allzumenschliches*, and *Morgenröthe*: "this determined self-limitation to what was bitter, harsh and hurtful to know, prescribed by the *nausea* that had gradually developed out of an incautious and pampering spiritual diet, called romanticism." He here describes this middle positivistic phase as "This stretch of desert, exhaustion, disbelief, icing up in the midst of youth, this interlude of old age at the wrong time, this tyranny of pain" (*Die fröhliche Wissenschaft*, Preface, 1).

50 In an earlier version of section 5, see KSA 14, pp. 496–98, Nietzsche repeatedly speaks of "the good," "the virtuous," and "the just," which he planned to criticize in the third volume of *Umwerthung aller Werthe*.

51 This information is not given in KSA 14, but is visible in the *Ecce homo* manuscript. The numbering of the sections as "1" and "2" was done later, and with lead pencil. It is not clear to me if this was done by Nietzsche, Gast (who made his revisions on the manuscript with pencil), or someone else. Probably it is not known, since two single digits are too little to identify handwriting.

52 The results of my examination of Nietzsche's intentions and notes during this period seem to confirm this. See my article "Nietzsche's *magnum opus*," *History of European Ideas* 32 (September 2006), 278–94.

53 Nietzsche's comments as to the place of *Götzen-Dämmerung* in this scheme, as being part of or as not being part of (or closely related to) the *Umwerthung aller Werthe*, are ambiguous. See the discussion below.

54 This section in *Jenseits von Gut und Böse*, 295, where Nietzsche already calls himself "the last disciple and initiate of the god Dionysos" and he claims, since *Die Geburt der Tragödie* to have "learned much, all too much more about the philosophy of this god" and states that "perhaps I might at last begin to give you, my friends, a little taste of this philosophy"—probably referring to the project *Umwerthung aller Werthe* that Nietzsche had also worked on already then as his *magnum opus*. That this is a promise to tell more in the future (i.e., in his planned four-volume *magnum opus*) is still more visible in the early draft of this section, where he writes: "vielleicht kommt mir auch ein Tag von so viel Stille und halkyonischem Glück [. . .]

daß ich Euch, meine Freunde, die Philosophie des Dionysos erzähle" (KSA 14, p. 374). The very last section, 296, is possibly also a reference to his coming *magnum opus*, in that its theme is the difference between old thoughts and truths (which is what is presented in *Jenseits von Gut und Böse*) and the new "many-coloured, young and malicious" thoughts which these had once been, and others such as these, which he now worked on to structure and present in his *magnum opus*.

55 See Montinari, 103, and also KSA 14, pp. 345f.: "Dass *Jenseits von Gut und Böse* sich *nicht* aus dem Material des sogenannten *Willens zur Macht* abgelöst hat, erhellt aus dieser Entstehungsgeschichte. Es war tatsächlich eine Vorbereitung, ein 'Vorspiel' für etwas, das noch kommen sollte und—zumindest als *Wille zur Macht*—nicht kam."

56 As one minor example of the fact that Nietzsche in his reviews is not concerned with discussing the books as such, but does so from the much more limited perspective of how they relate to his present plans and project, that is, to the *Umwerthung aller Werthe*, we can note that much important general information is simply left out. For example, on the cover of *Zur Genealogie der Moral* he had written that it served the purpose "to supplement and clarify his last published book, *Jenseits von Gut und Böse*," but such information was now in 1888 secondary and not included.

57 Such a description seems correct in the sense that *Zur Genealogie der Moral* appears to be more based on contemporary notes and work he did in 1887 while developing his four-volume *magnum opus*. In a letter to Overbeck from shortly after having finished *Zur Genealogie der Moral*, dated September 17, 1887, he writes: "With this book (containing three dissertations), is, by the way, my preparatory activity brought to conclusion: fundamentally exactly *such* as it should according to the programme of my life, *just barely at the right time*, in spite of the most terrible obstacles and headwinds: but for the brave everything turns to an advantage."

58 The most important and controversial sentence of the third section is the one which begins: "On 30 September" and which, in some versions, contains an explicit reference to the *Umwerthung aller Werthe*. Three versions of this sentence have been published in the different German editions of *Ecce homo*. In the actual, that is, in Nietzsche's handwritten *Ecce homo*, manuscript, the controversial words are missing: "On 30 September great triumph; seventh day; a god at his leisure beside the Po." However, it seems as if Nietzsche later sent in by post a short revision, where "seventh day" was to be exchanged for "completion of the *Revaluation*" (however, no such note or letter is extant). This is the text used in the critical edition of Nietzsche's works today (KSA and KGW). An alternative to this is "completion of the first book of the *Revaluation*" (used in most editions until KSA). However, Montinari argues, with what seems to be convincing arguments, that it was Peter Gast who himself added those extra words: "the first book of" to the manuscript. See KSA 14, p. 500f.

Compare the almost identical uncertainty as regards "*Revaluation*" or "the first book of the *Revaluation*" in the short prelude to *Ecce Homo*. I accept Montinari's conclusions, but assume that when Nietzsche says the *Revaluation*, he actually (and obviously) means the first book of it (in accordance with what he had written in the preface to *Götzen-Dämmerung* and as the subtitle to *Der Antichrist*). All three versions then become very similar, in fact, essentially identical.

59 "This book too—the title betrays it—is above all a relaxation, a sunspot, an escape into the idle hours of a psychologist." However, already in the preface to *Götzen-Dämmerung*, this ambivalence as to the role of the book is present, for he continues after the quoted sentence by claiming that "this little book is a *grand declaration of war*," which implies that it is part of the revaluation rather than a resting place from it.

60 I am working on a manuscript called *Nietzsche's Philosophy in a "Nutshell": A Discussion of and Commentary to Nietzsche's* Twilight of the Idols.

61 The reference to "the *good* man" in the second half of the second section is probably a reference to the third volume of *Umwerthung aller Werthe,* where he intended to discuss this concept and theme extensively.

62 The third section of the review of *Götzen-Dämmerung* was added in late November.

63 This is probably the reason why Nietzsche reversed its position—that is, all the other books are discussed in chronological order, but *Der Fall Wagner*, which ought then to have been discussed before *Götzen-Dämmerung*, was, instead, placed after that book.

Chapter 4 (pages 81–96)

1 KSA 13, 23[3].

2 An earlier version of these first two sections can be found in KSA 13, 25[6], written in December 1888.

3 KSA 14, p. 451. That it would most likely be three pages long can be determined by the page-numbering of the next epilogue which continues three pages after the end of the *Ecce homo* text.

4 See KSA 13, 25[1 and 6] and Nietzsche's letter to Brandes, dated to early December 1888. Possibly also relevant are the notes KSA 13, 25[11, 13, and 14], but these appear to have been written after the middle of December, and thus after Nietzsche had originally written the "Declaration of War."

5 See KSA 13, 25[14 and 19].

6 This is based on Montinari's research and account, KSA 14, pp. 468–70.

7 I have used but modified Hollingdale's translation, p. 231f. In *Also sprach Zarathustra* this text is followed by the words: "Thus spoke Zarathustra," but these

are not included in the manuscript. Otherwise the text is virtually identical to that in *Also sprach Zarathustra*—no word has been added or subtracted—but in a few places Nietzsche has changed punctuation marks, and ß is used instead of ss, and he has added italics to "großen Mittage." Nietzsche has written immediately before the quoted text that it should be printed with the same distance between the lines as in the foreword.

8 The great noontide, noon-day, and midday are merely three different translations of the German *grosse Mittag*.

9 KSA 12, 6[26] and KSA 13, 13[2], 14[77], 15[102], 18[15], and 18[17].

10 The first quarter of the fourth section of the review of *Die Geburt der Tragödie* discusses what will happen if the revaluation succeeds. The whole of the second section of the review of *Morgenröthe* belongs to the introduction to the "Destiny" section, and would suit very well as a section inserted between sections 2 and 3. This is also largely true for the first section of the review of *Jenseits von Gut und Böse* and the second half of the second section of the review of *Götzen-Dämmerung*, and possibly section 3 (but it is different in style, and more concrete concerning the actual writing of volume 1, that is, *Der Antichrist*). The second section of the review of *Morgenröthe* is actually a rewriting of the connected text which constitutes sections 6, 7, and 8 of the "Destiny" chapter—together they constituted sections 21 to 23 of the original, October version of the manuscript. See KSA 14, p. 510.

11 Nietzsche mentions this opposition in the following notes from the first half of 1888, KSA 13, 14[89, 91, 137], and 16[16].

12 Note that Nietzsche's discussion of the future after a successful revaluation, at the beginning of the fourth section of his review of *Die Geburt der Tragödie*, seems to be closely related to this theme.

13 KSA 13, 23[4–7].

14 KSA 13, 23[3].

15 They are at least not included in the selections of later notes entitled *The Will to Power* and *Writings from the Late Notebooks*.

16 During October in the notes KSA 13, 19[8], 22[3, 14, and 24], and 23[13].

17 See, for example, KSA 13, 11[416], 19[8], and 22[3]. Before Nietzsche wrote *Der Antichrist* in 1888, many of the themes relating to Christianity were spread out and were to have been dealt with in several different volumes. Especially KSA 13, 12[1 and 2], from early 1888, contain much detailed information about the then planned content of the four volumes, but since this is before Nietzsche wrote *Der Antichrist*, the chapter divisions and the planned contents of the volumes differ. Here, discussions of nihilism are placed in volume 1, "Kritik des christlichen Ideals" in volume 2, and discussions of the will to truth in volume 3.

18 Most clearly, perhaps, at the end of section 7, where Nietzsche suggests that perhaps it is not so much mankind that is decadent but the priests, and in section 8, where

Nietzsche writes: "The concept 'God' invented as a counter-concept to life," and possibly the following ten lines.

19 In KSB 8, this draft (no. 1170) is dated to as early December 1888, but in the later and more detailed KGB IV.7/3.1, p 464, it is suggested that it probably was written shortly after November 24. The word translated as "fate" here is not "Schicksal" but "Mensch des Verhängnisses."

20 It is not obvious to me to what extent this whole theme was meant to be treated as an independent theme in volume 3, or be regarded as part of the general theme of morality and be subsumed under the theme of immoralism, or if it should be regarded as part of Nietzsche's general discussion of the whole revaluation project and theme.

21 For the second volume of *Zur Genealogie der Moral*, see KSA 12, 9[83]; for later discussions and it being incorporated into his *magnum opus*, see, for example, KSA 12, 10[57 and 58], and many further notes. See also his important letter to Overbeck, dated January 4, 1888: "Nur ein Wort hinsichtlich des Buchs [*Zur Genealogie der Moral*]: es war der Deutlichkeit wegen geboten, die verschiedenen Entstehungsheerde jenes complexen Gebildes, das Moral heißt, künstlich zu isoliren. Jede dieser 3 Abhandlungen bringt ein einzelnes primum mobile zum Ausdruck; es fehlt ein viertes, fünftes und sogar das wesentlichste ('der Heerdeninstinkt')— dasselbe mußte einstweilen, als zu umfänglich, bei Seite gelassen werden, wie auch die schließliche Zusammenrechnung aller verschiedenen Elemente und damit eine Art *Abrechnung mit der Moral*. Dafür sind wir eben noch im 'Vorspiele' meiner Philosophie. (Zur Genesis des Christenthums bringt jede Abhandlung einen Beitrag; nichts liegt mir ferner, als dasselbe mit Hülfe einer einzigen psychologischen Kategorie erklären zu wollen) Doch wozu schreibe ich das? Dergleichen versteht sich eigentlich zwischen Dir und mir von selbst. Treulich und dankbar Dein N.," and compare also his letter to Deussen, on January 3, 1888.

22 Such as *Entselbstung*, *Entpersönlichung*, *Selbstlos*, *Selbst-verleugnung*, and *Selbst-entfremdet*.

23 Nietzsche also briefly refers to "improvers" of humanity—as typical of moralists—earlier in *Ecce Homo*, in the second section of the preface, and in the review of the *Unzeitgemäße Betrachtungen*.

24 KSA 13, 22[25]. This note seems to suggest that volume 3 of the *Umwerthung aller Werthe* at this time was planned to contain three major themes: immoralism and a history and critique of morality, a critique of the "improvers" of mankind, and, finally, a critique of the "good."

25 I believe that this is also one of the reasons Montinari and many other commentators have assumed that Nietzsche gave up on the last three volumes of the *Umwerthung aller Werthe*—many of the final notes were incorporated into *Ecce Homo*. My argument, given below in the next section, is that we know that

Nietzsche continued to assume that he was going to publish the three further volumes much longer than Montinari claimed, but also that it is not surprising that Nietzsche used these notes for this chapter, which was pointing forward to that which was to come. Recall his letter to his publisher, on November 6, 1888, that the book was "a in the highest degree *preparatory* text" and his statement to Brandes, early December 1888, that "the last chapter gives a foretaste of *what will come*, and where I myself appear as a human fate." Most important, however, is the fact that Nietzsche continued to refer to *Umwerthung aller Werthe* as a four-volume work, at least until the middle of December 1888.

26 The first time Nietzsche seems to use the word "immoralism" is in the note KSA 12, 1[168]. The term "immoral" is used over 100 times in Nietzsche's notes.

27 *Zur Genealogie der Moral*, II, 2 (Douglas Smith's translation).

28 KSA 13, 23[3], from October 1888.

29 See my somewhat longer argument in the article "The Place and Role of *Der Antichrist* in Nietzsche's Four-Volume Project *Umwerthung aller Werthe*," *Nietzsche-Studien* 40 (2011), 244–55.

30 The last letters in which Nietzsche explicitly refers to *Der Antichrist* as "the first book" of the *Umwerthung aller Werthe* are letters to Gast, dated October 30, 1888; to Overbeck, dated October 18 and November 13; and to Meta von Salis, dated November 14, 1888.

31 However, *Der Antichrist* is also referred to, without being named, toward the end of the third section of the review of *Götzen-Dämmerung* (where the "Druckmanuskript" says "seventh day"). There are also a few general references in which it is not clear if the references are to the philosophical project, the complete four-volume literary project, or to the first volume, that is, *Der Antichrist*—this occurs in the sixth section of the review of *Menschliches, Allzumenschliches* (added to the manuscript in late December), at the beginning of the third section in the review of *Götzen-Dämmerung*, and in the fourth section of the review of *Der Fall Wagner*.

32 KSA 14, p. 459. See also the first page of the proofs, figure 4.1.

33 "das erste Buch der *Umwerthung aller Werthe*." Furthermore, Nietzsche sent in the second part of the proofs shortly before December 27, and then makes no comment on the prologue, obviously because the corrections from December 18 were still valid, with *Der Antichrist* as the first of four volumes.

34 See KSA 14, pp. 525f. In this addition to *Nietzsche contra Wagner*, "Wir Antipoden," Nietzsche wrote (sometime between the middle and end of December): " Dieser Satz, hart und schneidig geworden unter dem Hammerschlag der historischen Erkenntniß (—lisez: erstes Buch der *Umwerthung der Werthe*—)" etc. In the end, Nietzsche did not use this addition. Instead, he wrote, as one of his last additions to *Ecce Homo*, the sixth and last section of his review of *Menschliches, Allzumenschliches*—a very similar text, but this time without the words "erstes Buch."

35 See KSA 14, 460–3.
36 The fact that Nietzsche stops referring to *Der Antichrist* as the first volume of the *Umwerthung aller Werthe* and, instead, as the *Umwerthung aller Werthe* does not necessarily mean that he had given up on writing the further volumes. It is possible that he decided to refer only to that which was already written. Compare the case of *Also sprach Zarathustra* in four volumes. The first volume was merely called *Also sprach Zarathustra: Ein Buch für Alle und Keinen* (although he planned to write further ones), and only after the second volume, which was called *Also sprach Zarathustra*: Book 2 ("Zweiter Theil"), was a similar subtitle given to the first volume ("Erster Theil"), see KSA 14, p. 281.
37 The sentence continues: "—it should prevent any mischief-making with me . . . I don't want to be a saint." He is saying not only that the *Umwerthung aller Werthe* is to be published after *Ecce Homo*, but also that this work is by far his most important work and the one which will make him famous.
38 In the German original (KSA 6, p. 365): "*Umwerthung aller Werthe*: das ist meine Formel für einen Akt höchster Selbstbesinnung der Menschheit, der in mir Fleisch und Genie geworden ist."
39 We can note that *Der Antichrist* does not contain a single reference to the term "immoralist," and that that work, on the whole, is almost exclusively critical and destructive. For his more creative and affirmative views, one needs to go to the plans for the further volumes.
40 Further examples: in a letter to Gast, dated November 13, 1888, Nietzsche writes: "As to the appearance [of *Ecce Homo*], I have this time 'requested' the same as for the '*Revaluation*': to which it is a fire-spewing foreword" (compare also the similar letter to Naumann, November 6, quoted earlier in the first chapter). In a letter to Georg Brandes, dated November 20, 1888, Nietzsche describes his *Ecce Homo* and continues: "the whole thing is a prelude to the *Revaluation of All Values*, of the work that lies finished before me." In a letter to Naumann, dated November 25, 1888, he writes: "As soon as 'Ecce homo' has had effect—it will raise astonishment without equal—I will prepare the already mentioned steps toward a translation of the 'Revaluation' in 7 main languages by nothing but excellent European authors. The book shall be published in all languages simultaneously." In a letter to Deussen, dated November 26, 1888, Nietzsche speaks of *Götzen-Dämmerung* and claims that it is a very cheerful book "in comparison to that which will come" (obviously a reference to the *Umwerthung aller Werthe*), and while speaking of *Ecce Homo* he says: "I appear in it at the end with a world-historical mission."
41 "I shall have a great opportunity to demonstrate [. . .] the uncanny consequence of *optimism*" (EH, Destiny, 4).
42 In the reviews of *Menschliches, Allzumenschliches* and *Der Fall Wagner*: "This principle, hardened and sharpened under the hammer blows of historical knowledge (*lisez: revaluation of all values*), may perhaps at some future

point—1890!—serve as the ax which will be applied to the roots of humanity's 'metaphysical need'" and "And so, roughly two years before the shattering lightning-bolt of the *Revaluation*, which will have the earth in convulsions, I sent *Der Fall Wagner* out into the world" (EH, Books, *The Case of Wagner*, 4).

43 Also the words for "unselfing oneself," *Entselbstung, Entpersönlischung, Selbstlos*, etc., occur only on a single occasion in *Der Antichrist*.

44 Considering that already from the very beginning of his plans for a four-volume *magnum opus*, the idea of eternal recurrence was going to constitute a central theme of the book (it even constituted the title in one of the first drafts), it is somewhat surprising that it is not more prominent in this last chapter of *Ecce Homo*. It is not completely absent; it is alluded to in several sections, but only in a subdued or hidden manner. He refers to "an ascendant and yes-saying life," to "not being alienated" from reality, to "yes-saying, future-assured, future-confirming man," and to Dionysos, who like Zarathustra, is a teacher of eternal recurrence (in sections 4, 5, 8, and 9 of the last chapter). Earlier in *Ecce Homo*, the idea is mentioned more explicitly (in the chapter "Wise," 3; and in his reviews of *Die Geburt der Tragödie*, sections 2 and 3, and those of *Also sprach Zarathustra*, 1 and 6), but perhaps the reason the idea is not more prominent in the last chapter is that the chapter primarily points forward to volume 3, while eternal recurrence was meant to be treated in the final, most affirmative, volume 4. Nietzsche may also have felt that he had just given such a cliff-hanger at the end of his immediately previous book, *Götzen-Dämmerung*, in which the last sentence (except the final quotation from *Also sprach Zarathustra*) is "I, the last disciple of the philosopher Dionysos—I, the teacher of the eternal recurrence."

45 The last sentence of *Götzen-Dämmerung*, obviously pointing forward, states: "I, the teacher of eternal recurrence . . . ."

46 See the later notes, KSA 13, 19[8], from September 1888, and KSA 13, 22[14], from September–October, in both of which the fourth book of *Umwerthung aller Werthe* is described as "*Dionysos*' Philosophy of Eternal Recurrence."

Chapter 5 (pages 97–119)

1 A similar text to this chapter has also been published in Nietzsche's *Ecce Homo*, edited by Nicholas Martin and Duncan Large (Berlin, Boston, Walter de Gruyter, 2021), pp. 235–261.

2 Dionysos (and related words) are mentioned twenty-nine times in *Ecce Homo* while Zarathustra appears seventy-nine times.

3 Letter to Overbeck, dated February 1, 1883. In the letters from 1888, that view becomes common; see, for example, letter to Seydlitz, dated February 12, 1888: "ein non plus ultra."

4 Letter to Overbeck, March 8, 1884.

5 Already in the letter to Overbeck, dated March 8, 1884, Nietzsche writes that if the idea of eternal recurrence will be believed as true "then *everything* will change and turn, and *all* present values will be devalued."

6 According to Nietzsche's own statements in letters, it seems that he regarded it as the latter, that he was in or attempted to move into, a new phase.

7 KSA 9, 11[195]. The subtitle was immediately below changed to "*Draft for a New Way to Live.*"

8 KSA 9, 11[197]. Prometheus was quickly replaced by Zarathustra and/or Dionysos.

9 KSA 9, 12[225].

10 Furthermore Nietzsche says much later, while proofreading the fifth book which he added in 1887, that he has made a number of additions to it for the purpose of giving it "yet more the character of a *preparation* for *Also sprach Zarathustra*," in his letter to Fritzsch, April 29, 1887.

11 See KSA 11, 34[144 and 145], 35[39, 41, 73, 74, 75], and 39[3]. See also KSA 12, 2[129], where Zarathustra also dies, although this seems not to be a continuation of *Also sprach Zarathustra* but probably a draft for a book of poems.

12 In the last section, 51, of the chapter "Reconnaissance Raids of an Untimely Man" in *Götzen-Dämmerung* Nietzsche writes: "I have given humanity the most profound book it possesses, my *Zarathustra*: I shall shortly give it the most independent one." These words were originally meant to constitute the very end of the book.

13 *Der Antichrist*, 53 and 54.

14 The twenty-five quotations from, or specific references to, *Also sprach Zarathustra* in *Ecce Homo* are fairly equally distributed between the first three books of *Also sprach Zarathustra*: four to the first book, ten to the second, and eleven to the third book. There are no quotations from the fourth book, which had been published only in a tiny private edition, and only about ten copies distributed. He once refers to it, in section four of "Why I Am So Wise," here under the title "The Temptation of Zarathustra," under which title he considered a possible re-publication of it.

15 The two main reasons for this are likely to be that it contains some aspects of the goal and "task" which Nietzsche also now strives toward, and is related to the fact that *Also sprach Zarathustra* is to a remarkable degree autobiographical in the sense that by it and in it Nietzsche succeeded in overcoming much in himself and sublimate it into this mixture of art and philosophy (see, for example, letter to Overbeck, February 12, 1887). I discuss this in the chapter "*Thus Spoke Zarathustra* as Nietzsche's Autobiography," in *Before Sunrise: Nietzsche's* Thus Spoke Zarathustra, edited by James Luchte, Continuum Publishers (London, New York, 2008), 29–46.

16 It may seem that the reference to Zarathustra at the end of the second essay of *Zur Genealogie der Moral*, quoted earlier, is an exception which points forward, but in my reading, the purpose of this section is to point the reader to go and read *Also sprach Zarathustra*, that is, he points backward in time rather than forward.

17 Three notes also concern Nietzsche's plans to publish the fourth book of *Also sprach Zarathustra*, KSA 13, 22[13, 15, and 16].

18 Except in two problematic notes from September or October 1888, KSA 13, 22[23], and 23[10], in which the same statement is repeated: "The highest law of life, formulated by Zarathustra, demands that one is *without pity* towards all rejects and refuse of life,—that one *exterminate* [. . .] *Christianity* in a single word." It is problematic in the sense that at first it seems to be enormously ruthless, and shows contempt for the weak—but on closer reading he seems to mean life-denying values and ideologies, and therefore his only example is Christianity. It is also problematic because it is so untypical of him, he writes it down four times in a row, virtually identically, and in that it seems to go against his claim in *Götzen-Dämmerung* that one should affirm enemies (including Christianity), not eradicate them.

19 In a letter to Pinder, September 24, 1859, Nietzsche mentions a no longer extant German school essay he had written on a theme of ancient mythology, entitled "Ino und Athamas." This possibly constitutes Nietzsche's first encounter with the figure of Dionysos, which later will become so important for him, for Ino was the sister of Semele, Dionysos' mother, and the one to whom the god-child was entrusted. Also in 1859 Nietzsche began to occupy his mind—and writing—with the figure of Prometheus which would remain an important preoccupation for a number of the following years. It seems as if Nietzsche's interest in Prometheus foreshadows his later interest in Dionysos (for example, Nietzsche selected an etching of Prometheus for the cover of his first book, *Die Geburt der Tragödie*). Nietzsche's first work on Dionysos can be found in his commentary on the first choir-song of Sophocles' *King Oedipus* with the title "Primum Oedipodis regis carmen choricum," written as a school essay at Pforta in Latin, Greek, and German during the spring of 1864 (BAW 2, 364–99). Here Nietzsche discusses, among other things, the origins of Greek drama. He emphasizes the difference between German and Greek drama and the importance of the choir and music in ancient times; indeed, he argues that the Greek drama had its *origin* in lyric and music. He emphasizes the importance of both Apollo and Dionysos. We already here see many of the fundamental themes of Nietzsche's first book, *Die Geburt der Tragödie aus dem Geiste der Musik* (1872).

20 KSA 10, 8[14], summer of 1883. This note which begins "My *first solution*: **Dionysian wisdom**" seems to reflect Nietzsche's reawakened awareness of Dionysos, which occurs while he is closely reading and annotating Leopold Schmidt's *Die Ethik der alten Griechen*, 2 vols (1882), and planning to write a text on the Greeks as having profound knowledge of the human situation. While reading Schmidt, Nietzsche also for the first time connects his idea of eternal recurrence with the Greeks and their mysteries, KSA 10, 8[15], which comes to expression only in his published works at the end of *Götzen-Dämmerung* (emphasis as in original). Nietzsche was at this time working on the first book of *Also sprach Zarathustra*, and also liberating himself from his more "positivistic" free-spirit period, see, for example, KSA 10, 9[9].

21 KSA 11, 25[2], March 1884 and KSA 11, 29[65], from late 1884. The former note seems to refer to a book of poems, while for the latter there is no information whether it was planned as a book of prose or poetry.
Hödl's study contains interesting discussions of the Dionysian in relation to *Ecce Homo.*

22 The bookseller Lorentz, in two notes from October and November 1884, tells Nietzsche that he is searching for this book for him. See letter to Overbeck, March 3, 1888 and KGB III 7/3.1, p. 275.

23 These four volumes contain no annotations, though Nietzsche has dog-eared a number of pages as he often used to do to mark pages.

24 KSA 11, 34[181 and 182], where the first note is an early draft of *Jenseits von Gut und Böse*, 295.

25 KSA 11, 34[191, 192, 201, 248], 35[26, 47, 73], 36[6], and 42[6].

26 KSA 12, 1[187], 2[11 and 44], and 4[4].

27 KSA 11, 41[7]. See also KSA 11, 42[1].

28 KSA 12, 2[204].

29 KSA 12, 10[3].

30 KSA 12, 5[93]. Possibly connected to it are 9[115] and 10[95]. The first is a long note for a satyr-play about Theseus, Ariadne, and Dionysos.

31 KSA 12, 10[159].

32 KSA 13, 14[14]. I am quoting Kaufmann's translation of this note as *Der Wille zur Macht* 1050.

33 KSA 13, 14[24]. Compare also KSA 13, 14[33], 16[32], and 17[3]. Especially 16[32] is an important note, in which both *amor fati* and eternal recurrence are related to the Dionysian.

34 KSA 13, 19[8], 22[14], and 23[8 and 13].

35 KSA 13, 24[1].

36 Dionysos was also emphasized in part of the early draft of section 36, see KSA 11, 38[12] and KSA 14, p. 727.

37 *Jenseits von Gut und Böse*, 295. Nietzsche continues after the quoted text: "I would have to extol his courage as investigator and discoverer, his daring honesty, truthfulness and love of wisdom. [. . .] [Dionysos says about man] I like him: I often ponder how I might advance him and make him stronger, more evil and more profound than he is [. . .] also more beautiful." Important early versions of this text where Dionysos plays a prominent role are KSA 11, 34[181], 41[9], and KSA 12, 2[25].

38 Burnham and Lampert who in their often profound and insightful commentary and interpretation of *Jenseits von Gut und Böse* respectively fail to see that this book, and especially the final sections, point forward to the *Umwerthung aller Werthe.*

39 This is also a reference to Zarathustra, for that work begins with those three words (and that is also the case in the very last section of the fourth book of *Die fröhliche Wissenschaft* where Zarathustra is introduced).

40 In section 7 of the preface to *Zur Genealogie der Moral*: "An dem Tage aber, wo wir aus vollem Herzen sagen: 'vorwärts! auch unsre alte Moral gehört *in die Komödie*!' haben wir für das dionysische Drama vom 'Schicksal der Seele' eine neue Verwicklung und Möglichkeit entdeckt—: und er wird sie sich schon zu Nutze machen, darauf darf man wetten, er, der grosse alte ewige Komödiendichter unsers Daseins! . . .."

41 With eighteen occurrences in *Götzen-Dämmerung* and twenty-nine in *Ecce Homo* (for both Dionysos and Dionysian). He is not mentioned in *Der Fall Wagner* and *Der Antichrist*.

42 In a letter to Gast, dated October 30, 1888, he writes about this ending: "Sind Sie zufrieden, daß ich den Schluß mit der *Dionysos-Moral* gemacht habe? Es fiel mir ein, daß diese Reihe Begriffe um keinen Preis in diesem Vademecum meiner Philosophie fehlen dürfe. Mit den paar Sätzen über die Griechen darf ich Alles herausfordern, was über sie gesagt ist.—Zum Schluß jene Hammer-Rede aus dem Zarathustra—vielleicht, *nach* diesem Buche, *hörbar* . . . Ich selbst höre sie nicht ohne einen eiskalten Schauder durch den ganzen Leib."

43 Nietzsche seems to begin with self-critique of how he set up the two principles Apollonian and Dionysian and made them into metaphysical principles.

44 Nietzsche was actually working on finalizing three books for publication at the time when he collapsed—*Ecce Homo*, *Nietzsche contra Wagner*, and *Dionysos-Dithyramben* (and the *Der Antichrist* manuscript remained unpublished)—so strictly speaking, there can be no definite last published words by him—but there can be little doubt that he regarded *Ecce Homo* as much more important than the other two incomplete but almost completely finished works.

45 Nietzsche adds in a last sentence that he has also hung on the cross.

46 KSA 11, 29[65].

47 KSA 11, 35[73].

48 Compare also the letter to Brandes, dated January 8, 1888, where he expresses himself in a similar way. In the private edition of this book from 1885, it had the title: "The Fourth and Last Part." Nietzsche had also, when he finished the third part, regarded it as the last part. When Nietzsche republished *Also sprach Zarathustra* in 1887, he did not include the fourth book, but the other three parts were then bound together in one volume.

49 Another alternative would be that Nietzsche intended to let Zarathustra return, and thus planned to write either a fifth *Also sprach Zarathustra*, or another sort of work in which the figure Zarathustra appears, but there is no evidence whatsoever among Nietzsche's later notes that he had any such plans. Furthermore, the fact that he says "I name no names" implies that it is going to be someone other than Zarathustra. In the later preface to *Die Geburt der Tragödie*, section 3, Nietzsche refers to himself as "a follower of an as yet 'unknown god,'" which almost certainly is a reference to Dionysos. This is also H. G. Hödl's interpretation, p. 589.

50 *Die Geburt der Tragödie*, Preface, 1.
51 In a letter to Overbeck, dated February 10, 1883, he writes: "It contains in the greatest possible sharpness a picture of my essence, the way it is after I have thrown off my complete load" ("Es enthält in der grössten Schärfe ein Bild meines Wesens wie es ist, sobald ich einmal meine ganze Last abgeworfen habe").
52 Zarathustra as Nietzsche's son: KSA 11, 26[394], and 34[204], KSA 12, 6[4] and in many letters, for example, in the letter to Fritzsch, August 29, 1886. As father: KSA 12, 6[4] and letter to Gast, April 6, 1883. As being pregnant with Zarathustra: *Ecce Homo*, "Za," 1. Nietzsche also explicitly on several occasions refers to how "autobiographical" *Also sprach Zarathustra* is, for example, in letter to Overbeck, February 10, 1883, quoted earlier, and to Hillebrand, May 24, 1883: "Alles was ich gedacht, gelitten und gehofft habe, steht darin."
53 *Ecce Homo*, "GT," 4.
54 More can be said about this, but since our interest is *Ecce Homo* and its relation to the *Umwerthung aller Werthe*, we will move on to Dionysos.
55 KSA 13, 17[4]. Sections 16 to 19 of *Der Antichrist* are closely based on section 1 to 4 of this note. The last section, 5, has been published (and translated into English) as section 1038 of *Der Wille zur Macht*.
56 KSA 13, 17[4].
57 Letter to Elisabeth, May 7, 1885.
58 In the Anglo-Saxon world there has generally been a strong liking for *Zur Genealogie der Moral*, which is more akin to a normal academic text. Note that Montinari points out, and I think correctly, that Nietzsche seemed to plan to write his *Hauptwerk* more in the style of *Zur Genealogie der Moral* (and *Der Antichrist*) than the style of *Also sprach Zarathustra*.
59 Letter to Naumann, November 6, 1888.

Chapter 6 (pages 120–143)

1 I have identified and used about fifty descriptions of the revaluation in *Ecce Homo*.
2 A similar statement was already made in 1880, "das Christenthum machte Alles wieder interessant, indem es alle Werthurtheile umdrehte" (KSA 9, 3[116]).
3 See also *Ecce Homo*, Wise, 7, Destiny, 1 and 7. In his review of *Der Fall Wagner*, 3, he refers to "four millennia" but this is probably a mistake for "four centuries," for that is what he is speaking about (since the Renaissance), and furthermore, two millennia is what he frequently refers to in his post-*Also sprach Zarathustra* notes and writings.
4 KSA 12, 9[8], autumn 1887 (also published as *Der Wille zur Macht* 462).
5 KSA 13, 14[96], "den natürlichen Werth umzuwerthen"
6 KSA 13, 14[134], April–May 1888.
7 KSA 13, 14[138].

8 Compare also the Foreword, 3, to *Ecce Homo* where Nietzsche speaks of how his kind of values have so far been hidden and forbidden, and quotes Ovid's "we strive for what is forbidden" as a sign of his philosophy and of healthy values.
9 Sometimes, but not in *Ecce Homo*, he also refers more generally to paganism.
10 One can speculate about who and what Nietzsche regarded as those other "moments in history." Possibly he refers to the Greek sophists (whom he discussed in *Götzen-Dämmerung*), perhaps Alexander and Caesar, both of whom he sees as his ancestors (EH, Wise, 3), Frederick II (1194–1250), whom Nietzsche praises as anti-Christian in *Jenseits von Gut und Böse*, 200, *Der Antichrist*, 60, and in this work: "I wanted to go to *Aquila*, Rome's counter-concept, founded from hostility against Rome, as I shall one day found a place, in memory of an atheist and enemy of the church *comme il faut*, one of those most closely related to me, the great Hohenstaufen Emperor Frederick II" (EH, "Za," 4), perhaps the classicism of the French seventeenth century and perhaps Napoleon (see the main text below).

Nietzsche makes some interesting and now relevant statements regarding Alexander in his *Untimely Meditation* about Wagner (which he, now in *Ecce Homo*, regards as being more about himself than about Wagner): "The history of the evolution of our culture since the Greeks is short enough, if one takes into account the actual distance covered and ignores the halts, regressions, hesitations, and lingerings. The Hellenization of the world and, to make this possible, the orientalization of the Hellenic—the twofold task of the great Alexander—is still the last great event [. . .] Thus it is that we now have need of a series of *counter-Alexanders* possessing the mighty capacity to draw together and unite, to reach the remotest threads, and to preserve the web from being blown away. Not to cut the Gordian knot, as Alexander did, so that its ends fluttered to all the corners of the earth, but *to tie it again*—that is now the task. I recognize in Wagner such a counter-Alexander: he unites what was separate, feeble, and inactive [. . .] to this extent he is one of the truly great cultural masters."[UB. IV. 4]
11 See KSA 13, 14[138]: "The history of the *counter-movements*: Renaissance / Revolution / Emancipation of science." What Nietzsche signifies by "Revolution" here is ambiguous. Nietzsche was always highly critical of the French Revolution, also in notes from this time. However, possibly here he refers to Napoleon as a consequence of the revolution. In an earlier note, KSA 11, 35[47], he refers to Napoleon as an example of the "counter-movement." With this interpretation, this note closely corresponds to the text of his review of *Der Fall Wagner* in *Ecce Homo*.
12 See, for example, KSA 13, 14[72, 137, and 138], 15[20 and 102], and in numerous notes he refers to art as a counter-movement.
13 *Der Antichrist*, 61.
14 *Götzen-Dämmerung*, "Expeditions, " 37.

15 KSA 10, 7[44].

16 KSA 12, 16[111], also published as WM 881.

17 GM, I, 16. Throughout this section a dichotomy is made between Roman and Jewish values.
Another example of Nietzsche's positive association of the Renaissance with antiquity is given in KSA 9, 7[206], written at the end of 1880: "Ein Bild des *Griechenthums* als der Zeit, die die meisten Individualitäten hervorgebracht hat. Das Fortleben in der Renaissance!"

18 This is very visible in his references to science in *Der Antichrist* and other later books. He, for example, sets off three sections, *Der Antichrist* 47–9, for exclusively discussing the opposition between science and Christianity, where he claims that God and the priests are all afraid of and opposed to truth and science—and that faith, so essential to all religions, is questioned and destroyed by science. Lies and imaginary causes are necessary for religion. See my discussion of this in "Nietzsche's Last View of Science" in *Nietzsche und Wissenschaft*, edited by H. Heit, G. Abel, and M. Brusotti (New York, Berlin, Walter de Gruyter, 2012), 39–54.

19 See KSA 13, 14[138]. Compare *Der Antichrist*, 48 and KSA 12, 9[86].

20 Nietzsche lists as a title for a planned text or chapter for the *Hauptwerk* in the spring of 1888: "Science against philosophy" ["Wissenschaft gegen Philosophie"] (KSA 13, 14[169] and 16[51]), and writes a number of notes under this title; many further notes during the late spring of 1888 are obviously related to this theme (of especial importance are the notes 83, 103, 109, 115, 131, 132, 137, 138, 146, and 153 in notebook W II 5, as well as the notes 40, 79, 81, 82, 84, 92, 93, 94, 111, 116, 122, 129, 133, 134, 141, 142, 147, 152, 168, 184, 186–189, and 194). Table 6.1 is constructed from the contents of these notes.

21 Compare also "Like a last signpost to the *other* path ['supreme rights of the few'], Napoleon appeared, the most isolated and late-born man there has ever been, and in him the problem of the *noble ideal as such* made flesh—one might well ponder *what* kind of problem it is: Napoleon, this synthesis of the *inhuman* and *superhuman.*" [diese Synthesis von *Unmensch* and *Übermensch* . . .] (GM, First essay, 16) and "Finally, when on the bridge between two centuries of decadence, a *force majeure* of genius and will became visible, strong enough to create a unity of Europe, a political and *economic* unity for the sake of a world government—the Germans with their 'Wars of Liberation' did Europe out of the meaning, the miracle of meaning in the existence of Napoleon; hence they have on their conscience all that followed, that is with us today—this most *anti-cultural* sickness and unreason there is, nationalism" (EH, "The Case of Wagner," 2). It should be noted that it is Napoleon the man Nietzsche speaks of, not Napoleon the general or a military leader.

22 "Dieser Satz, hart und schneidig geworden unter dem Hammerschlag der historischen Erkenntniss (lisez: *Umwerthung aller Werthe*)."

23 KSA 13, 16[32], also published as WM, 1041: "ich suchte nach den Ansätzen dieser umgekehrten Idealbildung in der Geschichte (die Begriffe 'heidnisch,' 'klassisch,' 'vornehm' neu entdeckt und hingestellt—) —."
24 The same argument is present in the epilogue to *Der Fall Wagner*.
25 I have discussed this in my "*The Antichrist* as the First Volume of Nietzsche's *magnum opus*," *Ideas in History* 3 (2008), 83–106.
26 For an excellent work on Nietzsche and tragedy, and of *Also sprach Zarathustra* as a tragic work, see Keith M. May, *Nietzsche and the Spirit of Tragedy* (1990), especially chapter 7, "Zarathustra and the Rebirth of Tragedy." See also Kathleen Higgins' insightful chapter two: "Nietzsche's Conception of Tragedy and the Tragic Worldview" in *Nietzsche's Zarathustra* (1987).
27 *Ecce Homo*, Za, 1.
28 Nietzsche also adds this section as an epilogue to *Götzen-Dämmerung*. "Hard" here should probably be read primarily as meaning "having a strong will and much *sophrosyne* (self-control)."
29 *Ecce Homo*, "GM."
30 Nietzsche's evaluation of the Greek and traditional virtue of justice is more critical and complex.
31 A large number of concepts and traits closely related to psychology and morality are mentioned by Nietzsche, and he frequently makes judgments about them: the egoistic and the unegoistic as opposites (both are absurd); the ego (a swindle); that man strives for happiness (wrong); that happiness is virtue's reward (wrong); that love is unegoistic (wrong); and equal rights between man and woman (a mistake).
32 Nietzsche exemplifies the different psychological approaches by the psychology of Christianity (resentment) and the psychology of conscience (cruelty turned inward). This is mentioned in *Ecce Homo*, but carried out in *Zur Genealogie der Moral*.
33 A large number of concepts and traits closely related to Christianity are mentioned by Nietzsche: sin, pangs of conscience, God, immortality of the soul, redemption, the beyond, spirit, free will, soul, and virtue.
34 In his discussion of *Menschliches, Allzumenschliches* in *Ecce Homo* Nietzsche mentions a number of ideals which he exposes there: the genius, the saint, the hero, belief, conviction, pity, and the thing in itself.
35 KSA 10, 16[49].
36 KSA 13, 18[17].
37 See letter to Brandes, January 8, 1888. After having sent him a copy of the fourth part of *Also sprach Zarathustra* (in which pity constitutes the main theme), Nietzsche writes: "Vielleicht beantworte ich so am besten Ihre Frage in Betreff meines Mitleids-Problems. Außerdem hat es überhaupt einen guten Sinn, gerade

durch diese Geheim-Thür den Zugang zu 'mir' zu nehmen: vorausgesetzt, daß man mit Ihren Augen und Ohren durch die Thür tritt."

38 *Der Antichrist*, 7. Pity is also mentioned and discussed rather frequently in *Ecce Homo*, most extensively in section 4 of the first chapter ("Wise"). Pity is also a major theme in *Die fröhliche Wissenschaft*, 338, and the whole fourth part of *Also sprach Zarathustra*.

39 *Der Antichrist*, 7.

40 *Der Antichrist*, 7.

41 *Die fröhliche Wissenschaft*, 338. See also KSA 9, 7[285] and KSA 10, 15[14].

42 I discuss how Nietzsche's relation to and view of pity changes as he develops in "The Development of Nietzsche's Ethical Thinking," *Nietzsche and Ethics*, ed. by Gudrun von Tevenar (Bern, 2007), 283–310.

43 See, for example, his letters to Overbeck, December 25, 1882; letter to his sister, July 10, 1883; letter to Meysenbug, middle of July 1883; and letter to Overbeck, September 14, 1884.

44 KSA 13, 14[11]. This translation is taken from *Nietzsche: Writings from the Late Notebooks*, edited by Rüdiger Bittner (Cambridge, 2003), p. 242.

45 KSA 11, 26[284]. This is one of Nietzsche's very first uses of the expression "revaluation."

46 This is also recognized by J. Young, who writes in his discussion of *Ecce Homo* in his biography of Nietzsche: "what will a 'superman' propose in the way of cultural reform? In a nutshell, 'the imminent return of the Greek spirit'" (p. 523).

47 A fairly large number of good studies of different aspects of Nietzsche's relation to antiquity have been published lately. To mention just a few of the best: Christian Benne, *Nietzsche und die historisch-kritische Philologie* (2005); Enrico Müller, *Die Griechen im Denken Nietzsches* (2005); and Dale Wilkerson, *Nietzsche and the Greeks* (2006). However, none of them discusses Greek values in relation to Nietzsche's revaluation project.

48 See, for example, in the notes from 1883, KSA 10, 9[27 and 29], where Nietzsche speaks of the Dionysian as his entry to antiquity and the Greeks, and this in a context related to revaluation, where men should go beyond themselves "like the Greeks."

49 KSA 13, 16[32], also published as WM, 1041: "ich suchte nach den Ansätzen dieser umgekehrten Idealbildung in der Geschichte (die Begriffe 'heidnisch,' 'klassisch,' 'vornehm neu entdeckt und hingestellt—)." Compare also KSA 12, 10[3] which also in a similar way reflects Nietzsche's historical approach: "Conception einer höheren Art Wesen als eine 'unmoralische' nach den bisherigen Begriffen: die Ansätze dazu in der Geschichte (die heidnischen Götter, die Ideale der Renaissance)."

See also his note from April–June 1885, KSA 11, 34[176], where he discusses those before him who have thought in terms of "a reversal of values," and points at pessimists—dissatisfied with present values—artists (like Byron)—who believes in the rights of higher humans—and most relevant here, "philologists and historians," who work on the discovery of antiquity.

50 The continued description of the second, life-affirming side of the dichotomy makes it clear that it is also related to Nietzsche's own idea of the eternal recurrence (in being affirmative, scientifically proved, and no part of reality able to be discounted): "This latter, the most joyful, most effusively high-spirited 'yes' to life, is not only the highest insight, it is also the *most* profound, the one which is most rigorously confirmed and sustained by truth and science. Nothing that is can be discounted, nothing can be dispensed with." How Nietzsche can mean that it is a hypothesis that is "most confirmed and sustained by truth and science" is not obvious here, but in his "Lenzer Heide" essay on "*European Nihilism*" (KSA 12, 5[71]) he gives three explanations for what he means. In section 6 of the essay he gives two reasons for why eternal recurrence should be regarded as "the *most scientific* of all hypotheses" (and alludes to a third one later on in section 13, based on accepting causality). The text to the first one is misread in KSA, but a new reading is given in KGW IX.3: "Energie des Stoffes u der Kraft *zwingt* zu einem solchen Glauben": "energy of matter and force *compels* such a belief" (which probably is a reference to the relatively recently discovered first law of thermodynamics, the conservation of energy). The second argument is: "We deny final ends: if existence had one, it must have been reached."

51 A frequent theme in the writings of the early Nietzsche, but rare later, is the *revival* of Hellenic antiquity: "Let no one try to blight our faith in a yet-impending rebirth of Hellenic antiquity" ("der Glaube an die Wiedergeburt des hellenischen Altertums"), *Die Geburt der Tragödie*, 20, p. 123. Other examples are "Der deutsche Wiedergeburt der hellenischen Welt," KSA 7, 11[1]; "Die Wiedergeburt Griechenlands aus der Erneuerung des Deutschen Geistes," KSA 8, 6[44]; "Die höchste Bildung erkenne ich bis jetzt nur als Wieder-erweckung des Hellenentums," KSA 7, 14[25].

52 KSA 8, 3[68]. Translated into English in "We Classicists," in *Unmodern Observations*, p. 341.

53 "Die Griechen bisher die höchste Art," KSA 11, 35[47], also published as WM 979.

54 KSA 13, 11[138] November 87–März 88, also published as WM 341. Other examples of later references to Greece as an example and ideal are "The best turned out, most beautiful, most envied type of humanity to date, those most apt to seduce us to life, the Greeks." GT, Preface (1886), 1. "Oh, those Greeks! They knew how to live!" FW, Preface, 4. "The whole labour of the ancient world *in vain*: I have no word to express my feelings at something so dreadful." AC, 59. "In die Nähe der Griechen sich heimisch machen." KSA 11, 41[10]. "Den Menschen über sich hinaus steigern, gleich den Griechen." KSA 10, 9[29]. "Heimisch sein in der griechischen Welt!" KSA 11, 41[4], also published as WM 419.

55 KSA 8, 3[62].

56 *Nietzsche contra Wagner*, Epilogue, 2 (W. Kaufmann's translation).

57 KSA 11, 26[3]: "Die Kenntniß der großen Griechen hat mich erzogen: an Heraclit Empedocles Parmenides Anaxagoras Democrit ist mehr zu verehren, sie sind *voller*" [than the great philosophers like Kant, Hegel, Schopenhauer, and Spinoza].

58 *Der Antichrist*, 61. The same view is expressed in *Ecce Homo*, "Wagner," 2.

59 One can convincingly argue that Nietzsche favors an ethics of virtue rather than deontological or utilitarian ethics. See my studies *Nietzsche's Ethics of Character: A Study of Nietzsche's Ethics and its Place in the History of Moral Thinking* (Uppsala, 1995) and "Nietzsche's Affirmative Morality: An Ethics of Virtue," *Journal of Nietzsche Studies* 26 (2003), 64–78. Other studies that also discuss Nietzsche's ethics in terms of virtue ethics are, for example, Christine Swanton, 2005. "Nietzschean Virtue Ethics," in S. Gardiner (ed.), *Virtue Ethics, Old and New*, Ithaca, Cornell University Press.

60 KSA 13, 12[1] (43), early 1888. Compare the longer note KSA 12, 9[55], from autumn 1887, to which the shorter note is a summary and brief comment. Nietzsche has written IV next to it, signifying that the note was to be used for volume 4.

61 Letter to Peter Gast, July 23, 1885.

Bibliography of Nietzsche Literature

The German edition of Nietzsche's works used is the *Kritische Studienausgabe* (KSA) in fifteen volumes, edited by G. Colli and M. Montinari (Berlin & New York, 1980). The German edition of the letters used is the *Sämtliche Briefe: Kritische Studienausgabe* (KSB) in eight volumes, edited by G. Colli and M. Montinari (Berlin & New York, 1986). Letters to Nietzsche, and commentaries on the letters, are in KGB.

However, on a few occasions an older edition of Nietzsche's works in German has also been used:

Friedrich Nietzsche, Werke und Briefe, Historisch-kritische Gesamtausgabe, München, 1933ff., (BAW), edited by H. J. Mette. This unfinished edition covers the period from 1854 to 1869, that is, for the young Nietzsche.

Friedrich Nietzsches *Ecce Homo*: Faksimileausgabe der Handschrift. Transkription von Anneliese Clauss. Dr. Ludwig Reichert Verlag, Wiesbaden 1985 in the series Manu *script*, Band 2. Faksimileausgaben literarisches Handschriften. Herausgegeben von Karl-Heinz Hahn.

Selected Bibliography of Nietzsche's Works in English

I have chosen to utilize existing translations for quotations from Nietzsche's published works. The translations are almost all by Walter Kaufmann and R. J. Hollingdale. Where there has been a choice between the translations of Kaufmann and Hollingdale, I have usually preferred those of Hollingdale. Hollingdale has translated *Ecce Homo*, but I have used the excellent translation by Duncan Large (Oxford, 2007). For most of Nietzsche's books there are also other translations than those I refer to in what follows.

Die Geburt der Tragödie (1872), *The Birth of Tragedy*, translated by Walter Kaufmann (New York, 1967).

Unzeitgemäße Betrachtungen (1873–76), *Untimely Meditations* (Containing all four essays), translated by R. J. Hollingdale (Cambridge, 1983). Introduction by J. P. Stern. Also translated as *Unmodern Observations* (containing all four essays and the notes for *Wir Philologen*), by several translators. Edited by William Arrowsmith (New Haven & London, 1990).

Menschliches, Allzumenschliches (3 vols., 1878, 1879, 1880), *Human, All Too Human*, translated by R. J. Hollingdale (Cambridge, 1986). Introduction by Erich Heller (Containing all three volumes.)
Morgenröthe (1881), *Daybreak*, translated by R. J. Hollingdale (Cambridge, 1982). Introduction by Michael Tanner.
Die fröhliche Wissenschaft (1882), *The Gay Science*, translated by Walter Kaufmann (New York, 1974).
Also sprach Zarathustra (3 and 4 vols., 1883–85), *Thus Spoke Zarathustra*, translated by Walter Kaufmann (New York, 1974), In "The Portable Nietzsche." Also translated by R. J. Hollingdale (Harmondsworth, 1961, 1969) and by Graham Parkes (Oxford, 2005).
Jenseits von Gut und Böse (1886), *Beyond Good and Evil*, translated by Walter Kaufmann (New York, 1966). Also translated by R. J. Hollingdale (Harmondsworth, 1973).
Zur Genealogie der Moral (1887), *On the Genealogy of Morals*, translated by Walter Kaufmann (New York, 1969). Also translated by Douglas Smith (Oxford, 1996)
Der Fall Wagner (1888), *The Case of Wagner*, translated by Walter Kaufmann (New York, 1967).
Götzen-Dämmerung (1888), *Twilight of the Idols*, translated by Walter Kaufmann (New York, 1974), In "The Portable Nietzsche." Also translated by R. J. Hollingdale (Harmondsworth, 1968), as well as by Duncan Large (Oxford, 1997) and Judith Norman (Cambridge, 2005)
Der Antichrist (written in 1888, but published for the first time in 1895), *The Antichrist*, translated by Walter Kaufmann (New York, 1974), (In "The Portable Nietzsche.") Also translated by R. J. Hollingdale (Harmondsworth, 1968).
Nietzsche contra Wagner (1888), translated by Walter Kaufmann (New York, 1974), in "The Portable Nietzsche."
Der Wille zur Macht (1906), *The Will to Power*, translated by W. Kaufmann and R. J. Hollingdale (New York, 1974). This is a translation of the second edition (the larger and most frequently referred to) by Elisabeth Förster-Nietzsche and Peter Gast.
Ecce Homo (written in 1888, but published for the first time in 1908), *Ecce Homo*, translated by Walter Kaufmann (New York, 1974). Also translated by R. J. Hollingdale (Harmondsworth, 1979) and by Duncan Large (Oxford, 2007).
Philosophy and Truth: Selections from Nietzsche's Notebooks of the Early 1870s, edited and translated by Daniel Breazeale (London, 1979, 1991).
Nietzsche: Writings from the Late Notebooks, edited by Rüdiger Bittner (Cambridge, 2003)

General Bibliography

Benne, Christian, *Nietzsche und die historisch-kritische Philologie* (Berlin, New York, 2005).
Blue, Daniel, *The Making of Friedrich Nietzsche: The Quest for Identity, 1844–1869* (Cambridge: Cambridge University Press, 2016).

Brobjer, Thomas, *Nietzsche's Ethics of Character: A Study of Nietzsche's Ethics and Its Place in the History of Moral Thinking*, Dept. of the History of Science and Ideas, Uppsala University, 1995.

Brobjer, Thomas, "Nietzsche's Reading and Private Library 1885–89," *Journal of the History of Ideas* 58 (1997), 663–93.

Brobjer, Thomas, "An Undiscovered Short Published Autobiographical Presentation by Nietzsche from 1872," *Nietzsche-Studien* 27 (1998), 446 ff.

Brobjer, Thomas, "An Undiscovered Short Published Autobiographical Presentation by Nietzsche from 1869," *Journal of Nietzsche Studies* 17 (Spring1999), 68–69.

Brobjer, Thomas, "Götzen-Hammer: The Meaning of the Expression 'To Philosophize with a Hammer,'" *Nietzsche-Studien* 28 (1999), 38–41.

Brobjer, Thomas, "Nietzsche's Atheism," in *Nietzsche and the Divine*, edited by Jim Urpeth and John Lippitt (Clinamen Press, Manchester, 2000), 1–13.

Brobjer, Thomas, "Nietzsche's Changing Relation to Christianity: Nietzsche as Christian, Atheist and Antichrist," in *Nietzsche and the Gods* (SUNY), edited by Weaver Santaniello (New York: SUNY, 2001), 137–57.

Brobjer, Thomas, "Nietzsche's Affirmative Morality: An Ethics of Virtue," *Journal of Nietzsche Studies*, 26 (2003), 64–78.

Brobjer, Thomas, "Nietzsche's *magnum opus*," *History of European Ideas* 32 (2006), 278–94.

Brobjer, Thomas, "The Development of Nietzsche's Ethical Thinking," *Nietzsche and Ethics*, edited by Gudrun von Tevenar (Bern: Peter Lang, 2007), 283–310.

Brobjer, Thomas, *Nietzsche and the "English": The Influence of British and American Thinking on His Philosophy* (Humanity Books, 2008).

Brobjer, Thomas, *Nietzsche's Philosophical Context: An Intellectual Biography* (Urbana and Chicago: University of Illinois Press, 2008).

Brobjer, Thomas, "Thus Spoke Zarathustra as Nietzsche's Autobiography," in *Before Sunrise: Nietzsche's Thus Spoke Zarathustra*, edited by James Luchte (Continuum Publishers, London and New York, 2008), 29–46.

Brobjer, Thomas, "The Origin and Early Context of Nietzsche's Revaluation of All Values," *Journal of Nietzsche Studies*, 29 (2010), 12–29.

Brobjer, Thomas, "The Place and Role of *Der Antichrist* in Nietzsche's Four Volume Project *Umwerthung aller Werthe*," *Nietzsche-Studien* 40 (2011), 244–55.

Brobjer, Thomas, "Nietzsche's Last View of Science," in *Nietzsches Wissenschaftsphilosophie*, edited by H. Heit, G. Abel and M. Brusotti (Walter de Gruyter, New York, Berlin, 2012), 39–54.

Burnham, Douglas, *Reading Nietzsche: An Analysis of Beyond Good and Evil* (Montreal: McGill-Queen's University Press)

Cate, Curtis, *Friedrich Nietzsche* (London: Hutchinson, 2002).

Chamberlain, Lesley, *Nietzsche in Turin: The End of the Future* (London: Faber and Faber, 1996).

Creuzer, Friedrich, *Dionysus* (Heidelberg, 1809).

Creuzer, Friedrich, *Symbolik und Mythologie der alten Völker, besonders der Griechen*, 4 volumes (1836–43).

Davis-Acampora, Christa and Keith Ansell Pearson, *Nietzsche's Beyond Good and Evil* (London and New York: Continuum, 2011).

Ekerwald, Carl-Göran, *Nietzsche: Liv och tankesätt* (Stockholm, 1993).

Groddeck, Wolfgang, "Die Geburt der Tragödie" in "Ecce homo": Hinweise zu einer strukturalen Lektüre von Nietzsches "Ecce homo," *Nietzsche-Studien* 13 (1984), 325–33.

Hayman, Ronald, *Nietzsche: A Critical Life* (London, 1980).

Hellwald, Friedrich von, *Culturgeschichte in ihrer natürlichen Entstehung bis zur Gegenwart* (Augsburg, 1874).

Higgins, Kathleen, *Nietzsche's Zarathustra* (Philadelphia, 1987).

Hödl, Hans Gerald, *Der letzte Jünger des Philosophen Dionysos: Studien zur systematischen Bedeutung von Nietzsches Selbstthematisierungen im Kontext seiner Religionskritik* (Berlin, New York, 2009).

Hollingdale, R. J., "Introduction" to *Ecce Homo*, from 1977 (Penguin Classics).

Hollingdale, R. J., *Nietzsche: The Man and His Philosophy* (London, 1965, Cambridge, reprinted with additions, 1999).

Huang, Jing, "Did Nietzsche want his notes burned? Some reflections on the *Nachlass* problem," *British Journal of the History of Philosophy* 27 (2019), 1194–214.

Janz, Curt Paul, *Friedrich Nietzsche: Biographie*, 3 volumes (München, 1978, second revised edition, 1993).

Kaufmann, Walter, Introduction to his translation of *Ecce Homo* from 1966 (Vintage Books).

Lampert, Laurence, *Nietzsche's Task: An Interpretation of Beyond Good and Evil* (New Haven, London, 2001).

Large, Duncan, "Introduction" to *Ecce Homo, Oxford World's Classics* (Oxford, 2007).

Martin, Nicholas and Duncan Large, eds., *Nietzsche's Ecce Homo* (Walter de Gruyter, Berlin, Boston, 2021).

May, Keith M., *Nietzsche and the Spirit of Tragedy* (London, 1990).

Middleton, Christopher, *Selected Letters of Friedrich Nietzsche* (Indianapolis, 1969).

Montinari, Mazzino, "Nietzsches Nachlaß von 1885 bis 1888 oder Textkritik und Wille zur Macht," in *Nietzsche lesen* (Walter de Gruyter, Berlin, New York, 1982), 92–119, p. 114f.

Montinari, Mazzino, "Nietzsches Philosophie als 'Leidenschaft der Erkenntnis,'" in *Nietzsche lesen* (Berlin, New York, 1982), 64–78.

Montinari, Mazzino, *Nietzsche lesen* (Walter de Gruyter, Berlin, New York, 1982).

Montinari, Mazzino, "Ecce homo: Zur Textgeschichte," in *KSA* 14 (1967–77), pp. 454–512.

More, Nicholas, *Nietzsche's Last Laugh: Ecce Homo as Satire* (Cambridge, 2016).

Müller, Enrico, *Die Griechen im Denken Nietzsches* (Berlin, New York, 2005).

Prideaux, Sue, *I Am Dynamite!: A Life of Friedrich Nietzsche* (London, 2018).

Rattner, Josef, *Nietzsche: Leben—Werk—Wirkung* (Würzburg, 2000).
Rée, Paul, *Der Ursprung der moralischen Empfindungen* (Chemnitz, 1877).
Ross, Werner, *Der ängsliche Adler* (München, Stuttgart, 1980).
Safranski, Rüdiger, *Nietzsche: Biographie seines Denkens* (München, Wien, 2000).
Salis-Marschlins, Meta von, *Philosoph und Edelmensch: Ein Beitrag zur Charakteristik Friedrich Nietzsches* (Leipzig, 1897).
Samuel, Richard, "Friedrich Nietzsche's *Ecce Homo*: An Autobiography?," in *Deutung und Bedeutung*, edited by B. Schludermann et al. (Mouton, 1973), 210–27.
Schmidt, Leopold, *Die Ethik der alten Griechen*, 2 vols (Berlin, 1882).
Sommer, Andreas Urs, *Historischer und kritischer Kommentar zu Friedrich Nietzsches Werken*, published by the Heidelberger Akademie der Wissenschaft and Walter de Gruyer. Volume 6/2 contains commentaries to *Der Antichrist, Ecce homo, Dionysos-Dithyramben*, and *Nietzsche contra Wagner*, all written by Sommer (Berlin, Boston, 2013).
Swanton, Christine, "Nietzschean Virtue Ethics," in *Virtue Ethics, Old and New*, edited by S. Gardiner (Cornell University Press, Ithaca, 2005).
Tanner, Michael, Introduction to Hollingdale's translation, from 1991 and later (Penguin Classics).
Wikipedia, "Nietzsche, Ecce Homo" (July 2020).
Wilkerson, Dale, *Nietzsche and the Greeks* (London, New York, 2006).
Wuthenow, Ralph-Rainer, *Nietzsche als Leser* (Hamburg, 1994).
Young, Julian, *Friedrich Nietzsche: A Philosophical Biography* (Cambridge, 2010).

Index

Printed in the USA
CPSIA information can be obtained
at www.ICGtesting.com
LVHW011743221223
767237LV00004B/198

9 781350 194304